Contents

The Novell Connection

Wayne Rash Jr.
Peter R. Stephenson

Brady

New York   London   Toronto   Sydney   Tokyo   Singapore

BRADY

Simon & Schuster, Inc.
15 Columbus Circle
New York, NY 10023

Manufactured in the United States of America

10 9 8 7 6 5 4 3 2

Library of Congress Cataloging in Publication Data

Rash, Wayne.
    The Novell connection / Wayne Rash and Peter Stephenson.
        p.   cm.
    1. Business—Data processing. 2. Local area networks (Computer
networks) 3. Business—Communication systems—Data processing.
I. Stephenson, Peter, 1944-   . II. Title.
    HF5548.2,.R2863   1990
    004.6'8—dc20   90–1795
    ISBN 0-13-624024-0   CIP

Dedications

To Carolyn
Wayne Rash, Jr.

For Debbie who puts up with my writing addiction
Peter Stephenson

Acknowledgments

Patti Heiser—Novell: For her support and effort above and beyond the call of duty getting screen captures

Marion Knaus—Delrina Technology: For help with illustrations

Limits of Liability and Disclaimer of Warranty

The authors and publisher of this book have used their best efforts in preparing this book and the programs contained in it. These efforts include the development, research, and testing of the theories and programs to determine their effectiveness. The authors and publisher shall not be liable in any event for incidental or consequential damages in connection with, or arising out of, the furnishing, performance, or use of these programs.

Registered Trademarks

Chapter 8
Being the Network Supervisor

Chapter 9
Applications on Novell LANs   191

Glossary 351

Index 363

Introduction

There are two kinds of office computing environments. Those that are connected using a local area network, and those that soon will be. At their current rate of growth, LANs will be in most office environments in the very near future. Today, well over half the local area networks in the world are produced by Novell. That means that you have a very good chance of either installing or using a Novell LAN sometime in your career. This book is designed to help you attain a working familiarity with LANs in general and Novell NetWare LANs in particular.

Who Should Use This Book?

There are few, if any, assumptions of networking experience in this book. We have taken the approach that you are a reasonably experienced user of personal computers, but have little or no networking background. So, if you are considering a network for your office, planning to install a Novell LAN or being faced with learning how to use a Novell NetWare system, this book was written for you. In short, it was written to help you as an entry level user or administrator get your feet wet with Novell.

Over the course of the book we'll cover a variety of subjects including a description of LANs and **network operating systems (NOSs).** We'll discuss the Novell NetWare operating system. Early in the book you'll find an analysis of the costs and benefits of installing a network, including a discussion of the hidden costs of network installation such as learning curve and work disruption during installation. We'll set the stage for your network installation by providing some preinstallation advice and procedures. And we'll explore some of the theory and standards of network communications.

In Part II we'll roll up our sleeves and install a NetWare LAN, learn how to be the network supervisor and learn about the various NetWare commands. Later on in Part II we'll describe the various types of applications you're likely to want to run on your network since applications are the reason most of us use computers in the first place.

As an added benefit, we've included information about the latest release of NetWare, NetWare 386. This brings our coverage of NetWare products to ELS (Entry Level System), NetWare 286, SFT NetWare and NetWare 386. If you're looking for a complete introduction to the Novell NetWare product line, it's all right here.

Finally, so that you'll never get bogged down in the jargon of networks, we've included a Novell-English Glossary. Terms you can look up in the dictionary appear in **bold type.** In short, we've brought you a compendium of information for Novell beginners that will get you to the point where you are quite proficient with your NetWare LAN. You'll have the basis to go on and become a real Novell NetWare power user or administrator.

Conventions Used in This Book

Throughout this book we will use some conventions that will help you understand what the various procedures you will be using mean. Generally, these conventions relate to the way you interact with the instructions on the computer screen.

- Commands are in UPPERCASE CHARACTERS
- Terms defined in the Glossary are in **boldface type**
- Complete file names are in lowercase with the first character in uppercase: Netgen.exe
- When file names are used as a reference they are in UPPERCASE CHARACTERS: NETGEN
- Function Keys appear in square brackets: [F1]
- Keys such as Escape and Enter appear in square brackets enclosing the portion of the key's name that appears on the keyboard: [ESC]ape

Novell and Local Area Networking

Novell, as we said, controls well over half the world-wide local area network market. There are several reasons for this and, there are several significant differences between Novell's approach to networking and that of many of the company's competitors. Although we will discuss the specific technology of network communications in more depth later, here's what the differences amount to.

When IBM introduced early LAN operating software, they took the approach that the network operating system should integrate with the DOS operating system at some level. They created a special BIOS (Basic Input/Output System—the method the CPU uses to communicate with everything external to it) called NetBIOS. NetBIOS is a sort of interconnecting bridge between the various operating levels of a LAN operating system. In fact, NetBIOS was, at one time, actually part of the firmware on an IBM PC Network interface card. Today, most network application software does not require NetBIOS to run on most LANs.

However, when Novell started developing network operating systems, it avoided the use of NetBIOS altogether and opted for its own interface between the computer's internal operating system and the outside world. That interface is called IPX. We'll give you a detailed description of IPX later on, but for now you should simply understand that IPX is "the other way" to "do" a LAN. There are some very large advantages to IPX. The most important is size. IPX takes up relatively little memory space in the workstation, leaving more memory for running applications. Other operating systems, especially those that use NetBIOS or a NetBIOS emulator tend to use up substantially more memory in the workstation computer. The result, of course, is that applications that have room to run on a Novell NetWare LAN simply won't fit on other networks.

So Novell entered the networking marketplace with a different approach to other network systems. But, it was also careful to maintain close compatibility with applications that needed to run on their networks. Interestingly, Novell developed such a presence in the LAN market at an early point in the development of LAN technology that developers of network applications went to specific lengths to produce Novell compatible versions of their products.

This was important because although close compatibility was maintained between Novell's system and the so-called DOS 3.X compatible systems, that compatibility was largely in areas of functionality. Internally, applications developed for the IBM environment would not run directly on a NetWare LAN. Today, there are basically two levels of compatibility and those boundaries are becoming increasingly blurred. Those levels are Novell and IBM. Companies like 3Com adhere closely to the IBM/NetBIOS side while Novell now provides NetBIOS emulators. As we progress into the world of OS/2, the boundaries will become even more unclear. Novell now provides the Requestor for OS/2 that allows a Novell LAN to correctly support an OS/2 operating environment.

Besides the advantage of minimum memory use, NetWare has the additional advantage of bundling a lot of capabilities other developers consider options. These capabilities include such extensions as **bridges** (which we'll explain later). The architecture of the NetWare operating system encourages this because, as you will see in Chapter 10, we actually generate a custom network operating system for each individual Novell NetWare installation. This means that users can include the necessary internetworking capability in their installation instead of purchasing it as an extra cost item.

To sum up, Novell NetWare is the standard of the networking industry for many reasons. As you progress through this book, you'll see many of the justifications for NetWare becoming so important to the growth of local area networking. You'll also learn how to use your NetWare system and develop the skills that make a good Novell network administrator. When we've finished, you'll end up with a good understanding of the way a local area network functions from the inside.

In the first chapter we'll begin with a discussion of local area networks. We'll tell you what they are, where you would want to use one, what they're good for, and why you'll benefit from them. This is a fitting start for our excursion through the world of Novell local area networking. And, we hope, it will encourage you to continue on with a smorgasbord of goodies that you can use in your day to day interaction with your NetWare LAN. So, on to the feast, and *bon appetit!*

Part I

1

What Makes Up Your Local Area Network?

You (or somebody you work for) have just decided that you will install a local area network. Or, perhaps, you haven't decided, but you are sure that LANs are something you should investigate. You are overwhelmed with hype from the various network suppliers. And, you're not completely sure how to proceed. In short, yesterday you couldn't spell LAN. Today your boss wants you to design one. The word comes down from above that you should install a Novell LAN. What do you do?

The fact is that your boss specified the best selling LAN in the world when he or she specified Novell. Your boss also gave you a relatively easy task. As we progress in this book, we'll show you how to take your boss' recommendation and turn it into a solid network you can design, install and manage. Oh, by the way, if you happen to be the boss, we'll show you everything you need to know about specifying and installing a Novell LAN. But, before we install the first workstation, we must learn what Novell local area networks are all about.

A local area network, or LAN, can be many things to many types of users. At the end of the day, as our British friends might say, a LAN is little more than a method of sharing data within a defined workgroup. But, in many regards, the results are more than just data sharing. As we will see later in this book, LANs actually can provide a mechanism for manipulating data, providing users with simultaneous access to documents and interfacing with external networks and systems. But the LAN's real benefits always come down to data sharing. So, in that regard, our British friends are right. Networks are for sharing.

Sharing data means many different things to different people. For some, it means moving their information to someone else and someone else's information to them. For some, it means more than one person using the same information. It means two people creating and editing the same document. Or several people updating data in a database. Or, perhaps, several people performing analysis with a single spreadsheet.

Each of these definitions is within the scope of a local area network. But each places different requirements on the system. The ability for two people to read the same word processing document is very different (and far less complex) than the ability for 1,000 people to share, read, update and create records in a shared database.

Another definition of a local area network might include the ability to communicate between individual computers on the network. It might include the ability to communicate between networks. And, it might include the ability to communicate from one computer on a network to a host computer or from an external PC to the network. In short, a LAN must have the ability to allow users to communicate information as well as share it.

Part of communicating implies the ability to connect the LAN to the outside world. And, certainly, that aspect of communications is very important. But what does this new breed of system look like? How does it do its jobs? Although we'll go into much more detail in Chapter 3, here we'll talk a bit about the pieces of a Novell LAN.

Finally, why should we bother with a LAN? Are there some more esoteric reasons for installing a Novell local area network than the obvious objectives of data sharing and communications? In this chapter we'll look at the what and why of local area networks in general and Novell LANs in particular.

What, Exactly, Is a LAN?

Before we try to describe what's *in* a LAN, perhaps we'd better go into some more detail about what a LAN is and does. Remember, please, that we are providing an entry level excursion into Novell local area networking. So, although we have our elementary moments, we hope to take you from the barest of basics to the point where you can install and operate your own network.

A Means of Communicating Information

We said, at the beginning, that LANs are for sharing and communicating data. Perhaps we'd better start there in our odyssey through the complexities of Novell LANs. LANs generally occupy a rather compact physical area. Unlike a **wide area network** (WAN) a local area network is usually confined to a single building. In some cases, a local area network may be confined to a single **workgroup** in a single large office. Often, in order to take advantage of several LANs, we interconnect them using **bridges**.

In any event, LANs are just what their name implies—local. But that shouldn't give you the impression that all LANs are small. Although there are certainly LANs with only four or five users, there are also LANs with over a thousand. So, LANs should not be considered "wimpy" or "Mickey Mouse" solutions. They should be considered as special computer networks optimized for groups of users who need to communicate and share common data. In fact, we might call local area networks workgroup networks.

How LANs Communicate

Without plumbing the technical depths of network communications at this point, we should at least understand what kinds of network interactions can occur. Local area networks provide four levels of communication for users. They are user-to-user, network-to-network, network-to-**host** and user-to-network. Of course, these are two-way communications. Although we specify, for example, user-to-host, you should realize that we imply host-to-user as well.

User-to-user communications are the meat and potatoes of local area networks. Almost all of the constant moment-to-moment communications occur either between users or between users and the server. Actually, if we were to be painfully precise they really only occur between users and the server because the server acts as a sort of traffic cop for network communications.

In order to handle user-to-user communications, the network uses special communications procedures called **protocols**. These protocols are step-by-step instructions for conducting a communications session. All of the networks communications require some sort of protocol. The one for communicating between users on the LAN is, however, at the very core of the specification of the Novell LAN. We will describe in detail the way a LAN is defined using, in part, the protocols required for communications later in this book.

A more advanced protocol allows networks to communicate with each other. Since networks themselves usually have little to say to each other about anything, this implies that network-to-network communication is a sort of long distance telephone system which allows users on the individual networks to talk to each other. So it is.

Network-to-network protocols are a mere step above user-to-user in the sense that they need to know where (on what network) the recipient of a message resides. There are two steps to allowing this communication. First, we need a communications server that knows where the other LAN is. A **communications server** is a fancy name for a dedicated PC that sits on the LAN and has no other purpose beyond communicating with the outside world.

Second, we need the address of the recipient on the distant LAN. The communications server contains a program called a bridge that keeps track of all the networks to which it can connect and their protocols. If the distant protocol is different from the sending protocol, the bridge needs to be able to ascertain that and translate between the two. This process of communicating between two LANs is called **internetworking**.

The third type of network communications available to local area networks is network-to-host. In a network-to-host configuration, the bridge needs to translate between the LAN's protocol and the protocol of an external computer. The external, or host computer, is usually a mainframe or mini computer. When the LAN wants to talk to the host it usually pretends to be a terminal on the host.

For example, if you were an individual user on an IBM mainframe, you might use a **3270 terminal**. 3270 terminals have a special protocol for communicating with IBM mainframes. So if we are users on a LAN, and we want to communicate with the same IBM host, we could also use the 3270 protocol. And that is exactly how it works.

Our bridge contains what is known as a **protocol emulator** which, in simple terms, pretends to be a 3270 terminal. We communicate with the bridge over the LAN and our LAN protocol is converted into a 3270 protocol by the bridge. Now we can communicate with the mainframe in its own language, so to speak. The mainframe, of course, needs to return our communication, so when it talks to the bridge using 3270, the bridge converts that back to our LAN protocol and we have two-way communications.

We'll get into a bit more detail later on, but you can see that our LAN can give us a fair amount of flexibility over both internal and external communications. The fourth type of user/LAN interaction is user-to-network. This type of communication occurs when a user who is external to the LAN wants to communicate with users on the LAN.

We use a similar approach to the LAN-to-host approach. Only this time, we call the bridge by a different name. We call it a **gateway**. Gateways are methods of accessing some intermediate communications medium on the way to our ultimate destination. Recall that when our LAN communicated with the mainframe, we implied a direct connection. At least we implied that a connection existed that only had one protocol translation to it. We translated between the LAN protocol and IBM 3270 protocol.

When this occurs, the formatting of the data occurs only once in each direction. The bridge formats the data in 3270 format on its way out to the mainframe, and the LAN's protocol on its way back in to the LAN. A gateway packages data so that it can be transmitted only. The gateway doesn't care what the protocol at either end might be. It only cares that it must get the data from point A to point B.

Often, the gateway is an entry point into a **public data network** such as Tymnet. The emphasis on the data network, or wide area network, is simply efficient point-to-point communication. Protocol conversions that occur at either end of the wire are of no concern to the WAN. WAN protocols, such as CCITT X.25, are optimized for their ability to move large amounts of data efficiently.

When we want to talk to our LAN from a remote location, we might use a dial-up telephone line over a public or private data network. We will connect with our LAN's gateway which, in turn, will connect us to the LAN. If we are not using a communications protocol that the LAN can understand, we will reach the gateway, but won't be able to log on to the network. It simply won't understand us. So we will need to insure that we have a gateway that understands our data on one side and can present it to the network in some understandable manner.

If that sounds like our old friend the bridge, it almost is. But the big difference between the two is that the bridge connects two systems directly, translating their individual protocols, while the gateway takes whatever the communication link gives it and turns it into the LAN's protocol. That still seems a bit complicated so, if you like, we can look at it still another way.

Our user in the field probably uses a standard **asynchronous communications program** to talk to the data network. That means that the data network gets streams of characters from the field user's computer, which, if connected to another similar computer at the other end, would be intelligible. The data network has a device at each end called a **PAD (Packet Assembly / Disassembly)**. The PAD takes the stream of characters from the distant computer, packages it into an efficient communications format and ships it out over the phone lines. At the other end the PAD reassembles the data for the other computer and, voilà, we have communication.

Our gateway often takes the place of one of the PADs. It accepts the packaged data, unpackages it, and, instead of giving it to another computer, sends it to the network. The trick is that we usually must send our information out in a format the LAN will understand in the first place. Our data, in a LAN-understandable format hits the PAD, is packaged up and sent to the gateway which delivers it into the LAN. As far as users on the LAN are concerned, our distant user is in the next office instead of the next state.

The interesting thing about gateways is, since they are primarily external communications interfaces, they can actually connect from gateway to gateway. That means that if I have a user in France who wants to communicate with a LAN in Boise, Idaho, the link is fairly straightforward. Even though the public data networks (PDNs) in France are very different from those in the US, there is a gateway between the two (called an **international gateway**) which translates the data and keeps it moving. Remember, the transmission protocol on the PDN is just that—a means of moving data without regard to that data's original format. No matter how the data gets twisted up between gateways, it always comes out the way it went in.

A Means of Sharing Information

Now that we've moved information around a bit, let's briefly explore what we might do with the information. We have emphasized that sharing data is what LANs are all about. Of course, we have to be able to get the information to a convenient place for the sharing to occur. That's what we have done with our various communications methods.

There are some issues that we will confront throughout this book in terms of sharing information. We have, essentially, only two things we might want to do with information. We can look at it (read it) and we can change it (write it). It is around these two activities that all information-sharing considerations revolve.

The first issue is: Who will we allow to see our information? This is at the first rung of the ladder of sharing issues. By answering this question we will, first, define who can gain access to our LAN, and, ultimately, who can gain access to our particular information. The issue, of course, is security—and security is basic to all local area networks.

So, the first sharing issue is security. The second is actually a superset of network security—who can read our information. We need to be able to differentiate between public information and private information. And, we need to decide when we will allow more than one person to read information at the same time.

Next, we come to the level of who can write information. Writing includes adding, deleting, creating and changing data. Obviously, all of the "read" issues are of concern here plus several more. Again, we are talking about controlling different types of access. We are talking about security. Novell LANs provide security in a variety of ways.

At the most primitive level, they seek to restrict access to the network. Once access is granted, they then provide barriers to access on the file level (they force certain privilege levels on a file-by-file basis to gain access); on an activity level (they limit the types of access—read, write, etc.—on a file basis); and on the user level (they specify that a user has certain security "rights"). Obviously, sharing information cannot be allowed to proceed in a completely uncontrolled manner. Novell LANs do not permit information anarchy.

Within the context of these various forms of network and file security, however, Novell LANs allow great flexibility of information sharing. The network administrator can easily grant combinations of privileges that permit virtually anyone on the LAN to have the correct level of access to all the information he or she needs without intruding upon off-limits data. But there is another sharing issue with which LANs must deal.

That issue, **data integrity**, will occupy our attention several times later on in this book, so we should get some basics out of the way early on. Data integrity, in its simplest terms, is preventing uncontrolled changes to occur to data. The types of changes we're talking about here are those which can result when more than one user attempts to change data at the same time. When this occurs, there is the probability that the changes will overlap or cancel each other out and the resulting data won't be what either user expected or wanted. Maintaining data integrity is the joint job of the network and the application. It is, often, the thorniest of all the sharing issues.

Within these contexts, LANs are the easiest way we know of to allow several users to move and share information. But, there is more. LANs also promote interconnection to outside services. This is a kind of hybrid of communicating and sharing in that both occur and the result is that outside resources become as much a part of the LAN environment as the applications running thereon.

A Means of Accessing More Information

There is a wealth of resources in the world of information management. In addition to the organization's own networks, there are vast databases of useful data available at the other end of a network gateway. Although individual users can often access this opulence, when it is brought into the group computing environment it gains new power. Often the data is located on a large computer somewhere within the organization itself. Sometimes it is public information, accessed through a public network. Sometimes it is an array of programming power on machines many times larger than the PCs on the LAN.

In any event, LANs have the unique ability to tap and store large amounts of information from external sources and make it available for sharing among the network's users. Through protocol-specific bridges, users can access mainframe applications and work with them as if they were mainframe terminals, then capture data, leave the mainframe and manipulate the data on their PCs. The advent of applications that can reside simultaneously on a LAN and a mainframe brings big machine power into the small machine environment.

Further, many applications currently on mainframes and minis can provide data that is more easily manipulated off line, on the network. Then, all of the network users can work with the same data without tying up the mainframe. Finally, it is certainly less expensive to allow several users to access a mainframe through a bridge on the LAN than with individual computers, each with its own connection.

A Means of Attaining Workgroup Synergy

With all of this wonderful communication, sharing and access to mountains of external information and services, you might think that LANs have at least one more benefit—promoting workgroup interaction. That turns out to be the case for a variety of reasons. First, when users can share the same data there exists a certainty that results will spring from a common point. The frustrations that go along with dealing with several sets of information (which one is correct today?) are simply not present on a LAN.

Second, there are a variety of communication tools, such as Electronic Mail, scheduling and calendaring, that help a workgroup function smoothly. Messages get passed quickly and easily without the need to locate the recipients. The computer becomes a real productivity tool instead of an expensive typewriter or calculator. But the productivity comes only in part from the computer. A lot of the increase is due to the forced (at first) interaction between workgroup members.

Another benefit of network computing is that data, kept in a common place, does not get lost or corrupted. Proper controls on network security will help insure that data is universally available to those who need it. Finally, most network applications will end up being reasonably consistent from user to user. On a LAN all users tend to use the same word processor or the same database program. The consistency results in improvements in user-proficiency since there is always plenty of experienced help around for the novice on any given program.

In short, LANs improve communication, data sharing, ability to access outside resources and workgroup cooperation. They generally are contained within a confined area such as a building and have a variety of ways of connecting to the outside world including other LANs.

What's *In* a LAN ?

Now that we know what a LAN *does*, let's find out what a LAN *is*. Although we'll go into this subject in depth in Chapter 3, we should get a general idea of the components that make up local area networks.

We'll start with a few definitions. LANs consist, in the simplest configurations, of one or more **file servers** and several **workstations** connected by cable and one or more printing devices. There are several different ways of connecting servers, workstations and printers depending upon how large the LAN is, how many users it has and with what it needs to interconnect.

A file server is, simply, a large, hard drive with some intelligence that allows it to operate the network. The server is, at once, a large filing cabinet and traffic cop. Files and applications reside on the server and the users at their workstations access them just as if they were on individual hard drives on stand-alone PCs. The only way a network user knows he or she is on the network is that there is a special log on procedure and some security present that would not usually be found on single-user machines.

Workstations can be of several types. They can be simple, floppy-drive-only PCs, more sophisticated ATs or the new breed of **diskless workstation**. Diskless workstations have the advantage that they usually are configured to be able to run larger programs (programs needing more memory). They have the disadvantage that they must be started (booted) from the server or from a special firmware program within them. They also tend to be a bit expensive.

Cable can be anything from telephone wire to coaxial cable to fiber optics. The choice of network configuration determines the type of cable you can use to hook up your system. Printers can be anything you would use as a stand-alone printer with the following caveat. Pick a printer that has some backbone. A wimpy printer simply won't stand up to the heavy usage that several network users will force upon it. Remember that a LAN is like a computer—with, perhaps, a hundred users. Pick robust hardware and software. If you don't, it won't stand up under the strain of heavy use.

Standards Make the LAN

Another way we can define what is in a LAN is to set some standards. We'll go into detail on standards in Chapter 4, but here are some thoughts to get you ready. Any LAN that doesn't meet at least some accepted standard is a recipe for trouble.

We have gone into a lot of detail on the subjects of communication and data sharing. LANs simply won't communicate and share if they don't adhere to a consistent set of standards. Fortunately, there are such standards. These standards define a bewildering array of network aspects. Let's start with physical standards.

Physical standards describe the network configuration or topology. There are such descriptive standards as star, ring and bus. Make sure that the LAN you choose adheres to a predefined physical standard. Novell allows you to mix various topologies and consistently follows popular standards for configuration and interconnection.

Electrical standards define the signals present on the LAN. You can have signals that range from fairly slow data rates to fiber optic transmission speeds. A subset of electrical standards is communication standards. Communication standards are defined in terms of protocols. Either stick to the same protocol throughout your LAN, or insure that you have made provision for the proper bridge. Bridges are always required if you wish to interconnect dissimilar protocols and **topologies**.

The key is that standards can be your best friends. If you are putting workstations on a Novell **Ethernet** bus, you know that any standard Ethernet bus card that is Novell-compatible will work out of the box. Since Novell no longer supplies hardware, this is very important. You will need to insure that your hardware meets the same standards as your Novell NetWare. Fortunately, NetWare itself has become a de facto standard throughout the network industry.

Summary

In this chapter we explored what a Novell LAN does and what it consists of. We saw that there are many benefits to be derived from LANs, many of which we will discuss in greater detail in Chapter 6.

We discussed the components of a LAN in the simplest terms and laid out the importance of standards. In the next chapter, we'll apply our general discussion of LANs to a more specific view of Novell NetWare including the various types of NetWare available, what each type is and does, and how they differ. We'll also touch on mixing the MS-DOS environment with the Apple Macintosh environment over a NetWare LAN.

2

Novell NetWare and Novell Networking

In this chapter we will examine local area networking in a bit more detail. Specifically, we will see the role that NetWare plays in our LAN. We will introduce some of the NetWare products and, finally, discuss using your Apple Macintosh in a NetWare LAN with PCs.

Before we get too deep into the specifics of Novell NetWare, however, we need a little general background on **network operating systems (NOSs)**. Although we will go into the NOS in greater detail in Chapter 4, at this point it's important to grasp a few basics.

The Network Operating System— Controlling Network Activity

When we are using a single-user PC we have no need of multiuser capabilities. Obviously, since only one person at a time is using our PC, we won't have any of the potential conflicts that require a sophisticated system of collision avoidance or security. Our DOS operating system is probably enough.

If we want to perform several functions on the PC at the same time, we have a need for a multitasking operating system. So, we might select an operating system such as OS/2. OS/2, unlike DOS, permits several tasks to operate at the same time. But, if we need the ability for several users to share the same information on several workstations tied together on a network, we need an operating system for the network.

Here's where things get a little more complex than in the single user computer, though. It is possible for us to have several operating systems on the same network at the same time because there are several computers in the network. These operating systems each have their place and the network operating system must be able to coexist with all of them.

Let's get these various operating systems into perspective. First, at the individual workstation we have the workstation's single-user operating system. That system could be, as in our examples above, DOS or OS/2, depending upon the computer being used as a workstation. The workstation operating system is at the heart of the computer. If you are not logged onto the LAN, your computer continues to function just as you would expect a stand-alone PC to function. But the moment you log onto the LAN, some new facets are added to your operating ability although you may not be aware of it.

The workstation's operating system doesn't go anywhere. It still functions just as it always did—controlling the activities of your workstation computer. After all, most of the application processing still takes place in your workstation's memory. In that regard there is no difference between your PC on or off the LAN. But the workstation must now recognize that the hard drives that contain the files it needs are no longer just local. In fact, in most cases, the workstation has its own local drives (except in the case of diskless workstations) and it has access to the various network drives. The DOS or OS/2 operating system on the workstation has no way of dealing with all of these drives.

The other thing the workstation has no way of dealing with is communication with other network users. So in order to "un-isolate" our workstation we need a second operating system at the network level for the workstation to talk to. That operating system is the NOS. The operating system itself resides on the network server and controls the network from there. The administrator or server operator communicates with the NOS directly using a keyboard and screen attached to the server called a console. An external computer on the network can also serve as a console if the administrator finds that more convenient.

The NOS has many functions besides controlling the network's activities. It must facilitate communications between the workstations and the server or servers, the workstations and each other; and it must interface with peripherals and peripheral software such as bridges and gateways. However, the NOS does not communicate directly with the workstation's operating system. It can't because the workstation operating system has no direct method of communicating with the network.

So we install a network interface card in each workstation and one in the server. The network interface cards are configured to conform to a particu-

Brady Books
15 Columbus Circle
New York, NY 10023

ATT: J. Padlad

lar physical and communications standard and we have a special software program that the workstation uses to communicate through the interface card with the NOS. We load this intermediate program as a memory resident application on the workstation when we log onto the network.

Many networks require several such programs, sometimes called **drivers**, to handle many of the network-workstation interactions. Some of these interactions are: message routing; operating system interface; address locating; and other network level functions. The problem with this approach is that these programs all take up space in the workstation's memory. That reduces the amount of space available for running large applications such as databases and today's word processors.

Novell has greatly reduced the number and size of the programs the workstation must retain in its memory in order to interact with the LAN. Novell, it turns out, is about the most memory efficient of all popular networks in terms of workstation memory usage.

Back to the NOS. The NOS has, as we said, several tasks. The first is to communicate with the workstations. Second, the NOS must control network security. It must be able to locate addresses on the network and issue requests to other networks for communications with their users' addresses. It must have a variety of network management tools for the network administrator. Finally, it must provide support for peripherals such as printers, bridges, gateways and other network devices.

The NOS resides on the server and communicates over the network with the adapter or interface cards in the workstations, which communicate through the workstation shell to the workstation's operating system. In Novell NetWare, the NetWare operating system communicates with the interface card which in turn communicates with the network Shell through IPX (NetWare's communications utility) to NET2, NET3 or NET4. The NET files provide direct interface with the workstation operating system. Which of the three you use depends upon which version of DOS your workstation uses. The NET file analyzes the workstation activity and decides whether it should be redirected to the LAN or kept for the workstation to process.

The memory-resident NET file, then, is really an internal workstation traffic cop, directing activity inward to the workstation or outward to the network. The IPX file is the specific means NetWare uses to achieve workstation to network communication. The whole thing looks like Figure 2-1.

Other Operating Systems for Other Workstations

We have discussed DOS as a workstation operating system, but there are at least two others with which we might be concerned. The first of these,

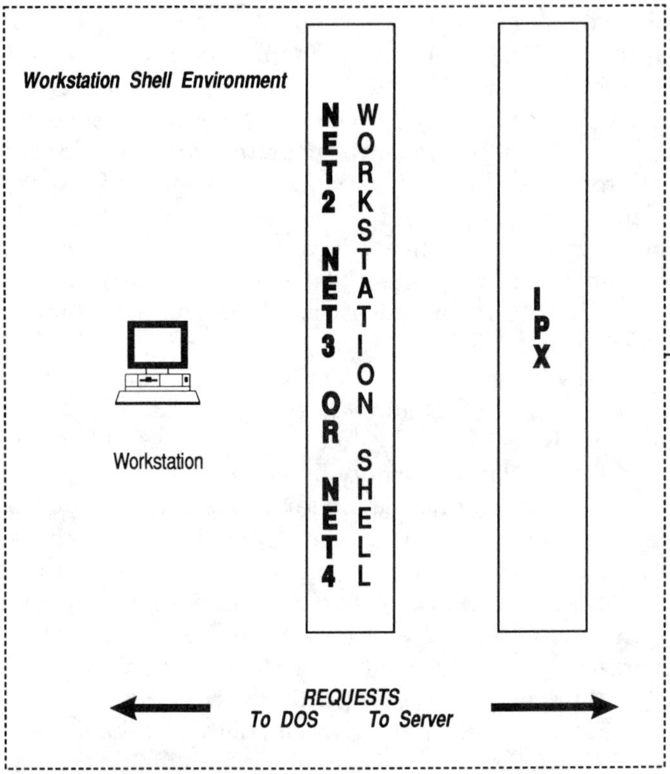

Figure 2-1   The Workstation Shell

which we touched upon, is OS/2. There is a simple method of dealing with different workstation operating systems on a Novell LAN. We simply use a different workstation shell. The special shell for OS/2 is called the NetWare Requester for OS/2. The Requester for OS/2 is a special version of NetWare which allows NetWare to function in an OS/2 environment. As you may have noticed, most local area networks today still operate in the DOS environment. Since OS/2 is a virtual necessity for many large applications, Novell has created the Requester to allow you to move into the next generation of operating systems. NetWare itself is not a **NetBIOS** operating system and, thus, is not of itself OS/2 compatible.

The second possibility is that you may wish to run Windows/386 on your workstation. In that case you will need another shell (the Windows/386 Shell) which is supplied with NetWare. Finally, you might want to add a Macintosh to your LAN. You can do that, too, but it's a bit more complex. We'll go into that in more detail at the end of this chapter.

Occasionally, you'll run into an application that was designed specifically to run on an IBM PC Network. These applications require a special BIOS (Basic Input/Output System) for LANs called NetBIOS. NetWare includes a NetBIOS emulator for your workstation that will allow you to run these programs.

The Physical Structure of the Network

The NetWare network is organized like any other network in many respects. In fact, there are a number of surface similarities between the way the LAN server is organized and the way your individual PC is organized. Both consist, fundamentally, of an operating system, an I/O (Input/Output) system and disk drives with directories and files for data.

We have discussed the operating system and we really have no need to get too involved with the I/O. But, we must understand how information is stored and organized on the server. Some of the terms we will use come from the mainframe world. Most come from the realm of personal computing. The first level of mass storage (hard disk drives) is the physical disk drive itself. A hard disk drive on a network server is far larger than any single file or directory could ever use on a stand-alone PC. We make it that large for a very good reason. We are going to subdivide this very large (300 MB and larger in most cases) drive into several smaller logical drives called volumes.

To understand volumes (a term from mainframes) we can take a simple example from your PC. Let's say that you have a 40 MB fixed drive on your AT. You divide that drive into a C: drive and a D: drive. You have created two logical drives or volumes on your PC. Simply, a volume is a logical drive—a portion of a physical drive.

We do the same thing with our network drive. We subdivide a very large drive into a large number of volumes. Each volume can be any size we want. The various volumes can be public or private. We decide which volumes are public and which are private based largely on what our needs as network administrator are. We may want to keep the volume that contains NOS files private for example.

On each volume, we create directories with their individual subdirectories. Those directories and subdirectories contain the various files we'll use on the LAN. Here's where it gets a bit complicated though. In order to simplify operating and improve network security, Novell allows us to treat directories as if they were drives. We call this process **mapping**. We can map a directory to a drive using the MAP command (part of the NOS support). Now our directory no longer has a directory name. It has, instead, a drive designation. Users don't have direct access the physical drive or logical volumes on the network by name. Instead, they have access to the mapped drives.

Here's an example of how mapping works. Suppose your network administrator puts a copy of WordPerfect in the WP directory on the H: volume. On your PC, if you were using WordPerfect from your own hard disk as a stand-alone computer, you might type CD H:\editors\wp (if you had an H: drive) to get to the program. That says that you have put the program in the WP subdirectory of the EDITORS directory on the H: drive. Then you would type WP to start it. On the Novell LAN it's much easier than that. You map the directory (using the MAP command) to any drive you wish—let's say your E: drive—and then when you switch to the E:\ drive you are really in the subdirectory containing WordPerfect.

The beauty of this is that if you don't use WordPerfect very often, you can unmap it (using the MAP DEL or MAP REM command) from the E:\ drive and use E:\ for something else. Unlike physical drives, mapped drives don't need to run out of space. When you see that the E:\ drive is filling up, you unmap something and free up space. You don't need to uninstall or unload the programs you unmapped, either. They are still installed on the logical volume. They don't need reinstalling, just remapping with a single command. We will discuss the MAP command along with the other NetWare commands in Chapter 7.

Getting Down to Details—Novell NetWare

We have touched upon the tasks that NetWare carries out on the LAN. Now let's go into a bit more detail. NetWare, as we have said, is an advanced network operating system. By that we mean that the operating system for the network server and the workstations and services it supports is NetWare in the same way that the operating system for your PC is MS-DOS or OS/2.

Your DOS workstation's operating system provides you with a number of services, though you may not think of them that way. Some of those services are copying files, making and deleting directories and subdirectories, deleting and renaming files, communicating with COM and printer ports and many other functions you probably use on a day-to-day basis.

The network operating system, in this case NetWare, provides many of those same services plus a great many more that are unique to LANs. In broad terms here are some of the things NetWare does for the network:

- Manages the network's multiuser file structure
- Controls data movement on the network
- Dictates communication both within and into and out of the network
- Keeps track of user addresses
- Keeps track of file locations within the network file structure
- Manages peripherals such as printers, bridges and gateways
- Controls user security
- Keeps track of user activity and produces accounting records
- Provides utilities to help the Administrator manage the network
- Manages special attached programs called VAPs (Value Added Processes)
- Provides fault tolerance to protect against data loss
- Provides server memory and cache management
- Manages command line utilities

These are a few of the specific functions of a NetWare network operating system. As you can see, NetWare provides services to the network in much the same way your PC's DOS operating system provides them to your single user computer. The only difference is that the network requires services that are a great deal more sophisticated than your single-user PC.

The Different Types of NetWare—Building from the Ground Up

The best way to understand the specific capabilities of a Novell LAN is to examine each NetWare product in some depth. Since there are several levels of NetWare, from the simplest ELS system to the most complex SFT LAN with bridges and gateways, if we start out by describing the individual capabilities of these products you'll not only gain some insight into NetWare, you'll also get some idea of which level of NetWare might be appropriate to your application. We'll start with the ELS products.

ELS NetWare—The Entry Level System

ELS NetWare stands for Entry Level System. In Novell terminology, the entry level system refers to not only a particular product, but also a philosophy. Entry Level Systems are designed to support smaller numbers of users; be simple to install; and be upgradable to larger NetWare LANs when the user is ready for more power. ELS comes in two versions—Level I and Level II. There are quite a few differences between the two besides price, but the most significant is the number of users permitted. Level I comes configured for up to four users and Level II comes configured for up to eight. Some other differences are the additional services available, the ability to support the Macintosh; additional bundled software; and other features. Basically the differences boil down to the following:

	Level I	Level II
Maximum Users	4	8
Supports Windows/386		X
Supports OS/2		X
Topologies Supported	3	12
Additional LAN Drivers		X
Internetworking		X
Password Encryption		X
Resource Accounting		X
Enhanced Security		X
Supports Macintosh		X (ver 2.15)
Diagnostics and network management		X
NetBIOS across bridges		X

As you can see, there are some serious differences between the two products. However, it is possible to start with ELS I and advance through upgrades all the way to Novell's most advanced product, SFT NetWare. You should start with ELS NetWare if you have a small office, professional group or other workgroup with eight or fewer members. There are significant reasons to network, even if you don't have a very large group of users. We will discuss many of those reasons in Chapter 6.

The file server requirements for a Level I system are 640K of base memory plus 512K of extended memory. An 80286 class AT with either an Ethernet, RX-Net or Arcnet interface card is also required. But installing ELS I is extremely easy since it comes preconfigured for four users, one internal fixed drive and one spooled printer. With utility programs supplied, you can upgrade your ELS I system to handle up to five printers and an additional hard drive. Both AT bus and micro channel (PS/2) bus machines are supported.

Now we come to a useful feature of ELS I NetWare. Although we haven't discussed it yet, there are two basic LAN configurations. We can set up our server as dedicated or nondedicated. What this means is simply that in a dedicated server LAN, the server must function as a server and nothing else. Thus, if we were to make our ELS I system a dedicated server system, we could really only have three users plus the server.

Fortunately, there is also a configuration referred to as nondedicated. This means that you can use the server both as a network server and as a user workstation. ELS I allows such configurations. There is another bonus with ELS I. You can have more than four users for the system. You just can't have more than four on at any given time. So, if you are running multiple workshifts, where shift workers share workstations, you could have three shifts of four users, or twelve users with network accounts since only four would be working at any one time.

ELS II has all of the features of ELS I plus the additional features we enumerated above. Unlike Level I, the Level II server can be either dedicated or nondedicated. Level II also allows older 8086 machines to be used as file servers. These older machines must, however, be dedicated servers. Nondedicated servers must be 80286 or 80386 class computers.

Selecting ELS NetWare as Your LAN Operating System

Under what conditions would you select the Entry Level Systems as you LAN of choice? First, if you have a small workgroup that will never grow beyond the number of users the LAN can support, the choice is an obvious one. Actually, the question at that point comes down to whether you need a LAN at all. We'll take a moment out here and discuss that point a bit.

There are a lot of good reasons for networking. But don't let the LAN salesperson talk you into something you really don't need. Here are some of the reasons for networking a very small workgroup.

- All members of the workgroup use the same software applications
- All members of the workgroup need to share common data
- You need to keep hardware costs down
- You want to centralize control of workgroup computing

Let's explore those four reasons. First, if all members of the workgroup use the same software applications, such as a single type of word processor in a typing pool or small legal office, you will save money by buying one network version instead of four single-user versions of software.

If you have a small workgroup that needs to share data, such as a large database or an accounting office that shares accounting files, you can benefit substantially by having common access to one set of data at a single source. There are a lot of technical reasons for this, but, for the moment, take our word that it's a fact. If you want more information now, refer to Chapter 6.

If keeping hardware costs down is a serious consideration, there are two big ways to save hardware dollars, even on a small LAN. First, you will need only one 286 or 386 hard disk computer for the server. All the workstations need only be single floppy PCs. These cost about half what a serious AT costs. Second, you can have all the users on the LAN sharing the same printer. This is far less expensive than a printer for each user.

Finally, if you need to centralize your workgroup computing for security, management or any other reason, the only way to do so is to use a LAN with the proper security and management tools built in. All of these reasons are significant when you are asking whether your workgroup should network, regardless of size. There are a couple of reasons which your LAN salesperson would have you believe that simply are not universally true.

One is the "databases work better" myth. Unless you are using a database product optimized for LANs that is absolutely not true. In fact, most database products actually perform worse on LANs. There are a lot of reasons for this and we've discussed most of them in Chapter 9.

The next reason is the speed myth. This myth says that, since the file server is a fast, high-performance machine, you'll get better performance than with your older, stand-alone PCs. The fact is that the server has little to do with performance on the LAN except as it specifically relates to disk I/O. If the bus speed on the workstations is 4.7MHz, even a 33MHZ server won't improve that user's performance. The processing still takes place at the workstation. With LANs the size of ELS networks, you'll never benefit by a fast server unless you also have fast workstations.

The plain facts are that a LAN won't solve your problems at this level. They only give you the tools to solve them yourself. If that's what you need, go get a Novell ELS LAN. You'll benefit a lot. But, if you and your staff have sloppy work habits, use vastly different products for the same applications, don't share any data in common and are dedicated to autonomous anarchy, save your money. The LAN will just frustrate you. Because, you see, LANs impose order on chaos, controls on independence, and make computing anarchy virtually impossible. You'll find that this is most especially true at the level where an ELS network is most likely to be useful.

Having said all that, we most heartily recommend that if any of the four reasons for networking we posed earlier apply to you, you consider strongly the benefits of networking with an ELS LAN. ELS LANs are perfectly suited to the user group that is small but efficient. They give the small office access to vast amounts of storage, common data, similar applications and workgroup efficiency that comes in no other way. But, at first, you'll need to work at it. Networking is a different way of computing life for most small organizations.

More ELS Details

ELS is completely upgradable to the larger NetWare installations. This means that from the beginning you'll be working with a real Novell NetWare operating system. This is a system that has proven itself with over two million users worldwide over the years. There is almost no standard PC hardware or software that won't run on NetWare. In fact, most developers test their multiuser products on NetWare prior to introduction making it a de facto standard for the PC industry.

Both Level I and Level II ELS NetWare have basic **fault tolerance**. That means that the network takes care of preserving data in the event of certain catastrophes. Although this capability is not as sophisticated as in Novell's most advanced product, SFT NetWare, it is the same as that found in the next step below, Advanced NetWare.

The fault tolerance function found at this level is safe storage of data in the event of a defect in the hard disk. It accomplishes this by using what is known as a hot fix. When data is written to the hard drive, the operating system attempts to read it immediately. If it finds a bad spot on the drive, it relocates the data to the hot fix area of the disk where it can be written safely. The bad area is then marked so that no further attempts will be made to use it.

ELS also duplicates the directory and FAT areas of the hard drive and checks these areas on powerup. If it finds an error in the FAT (File Allocation Table) or directory, it switches automatically to the backup file.

Another unique benefit of ELS II and higher is the **Value Added Process** or VAP. In simple terms, a VAP is an application, such as a database program, that has been written specifically for use with NetWare. The application has 'hooks' that connect directly to the NetWare operating system. Although VAPs appear on the surface to be for programmers, applications written for VAPs are, most definitely, for users of NetWare. Without going into the details of how VAPs work, we can simply say that applications written for VAPs run more smoothly, more reliably and faster than stand-alone applications simply because VAP applications are tied directly to the network operating system. VAPs act, in some respects, like users. They take advantage of some of the special **network services**, especially when they communicate with the network server or users. There is bad news, though. For ELS users the number of user positions taken up by a

VAP can materially reduce the number of users on your small network. For example, if you use the Btrieve VAP, you'll eliminate four potential users on an ELS II LAN. Every benefit has its price.

Advanced Netware—A Serious Local Area Network

If you're ready for a serious LAN that can support up to 100 simultaneous log ons, you're ready for **Advanced NetWare**. Advanced NetWare is the first of two levels of network operating systems, the top of the line being **SFT NetWare**. Advanced NetWare adds more than just more users, though. The whole networking scheme opens up to allow a vast array of network services and interfaces.

For example, Advanced NetWare offers both dedicated and nondedicated DOS servers as well as nondedicated OS/2 operation. It offers up to 32 different possible topologies of which 12 are standard. Unlike ELS, Advanced NetWare provides support for MHS (Message Handling Service) which replaces older E-Mail systems that were present in versions prior to 2.11. All external bridge software comes bundled with Advanced NetWare as does full support for VAPs, VADDs (Value Added Disk Drivers), diagnostic and management tools, and resource accounting tools. In short, the only real difference between Advanced NetWare and top-of-the-line SFT NetWare is the way SFT NetWare handles fault tolerance.

And Now, The Details

First, let's decide who needs Advanced NetWare. Potential users will fall into two categories. The first, and most obvious, category is the ELS II user who is starting to outgrow the ELS network. The first sign of that is the need for more simultaneous log ons than ELS can support. But there are some clues that you're heading for Advanced NetWare long before you get to eight ELS users. If you are beginning to see logjams at the network drives due to heavy use of disk-bound programs such as databases, it may be time to consider a bit more horsepower in your LAN. If network printers are getting too much use, the same may be true. Most important, if you need to do sophisticated internetworking it's time to move up to a bigger system. Even though ELS II has limited support for asynchronous internetworking, you take up a workstation as a bridge and the kinds of internetworking you can do are extremely limited.

The second potential Advanced NetWare user is the mid- to large-sized organization which needs more than eight stations from day one. In this case, the choice is obvious. You'll either want Advanced NetWare or SFT NetWare. We'll show you the difference later in this chapter.

One of the additional capabilities you'll find in Advanced NetWare over ELS NetWare is a suite of file and disk management capabilities that enhance efficiency when working with large applications such as databases. One of the most useful of these is indexed file allocation tables. By using indexed FATs some large database functions can be cut to as much as 25% of their original time to complete.

The most needed features in Advanced NetWare fall into the area of supervisor utilities. Managing a large LAN requires significant administrator tools and Advanced NetWare has a good selection. Especially welcome are the diagnostic functions and the ability for the supervisor to turn on and off the specific functions available in Advanced NetWare to suit the requirements of the individual installation.

Advanced NetWare allows a variety of add-on LAN drivers and supports NetBIOS across bridges. This brings up another of the real strengths of this level of Novell NOS. Internetworking is heavily supported with bundled bridging software. This support extends to LAN-to-LAN, LAN-to-Host, asynchronous bridges and gateways, TCP/IP gateways, X.25 remote bridges, remote PC to LAN and a full complement of IBM SNA connectivity. If you need to internetwork, you will need Advanced NetWare.

With all of these enhancements you might expect some performance degradation. However, that is not the case. In fact, the Advanced NetWare system outperforms the ELS systems in every respect. Workstation overhead is not significantly affected either.

Another convenience present in Advanced NetWare is field serialization for upgrades. Now, when you upgrade from ELS or an older Advanced NetWare system you simply use the NETGEN utility and your new installation is compatible with resources on the earlier one.

Perhaps the most important aspect of Advanced NetWare from the corporate standpoint is its enhanced security. An extremely wide variety of administrator security tools is part of the Advanced NetWare package. Some of these tools not only allow the administrator to place limits on the users of network resources, data and applications, they also allow limits to be placed on how long users can stay logged on to the LAN, when they can log on, how many users can access an application at one time, and how many users can log on at any given time.

Some of the other security features of Advanced NetWare are the ability of the supervisor to control the user accounts, their expiration dates, and passwords. Users can be restricted to specific workstations and limits can be placed on the amount of network resource, such as disk space, available to them.

In addition, passwords are encrypted so that the likelihood of password compromise is slim, indeed. NetWare also makes automatic security checks every half hour to validate the users on the LAN. If the system finds unauthorized users, a five-minute warning is issued after which the user is logged off the network. This is useful when users are being charged for use of network resources and their credit has expired or the user's account has been disabled for any reason.

Administrators also have access to tools such as the SECURITY command that assist in security audits. Workstation clocks are synchronized with the file server to insure that users don't alter workstation time to allow increased logon periods. Of course, there are the usual rights—granting and revoking commands for determining trustee rights and security levels required for access to files and applications.

There are also extensive resource accounting features available in Advanced NetWare. These features provide a complete audit trail of users on the LAN, the applications and data they use and how long they spend in various network areas. The next step of the resource-accounting function allows administrators to charge users for accessing network services and resources. There is a wide variety of charge options from disk space used to length of time logged on to a given application.

Administrator Tools

As we said earlier, administrator tools are among the key benefits you'll receive from Advanced NetWare. One of the most useful of these is the FCONSOLE virtual console utility. As you will see as we describe NetWare in more technical detail, the administrator does most of his or her work from a keyboard referred to as the **system console**. Usually the console is the server itself. But, if the administrator is located at some distance from the server location, it may be inconvenient to go back and forth to the console device every time service or administrative duties require.

The answer is the **virtual console utility**. With FCONSOLE the administrator can access the system console from any network workstation. Administrators on Advanced NetWare systems can control the file server, including shutting it down if necessary; broadcast messages to users; monitor a variety of server, drive, file and user data; and manage certain levels of security functions—all from any workstation on the network.

In addition, from the network console, administrators can maintain the **bindery** (a database, available only to administrators, that lists information about users, resources, charge rates and file servers), analyze drive problems and repair them and modify disk information. They can manage files, create and delete users, repair corrupted file systems, modify security parameters and enable resource accounting.

VAPs on Advanced NetWare

We touched on VAPs earlier in this chapter since VAPs are available to a limited degree on ELS II. But on larger systems, such as Advanced NetWare, VAPs can be a significant plus in terms of application performance. To review, briefly, a VAP is a Value Added Process. When we consider VAPs we must also consider APIs. An API is an application programming interface. What this means is that 'hooks' into the NOS are provided for programmers who wish to design applications that work with the network directly.

When a programmer designs an application for connection to an API, he or she bypasses the usual steps the application goes through as it executes and communicates with the network. That's the key, by the way. The way an application communicates with the network determines the performance and efficiency of the application in the network environment.

If there is no direct network connection, the application communicates using the usual calls to the NOS. It takes advantage of the NOS services such as file and record locking and it lets the NOS do the communicating for it. Thus, if a user wants to access the application, it is, as you might expect, a somewhat complex series of communications interactions between the user, the NOS and the application.

If, on the other hand, the application is connected directly to the NOS, a lot of that communication is biased. The application deals directly with network services instead of issuing requests to the NOS for operating system execution. When a developer writes an application which connects to a NetWare API, the application is called a Value Added Process or VAP. If the Application is a special disk driver, it is called, not surprisingly, a **Value Added Disk Driver** or **VADD**. VADDs allow special drivers for fixed drives to connect directly to the NOS without going through the usual I/O routines. This has the dual advantage of speeding up user access to network drives and reducing the I/O load on the server by allowing direct control of the fixed disks.

Going yet a bit deeper into VAPs, one of the big advantages is the ability of network servers on one LAN to use IPX (Internetwork Packet Exchange—the NetWare method of internetwork communication) to provide services and applications across internet bridges. Virtually any type of application from large scale systems like the Btrieve database management system to file and memory management utilities.

The main thing to remember about VAPs, VADDs and APIs is that they allow applications, utilities and drivers to run as if they were actually part of the network operating system instead of applications approaching the NOS externally and requesting services over the LAN.

The final big bonus in Advanced NetWare is the HELP system. Virtually all of the NetWare manuals have been placed into the HELP files and are, essentially, on-line manuals for access by any user on the network. As to other performance features of Advanced NetWare, you will be able to take advantage of fixed drives larger that 256MB and PS/2 computers as both workstations and servers. Advanced NetWare supports embedded SCSI drives and is completely Ethernet-compatible. All in all, Advanced NetWare has everything a serious LAN needs except fully redundant fault tolerance. And SFT NetWare has that.

SFT NetWare—The Top of the Line

If you're looking for the best available LAN operating system, you'll end up eventually with SFT NetWare. SFT is identical in most respects to Advanced NetWare with a few enhancements in the area of fault tolerance. So, before we go into how SFT keeps your data safe from catastrophe, let's explore some of the concepts of a fault tolerant system.

Why do we need fault tolerance? There are some areas of hard disk and data management that are very sensitive to failures in certain hardware components of a local area network—and, it turns out, there are several types of rather common failures that can jeopardize that data. The most sensitive parts of the fixed disk are the file allocation tables (FATs) and the directories.

Loss of or damage to either of those areas can make it difficult if not impossible to recover data stored elsewhere on the drive. When you add a file to a hard disk the operating system makes entries in the FAT and the directory so that it can find your file again when you ask for it. In addition, FAT entries are made for database files to help the system and the application locate records in the data files. So, if either the directory or the FAT gets damaged you simply won't be able to get at your data, even if it is undamaged.

Further, every time you modify existing data on your hard drive, the operating system makes changes in both the directory and the FAT. These changes require that the operating system rewrite the entire FAT and directory files. If you experience a failure during this process you can lose data or scramble your basic disk information to the point that the data on the drive can't be recovered. The types of failures that generally cause these data losses are power related. They can be power spikes, sags and surges, or loss of power altogether.

A second type of potential data-loss directly affects the data instead of the FAT or directory. This type of loss occurs primarily in databases when a transaction (file update) is interrupted in the middle by a hardware failure. If a software failure occurs, these applications usually have a mechanism to deal with the interruption. But, in an unplanned hardware failure the application usually has trouble defending against data loss.

All of these failure types or modes as they are sometimes called, can affect data, hard disk file and directory management, and network management as well since much network information is kept in data files such as the bindery. Fortunately, there are solid defenses against such data losses in SFT NetWare.

Guarding Against Data Loss

Let's start with the first line of defense against the most common type of failure—power loss. The best way to protect against power loss is to isolate the LAN from the power that could be lost. The most important LAN component, of course, is the server—and the way to isolate it is with an uninterruptable power supply (UPS). A UPS is a device that plugs into the primary power and into which, in turn, you plug the computer you wish to protect. In a large network installation, there is no excuse for not installing a UPS. If you have a LAN the size of most Advanced NetWare installations, you have enough data stored to cause you a lot of trouble if you have to rebuild a damaged drive. The term "rebuild" here refers primarily to recreating the data on the drive from scratch.

What that means is, invariably, low-level formatting the drive, reformatting it for the operating system, reinstalling the LAN operating software, and restoring the data and applications from the most recent backup. Depending upon the size of the network, this process may take anything from hours to days to complete. In addition, you will never recover all of your data since the most recent backup was invariably created hours or days earlier.

So, the first level of defense is the UPS. In order for the UPS to be effective it must communicate directly with the LAN. Here's why. A UPS is, basically, a heavy duty battery with some circuitry attached that senses a pending failure. When a failure is about to occur, the UPS switches off of the AC power line and uses the batteries to power whatever is connected to it (the server in this case). Obviously, if the power stays off long enough the batteries will drain and data will be lost anyway. So a good UPS/LAN combination should recognize that primary power has been lost, make the switch, and then get the network shut down in as orderly and undisruptive a manner as possible.

The next level of defense is to make sure that FAT and directory entries can't be completely lost. Now we get into another possible area of data loss, the disk itself. A fixed drive is made up of platters coated with a metallic substance. It looks a bit like several floppy disks, without their envelopes, stacked one on the other with a set of heads for reading and writing on each one. These disks spin at very high speeds and, occasionally, get small bits of surface damage due to rough handling, dirt or other physical contact with the heads (which does not occur under normal use).

Also, there can be small manufacturing flaws in the surface coating of the platter. Any of these defects can result in a bad spot on the disk where data can't be written. When you first format the disk, most operating systems allow you to mark the bad sectors and keep track of them in what is called a bad track table on the disk. But, if you miss one, get a new one, or have a marginal one that turns bad after you format, it won't appear in the bad track table. So, you might try to write to that sector and, as a result, lose or corrupt data. A good fault-tolerant system will monitor this and take appropriate measures.

Finally, you can actually lose data as you write it to the disk or you can experience a total disk failure or disk crash. In this case, all bets are off. All your data is gone. The FAT and directories are worthless. You may be able to rebuild the disk or the hardware itself may be damaged beyond repair. The last line of defense in this case is the backup. But backups, as we mentioned earlier, never occur just prior to a failure, so you have anywhere from a few hours to who-knows-how-much unbacked-up work which you will have to recreate. What we need is a constant backup in process every time we write data to our drive. That type of backup is called **hard disk redundancy** or **drive mirroring**. Figure 2-2 shows the various ways to protect against data loss on your LAN:

PROBLEM	SOLUTION
Power Loss	UPS
Loss of FAT and Directory	UPS and Disk Mirroring
Disk Crash	Disk Mirroring and Backup

Figure 2-2   Preventative Medicine for Data Loss

The SFT NetWare Solution to Disaster Control

Let's start with the UPS problem. SFT monitors the UPS and, in the event that the UPS takes over power on the LAN, starts an orderly shutdown of the network. This preserves all data and allows users to close their applications before the UPS batteries fail. All of this activity, as with all SFT fault tolerance, is automatic and transparent to the network users.

The next level, protection against damage to FATs and directories, is solved by keeping duplicates of both the FATs and the directories and updating them simultaneously. In addition, the operating system performs a check for consistency on the directories and file allocation table on powerup.

To protect against attempted writes to damaged disk sectors, SFT performs a read-after-write test. If an error is found, the data is written to a hot-fix area on the drive and the operating system adds the damaged sector to the bad sector table. These functions are present in what Novell calls Level I Fault Tolerance. Level I is present in ELS and Advanced NetWare as well as SFT NetWare. However, SFT has a few more features that add to Level I, bringing it up to Level II and protecting against data loss from virtually any cause.

We described a type of data loss, peculiar to database files, that occurs when a file or record is updating during a hardware failure. We told you that most applications have trouble dealing with this type of failure on a LAN, so, SFT adds a feature called the **Transaction Tracking System** or TTS. The TTS keeps track of information involved in a database update and, in the event of a hardware failure, allows the database to either **roll back** (abandon) or **roll forward** (complete) the transaction.

TTS does not require that an application be written to take advantage of its capabilities. It can operate either in the explicit mode (the application is designed to flag TTS at the start or end of the transaction) or in the implicit mode (it senses normal record locking and implies the beginning and ending of a transaction). Here's how these two approaches work:

In the explicit mode of operation, the operating system must be told that TTS is in operation. When the application developer writes the application to be protected under TTS, he or she sets flags at the beginning and end of each database transaction. TTS senses those flags and does its work.

In the implicit mode of operation, the application does not need to be written for TTS. All network-aware database applications perform what is called record-and-file-locking during certain types of transactions. Record-locking occurs when a user is performing a write to a single record in the database. That record is locked so that another user cannot access the same record at the same time. When the first user is finished with the record, the application removes the lock and the record is available again for other users. File-locking accomplishes the same thing during database operations that involve writes to an entire file of database records. In the implicit mode, TTS senses these locks and unlocks and performs its duties accordingly.

What all of this locking and unlocking, rolling back and rolling forward amounts to is NetWare's ability to sense that a database transaction is or is not complete. It allows the data to be written to the database in final form only if the transaction is complete and the data is good. Because of this, the likelihood of losing or scrambling data because of a hardware failure is minimized.

The final line of defense we discussed required disk mirroring. SFT supports full disk mirroring. Now, of course, this means you need a duplicate fixed drive since disk mirroring requires that you constantly back up one drive onto another, separate, drive. In addition, all of the other SFT fault tolerant functions are carried out on both drives. The operating system senses if a failure has occurred on the primary disk and automatically switches to the backup (mirror) drive.

SFT lets you go one step further, though. Not only does the system provide for disk mirroring, but you can create **complete network redundancy** with duplicated controllers, drivers, interfaces and power supplies. In short, SFT NetWare allows you to have two complete, identical systems, constantly kept updated and in synch with each other, and ready to switch automatically when a failure occurs. No data will be lost and operation will continue as if no failure had occurred. In fact, we know of at least one installation where every hardware and software element of the network has an automatic mirror. Although this is a fairly expensive solution, data loss is virtually impossible, and users of installations of this type have determined that any loss of data or operating time would be far more expensive than the cost of redundancy throughout the network.

SFT NetWare requires at least an 80286 class machine for a server with a minimum of 2MB of memory. It supports up to 100 concurrent logons, 32 volumes of 256MB each per server, 12MB of memory and 2GB of disk storage.

Using Your Macintosh on a Novell LAN

Corporate users are discovering that the Apple Macintosh can be a serious business computer, especially in some applications for which there are excellent software offerings unique to the Mac. However, the Macintosh operating system is foreign to the DOS or OS/2 operating systems which make up the IBM world. Of course, NetWare was designed specifically for that DOS or OS/2 environment. So, how do you use your Macintosh in an IBM environment on a LAN that was created specifically to serve that environment? The answer, if the LAN is a NetWare LAN, is very easily.

In all NetWare systems except ELS Level I you can add the Macintosh as an option if the NetWare release level is 2.15 or higher. There are three issues involved in connecting a Mac to a PC LAN. Those issues are file system differences, native networking architecture, and network communications protocols.

The file structure issue is the first barrier to integration. PCs use eleven character filenames while the Mac allows 32 character names. The Mac also uses a very different method of storing data. Apple's network architecture is AppleTalk, a system integrated completely into all Macintosh computers. PC LANs use a set of network protocols that vary significantly from AppleTalk. Such protocols are by no means integrated into the PCs they support.

Novell subverts these barriers using what they refer to as an **open protocol technology**. Open protocol technology actually combines the two dissimilar protocols into a third, common environment. Before we imply that a new protocol is being created, let us reemphasize that we are referring to a new environment. In this regard, what we really have is a system similar to a bridge or gateway between two dissimilar systems.

This allows the Mac to operate in its native mode and the PC LAN to continue to operate in its native mode. Novell accomplishes this with their **Service Protocol Gateway**. The SPG provides a direct connection and translation between the NetWare services and the requirements of both NetWare and the Mac. In other words, the Mac's operating system and the PC LAN workstation's operating system both address the NetWare services on the server. The PC workstation does this the way it always does, using the NetWare Shell and IPX. The Mac does it through the Service Protocol Gateway. Behind the NetWare operating system on the server is a universal file system that can respond to both the needs of the Mac and the needs of the PC.

To accomplish all of this, Novell added to NetWare the protocols required to communicate directly with AppleShare. Next they modified the file system to accommodate the Apple file structure.

Remember that the purpose of the server is to provide an electronic file cabinet for data and manage the network. Since file and application processing takes place at the workstation, what must be present for the system to work is a way to get at the files on the server. What that boils down to is network communications protocol and file management. Once a system is in place to move both kinds of files conveniently and to allow the different protocols to communicate with each other, the basic hurdles are overcome. Of course, the Macintosh environment at the workstation level is preserved.

When you connect Macintosh computers to a Novell LAN you are, basically, adding an AppleTalk sub LAN to your network. You can do this either of two ways. The easiest is to put the NetWare for Macintosh software in the NetWare server that supports the PCs on the LAN. Alternatively, you can put Ethernet adapter cards into the Macs and mix them on the PC LAN with PCs containing Ethernet interface cards.

In either case you will have a fully integrated PC/Macintosh environment with all of the network services of the PC NetWare LAN available. That includes fault tolerance, the ability to internetwork with bridges and gateways even to the point of bridging between a full PC NetWare LAN and a full AppleTalk network. What that means is the ability to mix AppleTalk and NetWare servers and services. When you opt for the Ethernet solution, you will actually be using an Apple protocol called EtherTalk on the Macs. EtherTalk is a full Ethernet 802.3 (the Ethernet standard) implementation. The NetWare driver for the NetWare for Macintosh is compatible with both. Finally, a printer sharing across the two environments is completely transparent.

Summary

In this chapter we have broadened our discussions of generic local area networks to include the specifics of Novell NetWare. We explored the various levels of NetWare and pointed out their differences and individual benefits. We discussed when you might select one level of NetWare over another and we got into some detail on the whys and wherefores of fault tolerant systems. We concluded with a brief discussion of adding a Macintosh or AppleTalk subLAN to your NetWare PC LAN.

In the next chapter we will describe the specific components of a Novell LAN in detail and show you the beginnings of designing and installing your LAN.

3

The Sum of Its Parts: The Components of a Novell LAN

As you know by now, a Novell LAN, in essence, is a hard disk shared by several computers. For the sharing to be accomplished, there are a variety of components that form the physical network, and software that allows these components to be tied together into a network.

Novell networks are based on a central server design. That is, there is a computer somewhere in the network that contains the hard disk that is being shared by the other computers in the network. This central computer is called the file server, and this is where the Novell NetWare operating system resides. Connecting the server to the workstation computers is a cable, and each workstation computer contains a network interface card.

In addition to the workstations and the file server, a Novell network may contain other devices, including communications servers and gateways, printer and facsimile servers, and additional file servers. These devices are attached to the network so that all of the network users can have access to them.

The File Server

This is the central point of the network. In most networks, it is the reason the network exists at all, and in the case of all Novell networks, it is the source of control for network operations. Normally, the file server is an IBM-PC/AT or IBM-PS/2 compatible computer. A few Novell networks use a VAX minicomputer from Digital Equipment Corporation. With the advent of Portable NetWare, virtually any computer from Unix-based super microcomputers to IBM mainframes will be able to act as a file server.

Because the file server is intended as an area for centralized storage, it normally has at least one large hard disk. This hard disk supports the NetWare operating system, and provides space for storing files that need sharing. Normally, this disk space also supports an electronic mail system.

Strictly speaking, a Novell file server does not need a disk that is particularly large. There are file servers in existence with disks as small as 20 megabytes. A disk this small offers little space for sharing, however. Few Novell networks have hard disks on the server with a capacity of less than 60 megabytes, and the current trend is to move to even larger disks.

In any case, the file server's hard disk is probably its single most important component. More than anything else, it is the disk's speed that determines the speed of the file server. A relatively slow computer with a large fast hard disk will make a better file server than a fast computer with an ordinary hard disk. This is because relatively little of the computer's power is used for most operations, but the hard disk is used for nearly everything.

When selecting the hard disk for use in a file server, you're better off concentrating on getting the most disk you can afford. Even if you have to buy a little less capability in the computer, it's more cost-effective to put your resources into the hard disk. This is partly because of the disk's impact on performance, and partly because computers will continue to get faster and cheaper. If you get to the point where the computer's capacity is slowing down the network, one with more capacity will certainly cost less than it originally would have. Once you buy it, all you have to do is swap the hard disk, and you're ready to run.

While nearly any hard disk will work with Novell NetWare, you'll get better performance with disks designed for this use. A number of manufacturers, including Maximum Storage, Priam, and Seagate sell hard disks that have been certified by Novell for use with NetWare. Following are some items to keep in mind when deciding on the disk you want for your file server.

- Disk speed—Look for an average access time of 28 milliseconds or less. Most large disks are much faster than this, but you should make sure. A slow access time will make your network operate more slowly.

- Disk controller—NetWare will use standard PC/AT style disks running on a standard controller. You'll get higher speed, though, with SCSI or EDSI interfaces. They transfer data faster, and, therefore, allow the network to operate faster.
- Disk size—Unless you're planning to use your network only for electronic mail and printer sharing, you'll need a disk with at least 100 megabytes. Part of this is because software has started requiring more disk space. In addition, users are learning about more software and will want it available on the file server.
- Disk quantity—Consider getting disk drives in pairs. Novell SFT supports continuous back up through disk mirroring. Other third party products also support this capability.

The Rest of the Server

Of course, there's more to a file server than simply a disk drive. A file server on a Novell network is, after all, a complete computer. Along with disks, you need memory, a monitor, and communications ports.

Novell NetWare uses an IBM-PC/AT's or PS/2's expanded memory. This means that it uses memory that is contiguous, rather than the paged memory that is found in the Lotus Intel Microsoft standard, such as that used by Lotus 1-2-3. NetWare will operate with 1.5 MB, but, unless your network is fairly small, it operates more effectively with more memory. If you are planning to run a large network, over 30 people, for example, you should consider having at least 4 MB of memory in the file server.

Novell NetWare uses this memory to hold information for each user working with the network at any time. The more users there are, the more memory required.

In addition to adequate memory, the file server should be equipped with at least one printer port. You can use either a parallel or a serial printer. NetWare will support either one. The printer attached to the file server can be used by anyone on the network. Normally, a fast printer such as a laser printer is attached to the file server for sharing by the users.

The Processor

Novell Advanced NetWare and Novell SFT NetWare are written to be used on an Intel 80286 microprocessor. This is the same processor that the IBM-PC/AT and its clones use. NetWare will also operate on the Intel

80386 and the Intel 80486. Because it is designed for the 80286, however, there is no inherent benefit in using the more advanced microprocessors. Of course, versions of the 80386 and 80486 will operate faster than the fastest 80286, but this is of relatively minor importance to the functioning of the file server. For processors with the same speed, there is no benefit at all as far as NetWare is concerned.

This means that if you have an 80286 available for use as a file server, there's no real reason why you shouldn't use it. On the other hand, there are some good reasons why you should look for a more advanced processor if you are buying a new computer for use as a file server.

The single most important reason for using an Intel 80386 or 80486 based computer for a file server is the future. The 80286 is already obsolescent if not obsolete. Novell is now shipping an 80386 version of NetWare, called NetWare 386, that will support up to 250 users. If you plan to be able to upgrade to this version, you will need to have that processor in your file server.

Peripherals

Once you have found the computer you plan to use as a file server, you need to decide what peripheral devices are necessary. A monitor, for example, is essential. Printer ports are probably required also, unless you plan to use some other arrangement for printing, such as a print server.

The monitor need not be anything special. You will only need to display text and block graphics on the monitor, so only the most basic monochrome monitor is required. A simple and inexpensive monochrome or Hercules video controller is all that is necessary to run the monitor. Once you get the system set up, the monitor will never show anything other than status information and text prompts, so a more expensive color graphics system would simply be wasted.

The file server is normally expected to provide the interface for the printers to be shared by the network. For this reason, you need to make sure that printer ports are available on the file server. Normally, these are the parallel ports that come as standard equipment on most computers. Novell NetWare will support up to three parallel ports on the file server and two serial ports. This means that you can have as many as five printers on a file server. Each of these is available to users attached to that file server.

In addition to printers, there are other items that can be attached to a file server. These items include magnetic tape drives, optical disk drives, and

CD-ROM players. Magnetic tapes are normally used for storing the information on the file server in a safe place. An optical disk is used when large amounts of information must be readily available. A CD-ROM reader is also used for large quantities of information; but is usually obtained from a commercial source, such as an encyclopedia company.

While the file server is the major component of a Novell network, there are a number of other components that must be chosen as well. They are no less important, for the network must have them to function, but they don't influence the operation as much as does the choice of the file server. Those items include the network interface cards, gateways; print and communications servers; server support devices; and, of course, the cabling. These items are, in turn, affected by the type of network you choose, and the manner in which it is arranged.

Network Topology

A network's topology is another way of explaining the relationship of the parts of the network. In other words, the topology specifies the layout of the network and describes where the items that comprise the network will go. These layouts are called bus, ring, and star.

Bus

The bus topology can be thought of as a straight line. The server, the workstations, and any other devices are attached to the bus at any point. Signals from any of these devices pass up and down the bus until they are identified by the device for which they are intended. When the signal is identified, the receiving station reads the information on it. See Figure 3-1.

The most common of the networks using the bus topology are the Ethernet networks. Ethernet was designed in the mid 1970s by the Xerox Corporation. Ethernet networks use a coaxial cable similar to the kind of cable used to connect an antenna to a CB radio. There is also a type of bus network called the token bus that works with broadband networks. A broadband network uses technology similar to that used for cable television, but may still run Novell NetWare.

Ring

"Ring" topology mean just what it says. The signals travel in a circle, until they are identified by the receiving station. This means that the signals

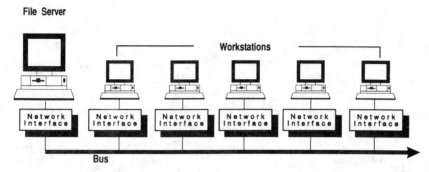

Figure 3-1   Bus Topology

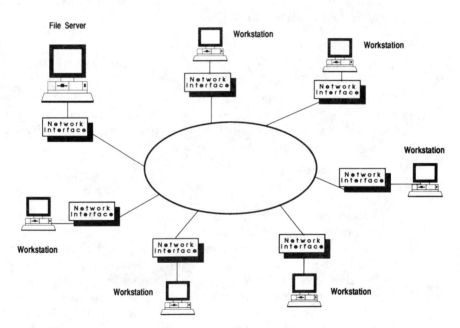

Figure 3-2   Ring Topology

first travel to one workstation and then to the next until they are identified. A missing or inoperative workstation can sometimes disrupt the network because it breaks the circle. See Figure 3-2.

The most popular network using ring topology is IBM's Token Ring.
The Token Ring is fairly new, but it is important because it forms an inte-
gral part of IBM's System Application Architecture, which is a way of inte-
grating and sharing information between computers. A Token Ring cable
may resemble telephone cable.

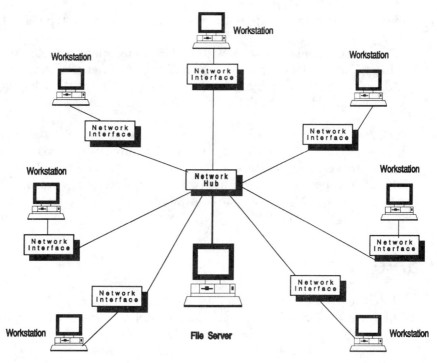

Figure 3-3   Star Topology

Star

The star topology is rapidly becoming very popular, especially in its form of the hierarchical star. Traditionally, a star network is thought of as having the file server in the center of the network, with cables radiating out to each workstation. In actual practice, the server is rarely in the center. Instead, there is a device for amplifying and passing signals, called a hub.

The star topology is becoming popular because most buildings are easiest to wire in that method. Normally, the utility services and telephone system are located in a central core of the building. The cables for those systems radiate outward from the center. The design works well for a LAN for the same reason. See Figure 3-3.

A hierarchical star starts out being like the star above, but some of the radials of the star terminate in another hub rather than at a workstation. This hub also supports a star of its own, and one or more of the radials from that may also support a hub. As you can see, adding to the network is easy with this type of arrangement. There is, of course, a limit to how long you can keep this up, but that limit depends on the type of network being used.

The most popular network with a star arrangement, and, in fact, the most popular LAN of any type, is ARCnet. ARCnet was developed by Datapoint shortly after Ethernet was developed. It has the advantage of being much easier to install than the other types of LAN, and is much less expensive.

There are other types of local area networks that use the star topology besides ARCnet. They include a version of Ethernet called StarLan, as well as another version of Ethernet that uses cabling similar to telephone wires. In addition, nearly all of the networks using fiber optics work in a star configuration. IBM's Token Ring, incidentally, looks like a star network, but electrically, it is a ring.

Cable Decisions

The choice of the cable for the LAN can be a critically important decision. The correct choice can help you build a LAN that will support you with little trouble or expense. The wrong choice can lead to both poor operation and a great deal of expense. The reason can be broken down to its simplest components—telephone cables.

Virtually all modern buildings are fitted with many more pairs of telephone cable that are likely ever to be required. They are installed during construction because there is relatively little difference in cost then, while installing them later would cost a fortune. If you can use these cables, you won't need to pay to have more cables installed.

Of course, there are other kinds of cable possibilities besides telephone cables, and each has its advantages. One of the problems with available telephone cable, for example, is that frequently the cable cannot be more than a few hundred feet long. The exact length depends on the type of LAN and the particular cable involved. If you need longer cable runs, or if you need immunity to electrical noise or security, then you probably can't use your telephone wiring.

For many years, the cabling of choice for LANs was coaxial cable. Ethernet started out using a thick cable called RG-8. Later, a thinner version, based on RG-58 was developed. Now, Ethernet can run on twisted pair (such as telephone) cables, fiber optic cables, and even television cable.

Likewise, ARCnet used the same RG-62 cable that had been used for IBM 3270 terminal wiring. Eventually, ARCnet was able to run on telephone cable as well as fiber optic cable. Like Ethernet above, ARCnet was adapted to the broadband LAN environment and its television cable.

IBM's Token Ring was designed around twisted-pair cable from the beginning. While IBM designed its LAN to run in a special kind of cable with a shield around it, LAN installers have found that telephone cables will also support Token Ring. As is the case with the other LANs, there is a fiber optic version of Token Ring.

Interface Cards

Between the cable and the computer, there is an interface. This is a card that receives the signals that are traveling along the network, translates them into something the computer can understand, and places them into the computer's memory so that the information can be used.

To some extent, the choice of the type of network will determine the card you will select. If you choose a Token Ring network, for example, you will only be able to buy interface cards from IBM and a few other vendors. ARCnet and Ethernet cards are more widely available, but the choice of card vendors is still limited by the choice of the type of network.

Normally, the network interface card is a circuit board that fits into the expansion bus on your personal computer. On an IBM-PC compatible computer, it is usually a half card and will fit into any slot. At this writing, Apple Macintosh computers will work with only their built-in AppleTalk interfaces or with Ethernet. Using Ethernet requires an expansion card, just as it does for IBM compatibles. One company, Xircom, puts out network interface cards that work by attaching to a computer's printer port.

Along with making sure you get the proper kind of network interface card, you need to make sure that it will work with your network. There are cards that are designed to work only in specific environments. Ethernet cards, for example, can be found that will work with twisted pair wiring, or with coaxial cables. There are also some cards that work only with fiber optic cable. If you have a coaxial cable network, a card designed for fiber optics will do you little good.

The choice of the type of cabling also can have other effects on the way your LAN is made. An Ethernet LAN, for example, is normally bus topology, but if you use twisted pair or fiber optics, it becomes a hierarchical star.

It pays to plan your cabling carefully. There are two reasons for this. First, once the cabling is in place, it's very difficult to change. Second, because of local fire codes, and the fact that it is very labor intensive, the cabling will probably be the single most expensive part of your LAN. We'll discuss the details of cable installation later, when we get to Chapter 5; but, if you have to pick just one part of the installation to hire someone else to do for you, this is it.

Supporting the LAN

We've already covered all of the necessary parts of a Novell LAN. Essentially, they are the workstation and its interface, the server and its related hardware, and the cabling. If you have these parts connected properly, your LAN will work.

That's not to say that we've covered everything that should be in a basic LAN, however. There are still areas that need to be considered, even though not all LANs will have them. They are communications hardware and support hardware.

Communications hardware allows information to be passed to and from the outside world by the users on the LAN. Some examples of communications hardware are asynchronous communications servers, 3270 gateways, and bridges to other LANs. Each of these devices communicates in a different way, but for the most part they simply consist of a card that is installed in a personal computer attached to the LAN. Normally, once a computer has been equipped with such a card it is dedicated to its task. While it is performing communications services, it cannot be used as a workstation.

The most common communications device is the asynchronous communications server (called an ACS). The ACS is used to provide a connection with such outside services as BIX, Dialog or CompuServe. This device can also be used to provide a pathway to a minicomputer or mainframe that has the capability to work with asynchronous terminals, such as a VAX from Digital Equipment Corporation. Finally, the ACS is needed when users who are away from the LAN want to call in and use it from a remote location.

Communications gateways are used to connect the LAN to another system, usually a mainframe computer. The most common gateway is to an IBM mainframe using 3270 terminal emulation. Normally, the gateway is connected to an IBM communications controller, which in turn connects it to the mainframe itself. Similar gateways exist for use with Honeywell and other mainframe systems. They normally allow several users to have access to the mainframe at any time.

A bridge is a device used to connect your LAN to another LAN. This bridging can be between LANs that are alike, such as two Ethernet LANs, or between different LANs such as an Ethernet and a Token Ring LAN. Novell provides for this capability within the file server. In addition, Novell allows for bridging using a workstation.

There are also bridges that can exist between parts of the same LAN. You can, for example, separate two sections of a LAN and connect them with a telephone line. You can in turn use a bridge to attach each section of the LAN to the phone line. Once this is done, the two sections of the LAN will appear as one, despite the physical separation.

Support hardware includes everything else that you might need to make your LAN work properly. Some examples of these include uninterruptable power supplies, transceivers or tape backup units. Two of these items, uninterruptable power supplies and tape backup units, probably should be installed on more LANs than they are now. These devices help insure that the information on the LAN will be safe. An uninterruptable power supply protects against power surges and outages. A tape backup unit preserves data against the failure of the file server. A transceiver is a device that can be used on some LANs to extend the distance that the LAN cable can reach. It is often necessary when the cable is expanded.

The Physical Plant

We've just looked at what LAN designers call the physical plant. These are the components that make up the local area network, and which support the operations of Novell NetWare and of the workstations. There are, of course, devices that could be attached to a LAN that we haven't discussed here. Some of these, such as FAX servers, are still in the early stages of development. Others, such as baseband to broadband bridges, are so esoteric that they play little role in the design and installation of most LANs.

The three major parts of the LAN are the workstation, the file server, and the cabling. You must have these if the LAN is to function. Other items, such as communications equipment and backup devices are frequently used and often considered essential to good LAN design, but are not strictly necessary. Now that you know what the parts of a LAN are, it's time for a closer look at them.

4

Unscrambling LANS—The Importance of Standards

With the profusion of LAN manufacturers and types in today's market, it's a sure bet that you'll want to connect your Novell network to someone else's system one day. And, since Novell supports virtually all popular protocols and topologies, you'll have some choices to make right from the start.

In this chapter we'll discuss protocols and standards. We'll get a detailed understanding of the basis of any network—communication.

Starting at the Beginning—A Data Communications Primer

In order to understand what goes on in a LAN, we need insight into the basics of how data can move between two points in a network. In Chapter 3 we saw how to connect hardware components in different topologies. We saw how we can interconnect those topologies to other systems using gateways. And, we saw how we can share network tools such as printers, fixed drives and devices for communicating with the outside world.

Now, we're going to discuss the software side of things. You won't need to know how these various standards translate to an actual operating system. But, you'll need to know how what kind of impact they have on the way you use your Novell LAN.

Novell offers a very wide choice of networking and communications options. Depending on how you plan to use your network, any one or a combination of options may be appropriate.

In order to simplify interconnection between networks, the industry has developed standards for communication. These standards allow users of one manufacturer's products to connect to users of systems from a different provider. Since local area networking is relatively new compared to other types of communication, it is no surprise that many of the data communication standards in effect for wide area networks (**WAN**s) apply to LANs. Nor is it surprising that methods of data transfer, the so-called "data highway" would also apply in LANs.

There are two ways to move data between points. If you wish to move a single channel of information you can choose the simplest method—baseband. If you want to move several channels at the same time, including, perhaps, video and audio, you might choose broadband. This last method is the method by which your local Cable TV company transmits information.

Before we give you the impression that broadband transmission implies several channels, let's simply say it "allows" several channels. The term "broadband" hints at the reason. Broadband systems allow a lot of bandwidth for information. Baseband systems do not.

Here is a simple example of the difference between broadband and baseband systems. When you put a cassette on your stereo system you need a bandwidth (frequency response) of about 20 to 25,000 Hz. That is a fairly narrow bandwidth. Narrow enough, in fact, that we can compare it to a baseband system.

But, suppose your local CATV system wants to send that music out, perhaps with several TV channels—they need to transmit it on a cable with several other signals. This requires several thousand times more bandwidth. The CATV system imposes the audio on the cable by a process called Frequency Modulation. Now we really have several signals— the TV channels and our audio channel. And, we have a broadband system.

Let's compare that to broad- and baseband data communications systems. All data is a series of ones and zeros. A byte or character of data is composed of electrical impulses that are either off or on. If we need to move data over a very simple network we can set up a baseband system that offers some method of identifying and moving those bits of data.

In most baseband systems there is no need to convert this stream of data bits into any other type of signal. The data is simply packaged by the network interface card and sent out in a serial signal appropriate to the network media. The method is simple and inexpensive—the equivalent of listening to your home stereo cassette player.

However, if we want to send several channels of information along the same media, we will need more bandwidth. We will also need to use network hardware that supports the greater bandwidth. In short, we will need a broadband system. In our baseband system, not only did the signal require less bandwidth, it took up the entire transmission medium. Therefore, regardless of how we sent the baseband signal or how much bandwidth the media could support, we could only put one data channel on it.

This means we need a method of getting several data channels on our broadband network without the signals getting in each other's way. The method we use is almost identical to the method your local cable TV system uses. The difference is that instead of sending several TV and audio signals over the cable, we can send several channels of data and, perhaps one of audio and one of video.

The technique we use to put several signals on the same cable is called Frequency Division Multiplex. In simple terms, we decide what the requirements of each channel of data are and we carve out a piece of the cable's bandwidth for that channel. We divide the broadband system's bandwidth into several smaller bands. Then we modulate those frequencies with our data signals.

There is a big difference in the actual data signals on a broadband and a baseband system. The baseband signal can be analog (one tone for a one, another for a zero) or it can be digital (current off for a one and on for a zero). But on a broadband network the signal is always analog. Usually, the two tones alter (shift) the carrier signal low by a fixed number of Hertz for a mark (one) and high for a space (zero). This is the same method a modem uses to send data over telephone lines. We carefully define the various bands and frequencies so that two systems will have no trouble communicating, even if they were built by different manufacturers.

Why is the distinction between the two types of systems important? Although some protocols are quite comfortable on both types of networks, clearly there are significant differences in cost and complexity. The broadband network is always more complicated and costly than the baseband network. But, it can cover a far larger physical area and allows several channels of information to operate on it simultaneously.

For this reason, broadband networks are often used as what is referred to as "backbone networks." A backbone network has the physical appearance of the human spine. The spinal cord (the 'backbone') is similar to the broadband network. Smaller LANs (the nerves branching off of the spine) attach to the backbone.

These smaller workgroup clusters are, often, complete in themselves. They communicate with each other over the backbone. Since the backbone is broadband, it can support several channels. The channels correspond to groups of the smaller clusters. Thus we could have an accounting department with payroll, accounts receivable, and accounts payable. Each accounting group is in a different office. Each has its own small LAN. The three groups communicate with each other and share data over the accounting channel of a broadband backbone.

Most Ethernet, Token Ring, and Starlan networks operate as baseband LANs. IBM's PC Net, Token Bus, Arcnet, and some Ethernet LANs can operate as broadband systems. Novell provides both broadband and baseband implementations of some of the protocols it supports.

Standards—The Glue That Holds Networks Together

Over time users of a class of products determine what they want in them. Manufacturers usually take note of the market's preferences and begin to include consistently implemented features in their products. As a market begins to mature these features become standardized so that users of one manufacturer's products can coexist with users of similar products from other manufacturers.

If a market is sophisticated it often will develop standards in advance of the appearance of products. In the data communications world there is a serious need for standardization in the way systems communicate both internally and externally. Over time a series of standards has evolved that allows great diversity in individual product capability while preserving the consistent ability to communicate.

The International Standards Organization Model

The basis for modern data communication standards is a layer model developed by the International Standards Organization (ISO). This model is the 'Reference Model for Open Systems Interconnection' or OSI. The OSI model is appropriate to virtually all wide and local area networks. One of the key benefits of the model is that even when a manufacturer chooses to depart from the standard within a product, as long as he provides an interface compatible with the OSI model, his product can fit into a standard network.

The concept of layers is both visually and actually descriptive. We can easily illustrate the layers as in Figure 4-1. And, we can build communications products that functionally adhere to each of the layer definitions.

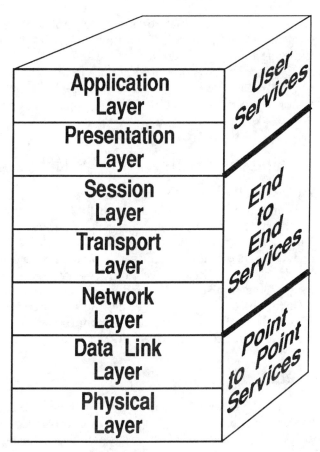

Figure 4-1   The 7-Layer OSI Model

In the OSI model, each layer contains a set of entities or attributes that support a coherent set of functions. These layers contain access points, defined by specific addresses, that allow two systems to communicate directly between the same access points. This one-to-one or peer-to-peer communication is possible only between two identical systems.

However, if two dissimilar systems want to communicate they must do so at the lowest common layer. Often that layer is the first or physical layer. As long as system developers adhere to the standard for the physical layer, then, they are assured of at least some degree of intersystem communication.

In some cases, where significant dissimilarities exist in higher layers, applications on one system cannot communicate with applications on another system. An example of this dilemma is Electronic Mail. Often

E-Mail between dissimilar networks will be impossible even though the networks themselves can communicate, because of incompatibilities in one of the high layers between the two systems.

The OSI model allows communications on a LAN in much the same way as on a WAN. However, LAN developers have established a set of communications protocols that are more appropriate for the closed, local nature of LANs.

Understanding the Layers—The Physical Layer

The physical layer of the OSI model is the lowest of the seven layers both physically and in the model. It is the layer that defines the interconnection between the system and the media. It covers four areas of physical interface.

The physical layer defines the mechanical interconnection between the system and the media. It also defines the nature of the electrical interconnection. In addition to the mechanical definition, the physical layer defines the signals present on the individual wires of the media if appropriate. Lastly, the physical layer specifies the sequence of communications events that allows two systems to interconnect on a peer-to-peer basis over the media. This sequence of events or procedures is called a protocol.

The Data Link Layer

The data link layer allows point-to-point communication between two open systems using the same protocol. It is in this layer that the system's protocol is defined and executed for systems using synchronous communications.

Asynchronous communication, such as normally used to access public bulletin boards and networks with a modem over dialup telephone lines, require certain error checking and hand-shaking capability to move information between two systems.

They are called asynchronous because the two systems are not synchronized. In fact, they are not interrelated in any way. In order to move the information, the communications application (program) packages the data in blocks of several characters along with some means of error checking and sends it out to the distant end. The distant end receives the block, unpackages it, checks for errors and requests the next block (or a resend if it finds errors).

In a synchronous system, all of those services (packaging, error checking, correction and request for the next package of data) are provided by the data link layer of the system. Thus the two ends are "synchronized."

In such a system, a protocol residing in the data link layer instructs the system to packetize data in packages or frames of a fixed number of bytes. In addition, the protocol dictates that the packet contains specific address information for both sender and destination. Finally, an error checking mechanism such as a CRC (cyclic redundancy check) is also embedded in the packet. The protocol instructs the sender to ask permission of (poll) the distant end to send a packet.

Upon receiving an acknowledgement, the sender dispatches the packet along the media. When the distant end receives the packet it extracts the data, checks it against the CRC and replies to the sender. Through flow control implemented at this layer, packets are dispatched in an orderly—synchronized—manner. The specific steps, functions, and specifications of the procedure vary depending on which protocol you use.

The Network Layer

The network layer has a seemingly simple task—sending the packets of data to their proper destinations. However, along with this function the network layer must track each packet as it moves along the network.

It is also in this layer that addresses on interconnected networks are kept. So we can simply say that all routing and tracking of network data is the province of the network layer.

The Transport Layer

The transport layer has a seemingly obscure function. In some regards it appears to provide the same services as the network layer. But there are some important differences.

In some cases, when a session is in process between two similar systems, the transport layer can establish a direct connection between the two systems. For example, if we establish a batch process between two systems the transport layer can take over the flow control, bypassing the network layer. This provides a more efficient means of intersystem connection.

The Session Layer

Remember that we referred to a session above? A session is a preplanned process which proceeds to its conclusion without interference from the operator. An example of a batch session might be a file transfer between two systems. The session layer of the OSI model controls session connections in conjunction with the transport layer. In short, the session and transport layer allow some efficiencies in certain types of processes by bypassing the network layer and controlling data flow independently.

The Presentation Layer

The presentation layer controls the syntax of data passing between two systems to insure that the systems understand each other. This can take the form of insuring that both systems are using the same character set, that data packets are correctly formatted, and that device support is correct.

Simply, this layer acts as a translator, insuring a one-to-one communication, regardless of the format of the individual systems' data.

The Application Layer

The application layer is the top level of the OSI model in the sense that it is at this level that all user and application interaction takes place. The interaction takes place on several levels within this layer. These levels accommodate user interaction, applications interaction, system interaction, programming within applications, and those functions that are visible to the operator.

In order for users and programs (applications) to interact at this layer a system of protocols has been defined. These protocols allow system management, applications management, system interaction, interaction with other industry standard systems, and interaction with locally defined systems.

Using these protocols, developers can interact through the OSI model at the DOS level, the application level, the user level, the system level and on a custom system or datafile level.

As we discuss the various protocols available as you configure your Novell LAN, we'll refer to the appropriate layers on the OSI model. You'll see why some networks are more appropriate to a particular protocol based upon the use to which you plan to put the network.

But, more important, as you interconnect networks using bridges and gateways you'll need to know at what level they interact with your LAN— and you'll need to be able to establish compatibility.

Within a LAN all interconnection takes place in the first two levels of the model. However, as you mix topologies and protocols in a complex system, you will need to insure that you have maintained compatibility up and down the model or you will lose some of the network services available to you.

Network Operating Systems—Internal Communications

In order for the systems to communicate on the LAN, the systems must communicate internally. The interface between the data link layer and the network layer takes the form of requests for service by the data link layer and responses by the network layer.

The interface between the transport layer and the layers above it is governed by the network operating system and DOS or NetBIOS. Novell networks emulate NetBIOS communications with an emulator called IPX. The IPX file resides in the network shell and allows an application on the workstation to communicate down the OSI model to the physical layer and out to another system, usually the file server.

Since NetBIOS has real meaning only within an IBM PC Net environment, we are primarily concerned with how our NetBIOS or DOS compatible application will run in a Novell environment. Here's how Novell runs the application transparently to the user:

When you start your Novell workstation, you load a program called the Shell. The Shell is simply an interface between the outside world and the internals of your workstation. The Shell has several parts which remain in your workstation's memory once you have loaded them.

The outermost layer of the Shell is the IPX file. IPX communicates with the network through the network adapter card. Deep inside the workstation's operating system (DOS), requests are sent out toward the Shell. At the innermost layer of the Shell is a file called NET2, NET3 or NET4 depending upon the version of DOS installed on the workstation. The NET file decides whether to direct the request back to the workstation for internal processing or to send it on to the network.

If the NET file sends the request to the network, it must first go to the network operating system, NetWare. NetWare then processes the request where it proceeds to the IPX file for transfer onto the LAN. Thus, if you wanted to see a directory of your local (workstation) drive, your request would be routed to DOS. But if you wished a directory of a network drive, the request would be routed to the NetWare operating system, through IPX and out to the server.

Although you still have the option to load NetBIOS if required for a specific application, in most cases the IPX NetBIOS emulator will provide all of the compatibility you need.

The NetWare network operating system is divided into two parts, each with its own functions. At the workstation end, NetWare acts as an interface between applications and IPX. At the server end, it provides server support and network services and utilities.

The IEEE Standards—Defining LAN Protocols

The IEEE has evolved a set of protocol standards which we can use to define compatibility within networks. The three most popular LAN protocols are Ethernet, Arcnet and Token Ring. There is a variation on the Ethernet standard called StarLAN.

While, technically, the standards define the network protocols, they also to some extent define the topologies as well. For example, IEEE 802.3 defines the Ethernet standard while IEEE 802.4 defines a token passing protocol on a bus and IEEE 802.5 defines token passing in a ring topology.

Before we stray too far in our discussion of protocols let's make an important distinction. In dealing with LANs we are dealing constantly with the protocol issue. Here it is very helpful to think in terms of the OSI model. There are protocols that move data up and down the layers of the model and there are protocols that move data between open systems.

For our purposes a system can be a server, a workstation, a bridge or any independent unit in a LAN. So when we want two workstations to communicate on a LAN, we say that we have two open systems and that they will communicate using the two bottom layers of the model.

On a LAN it is only necessary for the two lower layers to be able to interface to the higher layers for systems to be able to communicate. Thus all of the IEEE standards are constructed so as to maintain system compatibility at the physical and data link layers.

The importance of understanding the benefits and drawbacks of the various protocols lies in the versatility of the Novell system. Unlike many other LANs, Novell can be virtually any topology and run virtually any protocol. In fact, one of Novell's unique features is its ability to run up to four different protocols simultaneously on the same server. Thus you could have Token Ring, Arcnet, Ethernet and broadband LANs all communicating with the same server without the need for bridges as in most other networks.

Ethernet—The Granddaddy of LAN Protocols

Layer 1 and 2 protocols fall into two categories. These categories, contention, and non-contention, determine how data passes between two systems or stations on the LAN. In a contention protocol there must be some way for one station to know that another station has put data on the network in order to avoid collisions.

The earliest formal contention protocol standard was the Ethernet standard, IEEE 802.3. In its title, "Carrier Sense Multiple Access with Collision Detection," we get a hint of how stations on the LAN contend for the network. Although Ethernet started as a de facto protocol, it has evolved into a complete IEEE standard.

In an Ethernet system, it is possible for two stations to attempt to access the network simultaneously. When this occurs, a collision is said to have happened. Packets of data are placed on the media embedded with the addresses of their destination. They attempt to deliver their data to the destination address. If the address is busy or there is traffic already on the system they can't access the destination address. They have collided with other data packets and the results are at best unpredictable.

But in a collision avoidance scheme such as Ethernet, the second and subsequent packets would wait until there was no traffic on the media before attempting delivery. The method hinted at in the title of the standard is carrier detection. When an Ethernet card sends data, it sends it out as a shifting carrier signal, something like a broadband signal, but much lower in frequency. As long as the carrier is present on the media, other Ethernet cards know that they cannot attempt to transfer data.

Thus Ethernet has the effect of allowing only one piece of traffic at a time on the LAN. There are some other benefits to using Ethernet. Because of the use of a modulated carrier both greater length of the media and higher data transfer rates are possible. Ethernet's data transfer rate is 10 Mbps (Megabits per second). One drawback is the fact that since only one piece of data is allowed on the network at a time, certain server schemes can cause degradation of network performance.

As we have mentioned before, the speed of the workstations and the data rate of the network have far less to do with network performance than does the bottleneck at the network drives. When data cannot get on or off the drive fast enough the network slows down while packets wait their turns to be transferred. The performance degradation appears to be on the LAN but, in reality, it's at the server's fixed drive. One solution is to use a large cache.

A cache is, simply, a large block of memory that accepts data destined for the disk at RAM rates (around 9.5 Mbps +) instead of disk rates (less than 8 Mbps). This clears the activity on the media and permits the next packet of data to flow. Meanwhile, the cache transfers its load of data onto the fixed drive at a slower rate. Caches can also send data out from the drives in a similar manner, improving network drive read speeds.

Ethernet has a popular subset which has now become an IEEE standard. IEEE 802.3 Base 1 defines the AT&T StarLAN standard. StarLAN is a low cost, low performance variation on Ethernet which uses twisted pair (telephone) cable instead of the coaxial cable required for 802.3. StarLAN also uses a star topology which requires a hub as we described in Chapter 3.

Token Ring—A Protocol and Two Topologies

When we think of token passing protocols, we think generally of IBM's Token Ring. Actually, the Token Ring is a combination of the ring topology and the token passing protocol. This combination is defined by IEEE standard 802.5. But we can also have a token passing scheme on a bus as defined by IEEE 802.4.

The token passing approach to moving data on a LAN comes from the other side of the protocol family from Ethernet. While Ethernet is a contention protocol, token passing and polling protocols are non-contention protocols. This means that data packets are moved in a specific, predefined order and never need to contend for the network.

Polling is the forerunner of token passing schemes. In a polling situation, the sending station has a list of addresses it wishes to query or poll. These addresses are distant end systems. The originating end sends out a request over the network to the first address in its list for information. If the distant end has a message to send it does so. Then the originating end sends out any messages it may have for that address and moves on to the next address. This scheme often is used in wide area networks.

In a token passing protocol, the server creates a packet of data with a list of destination addresses and data for those addresses. This special packet (actually a sort of super packet since it contains packetized data) is called a token. The server sends the token to the first address. The token drops off its packets destined for that address, picks up any data packets the address wishes to send and moves on to the next address.

The token acts on the LAN like your letter carrier making his rounds, picking up and delivering mail at each house on the route in order. If you miss putting out your mail today, you'll have to wait until tomorrow. The same is true of the token. It visits each address in sequence, never at random as in a contention scheme like Ethernet.

Token passing networks, whether bus or ring, operate at slower data rates than Ethernet in part because they do not use the carrier method of transmission. They also do not require the expensive coaxial cable used by Ethernet. Token Ring LANs, for example, operate at speeds up to 4.0 Mbps. In general, Token Rings are smaller in terms of length of media, slower, and less expensive than Ethernet. A popular network configuration is several Token Ring workgroups connected to an Ethernet backbone.

Arcnet—The Non-Standard Standard

Although Arcnet closely follows IEEE 802.4, it really has no official status beyond being a de facto standard. But, some say, in coming years the bulk of all LANs will be Arcnet LANs.

Arcnet is a token passing protocol defined for a bus topology. Because of its relatively low data rate (2.5 Mbps) Arcnet can be quite inexpensive to install. It uses twisted pair cable such as telephone wire as its transmission medium. Arcnet is very popular in smaller networks where great distances, large numbers of workstations, and high data rates are not a factor.

Proprietary Standards and Fiber Optics

There are several proprietary protocols, many of which Novell supports. However, because protocol compatibility is a Level 1 and Level 2 function of the OSI Model, it is important to maintain compatibility at that level.

If you stick to the same protocol with consistency, you'll have no trouble communicating on your LAN. If you depart from this consistency, however, you'll either need special bridges or you'll need to make allowances within the server.

One notable exception is AppleTalk, the Macintosh network protocol. Novell handles AppleTalk in its native mode allowing Macintosh computers to act as workstations on a Novell DOS server. However, you can also connect your Mac to the network using Novell's Ethernet card for Macintosh if you are running Ethernet on your server. As so often with Novell, the choice here is yours.

One reason for using a proprietary protocol is data transfer rate. Although we have emphasized that the network bottlenecks are most likely to occur at the fixed disk instead of on the media, there is an advantage under certain circumstances to using a faster LAN.

Data transfer rate, when combined with fast drives or caching can allow more users on the network. What it boils down to is this. If the data transfer rate allows X number of users to move data in a fixed period of time, ten times the data rate will allow 10X users to move their data in the same period. If the drive can't accept the data of course, there is no benefit. There simply would be bigger gaps while the system waits for the drive. But, with fast caching and a fast drive some performance improvements can be achieved.

An example of this improvement is the caching controller used by Network Connection on their optimized servers. Benchmarks have shown up to a 40 times improvement in network performance using this large (4 MB) fast cache.

Another reason for using a proprietary protocol is the ability to use fiber optic media in portions of a network. Since Novell does not directly support fiber optics you will need to bridge to a fiber optic controller. But in areas where high security of data on the media is a factor or where high electrical noise interferes with LAN operation you may want to consider fiber optics.

Summary

The basis for simplifying network communication is the standardization of the protocols you use, both internal to a system and between systems on the LAN.

Understanding how external and internal protocols react with each other and on the various layers of the OSI Model can help you decide if you will experience compatibility problems.

The Novell implementation of the Shell allows workstations to maintain complete compatibility with DOS and NetBIOS while offering the improved performance associated with the NetWare network operating system.

Finally, understanding the strengths and weaknesses of the various standard protocols (Ethernet, Token Ring and Arcnet) will help you choose one or some combination for your LAN.

In the next chapter we'll discuss the specifics of installing a Novell LAN using the theory we've learned so far. We'll take you from requirements analysis through design and hardware/software/protocol selection to facility support and physical installation criteria.

5

Putting the LAN Together

Now that you know some of the background, it's time to look at how all of this goes together. Knowing something about the installation process is important, even if you plan to have someone else do the work, because the requirements of your particular installation can have a very significant effect on the LAN you choose. This is partly due to physical factors, such as the length of cable that will be required, and partly due to the requirements of your specific building.

Because it is so important, the installation process should follow a structured procedure. You will need to do part of this work yourself. Part of it can be assigned to a consultant, subcontractor, or LAN installer. The first stages are the ones that define the LAN so that it meets your needs, and these you have to do yourself.

Requirements Analysis

This is a term that consultants use to indicate that you must decide what you need, preferably before you make your purchase. To make your decision, you must decide exactly what you want your LAN to accomplish. Then you must decide what equipment you want to use for it to accomplish that, then you decide how you want to go about putting it together. In other words, you decide what you want to do, then make a plan to help you get there.

Deciding what you want is often the hardest part of a requirements analysis. By the time you discover that you need to look at your requirements, you've probably already decided to yourself that you want to buy a LAN. Now you're just thinking of a way to justify it. You will have to force yourself to look at your requirements objectively. It may be that you do indeed need a LAN. On the other hand, it may be that you haven't thought your needs through completely enough and you need something else entirely.

Once you arrive at the decision that you need a LAN, you need to decide what sort of LAN you need, how big it will be, and what sort of services the LAN will provide. While people in many companies prepare a formal paper for this process, it isn't really necessary. You can arrive at answers that are just as correct by writing your points on a legal pad, making sure that you look at the pluses and minuses of your decision.

It's important that you be fair with yourself. It's easy to ignore the minuses of something like a LAN. At first glance, it may seem that there aren't any, but be assured that there are always minuses. It's critical to the success of any decision like this to look at both sides.

To help you in the decision making process, here are some questions that you may want to ask about any proposed LAN installation, whether it's yours or someone else's:

- What is the LAN to accomplish?
- Do I currently have a need to share data? Do I project a need to share data? Are there resources that I need to share?
- Does the business currently have equipment that could be used on the LAN?
- Can I afford the initial investment? Will the investment be repaid through productivity? Why do I think so?
- How many people will need access to the LAN right away? What will the eventual requirement be?
- What kind of work do I expect to do on the LAN?
- What is the physical size of the area I have to cover? Is everyone in the same office? The same building?

Once you've arrived at answers to as many of these questions as possible, it's time to decide whether you need a LAN, and if so, what kind. Remember that it's possible that you may find out that your current requirements don't support your desire for a LAN. Or it may be that your future requirements do.

Once you know the answer to these questions, it's time to use the requirements to help design the LAN. The design will have to take into account what you want the LAN to accomplish, as well as what is required to make it work in your location.

Designing the LAN

LAN design has three parts. First you have to decide what LAN services you need, then you have to decide where the physical plant (cable and equipment) is going to go, and, finally, you have to decide how you're going to connect it all.

Deciding what the LAN services must be is where you use the list of requirements you made above. There's no need to specify an asynchronous communications server, for example, if you're not going to need to communicate with some asynchronous service such as BIX or Dow Jones. Likewise, there's no need to specify a baseband LAN if you know that you need to provide video services along with the data.

The simplest way to determine your requirements is to make a list of everything you would like the LAN to do. The requirements list will give you that information. Once you make this list, you go through it and eliminate those things that are not available, beyond the state of the art, or too expensive. You might decide, for example, not to run the network to the mail room, if it means raising the price by another fifteen thousand dollars.

Once you've crossed out the obvious items, take another look. You might decide that some items you've listed are not particularly vital. You may have listed a link to the IBM mainframe through the LAN, when only one person to be served by the LAN will actually use it—which is a case for making some other arrangement. Remember, the LAN is for sharing resources.

Now that you've gone over the list twice, you have probably narrowed it down to those things that you really need. It's time to see what you want, and how those requirements can be fulfilled.

Locations

Now that you have some idea of what types of equipment you want, you need to decide if you have some place to put it. Pay close attention to this. LANs need working space for the system administrator, ventilation, and they need electrical power. The lack of a proper power source has brought about the failure of many a local area network.

If possible, you should select a location for the file server which works properly with the type of LAN you've chosen. For example, if you've picked a token bus or Ethernet LAN, the server can be at one end. Even if the LAN has several floors, and therefore several LAN segments, you may

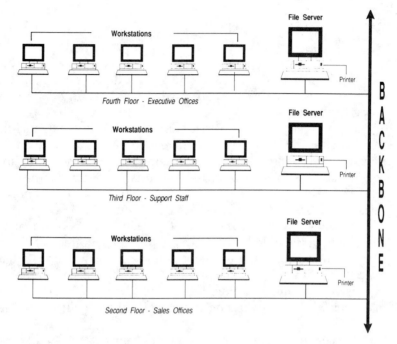

Figure 5-1   A Backbone LAN

find it most convenient to place all servers in the same or adjacent rooms. The reason is that it will require less travel by the LAN administrator for all of the servers to be supported.

In the case of LANs with a physical star topology, the servers will probably be somewhere near the center. The reason for the central location is the same as in the last paragraph. The LAN administrator needs to reach all of the servers for them to be supported.

Of course, the view here is somewhat simplistic. Very few buildings lend themselves to optimal LAN design, which means that it's usually worthwhile to obtain a copy of the blueprints of the building and lay the LAN out on paper well before the first piece of cable is installed.

In the case of multi-story buildings, the solution is more complicated. Not only must you install cable on each floor, you probably will have to run cable between floors. When you do this, you will be installing what is known as a backbone. The backbone LAN connects the LANs on each floor together. See Figure 5-1 for an example of how a backbone LAN would work in a typical office building.

Because Novell NetWare will support more than one type of LAN from the same server, you can use one type (such as Ethernet) for the backbone, while you use another type (such as Token Ring) on an individual floor. More importantly, you can tailor the LAN on each floor to meet its individual needs, regardless of whether it's the same as the LAN on the floor above or below. You do this by having one network adaptor card in the server for the backbone, and the others for the LAN on that floor.

As you can see, LAN design is a complex process, and there's a great deal more to it than defining your operational and physical requirements. You also have to select the hardware environment, the proper protocol, and the type of cable. These can have a great effect on the manner in which your requirements are met. Because of this, you need to be familiar with the entire process, and in the ways it affects other parts of the design process.

Hardware Selection

Novell NetWare is normally a PC-based network. This means that the file server is based on an IBM-PC/AT or compatible computer. There are exceptions, of course. Novell NetWare is also available for a DEC VAX running the VMS operating system. There is also a version of NetWare called Portable NetWare that can be customized to run on nearly any machine.

Because the vast majority of Novell servers are PC/AT compatible computers, we will concentrate on those. Where reference to the VAX version is appropriate, that will be mentioned specifically.

As we mentioned earlier, the primary emphasis in your choice of the file server must be on the disk drives. They must be fast enough and have enough capacity to support the anticipated workload of the network that's using them. Unfortunately, there are no solid rules that define exactly what is fast enough or what is enough capacity.

In spite of the lack of rules, you can still make some estimates. You know you need disk space to store all of the files required by Novell NetWare. In addition, you will need space for other applications and support software. Finally, you will need space for each user to have data files for the applications and for system utilities such as electronic mail.

It's fairly easy to figure the amount of disk space required by software. You simply add the space requirements of each application, utility, etc., to the approximately 5 megabytes required by NetWare. The remaining space is available for user files. If all or most of the users have some local disk storage, you can allocate less space than you would if they do not.

Exactly how much disk space is required for user files depends on what the users will be doing. If many of the users are working with large nonshared databases, the space requirements will be large. On the other hand, it they are mostly doing electronic mail, the requirements will be quite small.

Disk Sizing

A good rule of thumb for networks performing general office tasks that expect most users to be active is about two megabytes per user. This figure can be adjusted up or down according to the functions that the users normally perform. For example, if nearly all users are using only word processing and electronic mail, that figure can be reduced to one megabyte per user, or less.

To arrive at a figure for disk space requirements, you simply add the requirements for the network and application software to the space required for the users. If possible, you should allow some space for growth of the network. Here's an example of how this would work:

Let's assume that you are planning a file server to support 80 people. It will be running NetWare, with WordPerfect Office as the electronic mail system. In addition, there will be other applications including Lotus 1-2-3, WordPerfect 5.0 and others. The total disk space required for the software will be 15 megabytes. If the work environment includes a mix of users with word processing, spreadsheet and database programs being run, you should assume a requirement of two megabytes per user. This will require an additional 160 megabytes.

At this point, the identified uses require 175 megabytes. If you check the ads for hard disks, you will see that 220 megabytes is a fairly common size for fast reliable hard disks. This is a bit larger than you need for current requirements, but it will work, and will give room for growth. The 220 megabyte hard disk is probably the size we require for the server.

You can, of course, realize this much disk space in ways other than buying a single hard disk. Novell NetWare will allow you to assign two hard disks to a standard PC/AT disk controller. If you use a Novell Disk Coprocessor Board, you can have up to 16. If you are using SFT NetWare, you can have two identical hard disks, and assign one to mirror the other. This will give you complete and immediate backups.

NetWare will allow you to use any commonly available PC/AT hard disk controller. Or, you can select SCSI and ESDI disk controllers which will give you faster operation. Normally, large disks designed for use with networks will include the proper software to allow NetWare to make use of them.

Computer Selection

Once you've selected the hard disk, you should decide what platform it will be installed in. Because Novell no longer makes file servers itself, you'll need either an IBM-PC/AT or PS/2 compatible computer. While you will need to be careful in selecting the platform for your network server, specific brands are not particularly critical.

The most important factor in selecting a computer that will be used as a file server is reliability. Your LAN isn't any good to you if the server is inoperative. You will need to try to get a computer that can be repaired quickly at your location. Exactly what brand that turns out to be depends on where you are.

For this reason, you should check with more than one supplier in an effort to determine the quality of service, the level of reliability (expressed as mean time between failures), and the method of repair. You should avoid making the decision on the basis of the lowest price. A few dollars in initial cost is more than offset by difficulty in getting repairs performed if the support organization doesn't know its job, or doesn't provide on-site service.

Once you're satisfied that you have found a dealer who can support you, the time has come to select the proper model. While this may seem bewildering at first, you can generally narrow it down, especially since you don't need to be distracted by such things as hard disk drives—you're handling them separately, after all.

To narrow the selection, it helps to have a checklist. Here are some items that you might want to put on yours to start with:

- Intel 80386 or 80486 processor. While an 80286 will work fine, there's no point in limiting your future capabilities.
- Full-sized AT or PS/2 chassis. You need as many expansion slots as you can get. Compact or "baby" AT class computers may not have the expansion room you need.
- Space for six drives. While you won't need six half-height disk drives, remember that most servers use hard disks that are full height. On top of this, you will still need a floppy disk drive and perhaps a tape backup. That will account for six, if you have two hard disks.
- Motherboard memory expansion. While you can make use of a memory expansion card, remember that expansion slots are at a premium in some servers.
- Heavy duty power supply. 200 watts is a must. Try for 300 watts if you can find it.
- Keyboard lock. Believe it or not, there are computers without this. You must have it on your server to keep people from tampering.
- Monochrome video card. There's no point in paying for color. You won't need it.

- Reasonably high clock speed. 16 or 20 MHz will work fine with a file server. So will faster speeds, but the benefits will be minimal.

Support Hardware

Now that you've decided what you want for a server, you have more decisions to make on other support hardware. Fortunately, most of these decisions are reasonably simple, but they do have to be made.

Power backup can be critical if you use your LAN for support of important business activities. Since it's unlikely that you would have a LAN for trivial activities, we can assume that this is the case for you. The reason power backup is so important is that the file server needs some time to shut itself down in the event of power failure.

Presuming, therefore, that you are selecting an uninterruptable power supply, you'll need to make sure of two things. The first is that the UPS will support the server long enough to allow the shutdown to occur. The second is that the UPS must have a way to let NetWare know that a power failure has occurred, so that the software can begin shutting down the server. At this point, only SFT NetWare has the ability to sense this signal from the power supply, but there are third-party products that allow Advanced NetWare to sense the condition, and NetWare 386 will also support sensing the power-out alarm from the power supply.

Other support items include a monitor—there's no point in getting anything but monochrome—and printers, which normally are connected to the file server. Most likely, these will be high-speed expensive printers, such as laser printers. You probably should have a dot-matrix printer attached to the file server for printing drafts and listings, and for those occasions when the system administrator needs NetWare to print something. If you keep your server in a locked room, the printers are normally positioned outside of the room so that people can get to them.

You normally will not need special devices to spool text to printers, and you will not need to buy extra memory for your printer to serve as a print buffer. NetWare already buffers print queues, making external print buffering less of an advantage.

Protocol Selection

In the vast majority of LANs, the selection of the LAN protocol makes remarkably little difference. That's mainly because the traffic on the LAN is relatively low, and there are no external systems to which the LAN must be attached. That being the case, you might as well select something inexpensive and easy to install, such as ARCnet. For most LANs, the capacity of Ethernet or Token Ring is a waste.

That does not mean, of course, that you might not find yourself using Ethernet or Token Ring anyway. There are a large number of reasons to select a specific LAN protocol that have nothing to do with the amount of traffic that will be on the network.

Most likely, you will find your selection made for you. You will have some aspect of your LAN that eliminates one or more of your choices. You may have, for example, a location that is already wired for a LAN or for computer terminals. If you can use that wiring, you can save a great deal of the expense of installing a new LAN. You may find that you have cable runs long enough to exclude some types of wiring. Most importantly, you may find that some other computer, such as a company minicomputer, requires attachment to the LAN. Here are some items to help you make your selection:

- Do you need to connect to a mainframe or minicomputer? Most DEC- and Unix-based equipment will indicate Ethernet, IBM will indicate Token Ring, and Datapoint minis will work with ARCnet.
- Do you need to move large files frequently? A heavily-used computer-aided design operation will probably need Ethernet or 16 mbps Token Ring. Electronic mail and most word-processing users can use nearly anything.
- Is wiring already installed? If you have twisted pair wiring already in the building, you might want to use that. There are ways for Ethernet and ARCnet to work that way. Token Ring will frequently work with telephone twisted pair wiring, but IBM doesn't support that. If you have IBM 3270 terminal wiring in place, you may be able to use that with ARCnet, which uses the same cabling.
- Do you have some unusual condition? Electromagnetic interference or a security requirement may dictate the use of fiber-optic cables. While there are fiber versions of ARCnet and Token Ring available, fiber Ethernet is by far the most widely used. Extremely long distances may dictate fiber optics or a broadband backbone LAN.
- Is your building layout such that one type of LAN seems to fit better? For example, a building with a long central hall and offices on either side may fit better with the bus topology of Ethernet than with the physical star topology of either ARCnet or Token Ring.

Finally, there's cost. Under normal circumstances, ARCnet is the least expensive protocol to implement. Ethernet is next, and Token Ring is the most expensive. If all other points are equal, then expense becomes the controlling factor. ARCnet is admittedly slower than the others, but that is not apparent to the user, and probably not significant to the operation of the LAN. For most users, it's not the capability that matters, it's what they do with it every day.

Impact On Your Business

Before you settle on the final choice for your LAN, remember that it can have an impact on the way you do business. For that reason, it's important to look at the way you do business now, and what you plan for the future. You should plan ahead for possible additions in personal computers, as well as new needs for communications, or for connections to company mainframes or minicomputers.

It may be that you don't know exactly what your company's intentions are. If that's the case, you should plan as well as you can, and seek comfort in the fact that NetWare can support multiple LANs from the same server, and can communicate with most external systems.

There will be other effects on the business as well. If you are using the extra cable pairs in your telephone system to support the LAN, you will need to realize that this may reduce your ability to expand the phone system. If you are using existing 3270 wiring for ARCnet, then you won't be able to use it for IBM terminals. If you install all new cabling, it will have some effect on the budget, the exact effect will depend on the kind and amount of new cabling that is installed.

Cable Installation

Once you've decided exactly what sort of LAN you need for your business, you've come to the question of cabling. Since this may well be the single most expensive element in your LAN, and since it can have some far-reaching effects if it's installed improperly, it pays to plan your cable plant carefully, and have the most professional installation you can afford.

Once you've decided what sort of network you want, your next step is to find a set of accurate floor plans for the area you want to use. I stress the accuracy, because these plans will be used to figure cable lengths and the placement of faceplates in offices. If the cable plant is to meet your needs, you should start out with careful planning.

Once you have the floor plan, you will need to determine where the file
server or servers will be located. This will depend on the shape of the
building and the type of LAN to some extent. You may find that you will
have to create an area for the servers in order to have adequate electricity,
cooling, access for the supervisor, and access to the cable plant. Often,
you can simply select a convenient corner of a larger office. You should
make sure that the file server is in an area that can be locked, so that people aren't tempted to tamper with it.

As part of the process of selecting the location of the file servers, you
will need to decide where you want to put the system printers. They will
need to be close enough to the file servers that they can be attached; but,
available to workers in the office who need them. If you use print servers
on your network, you will also need to determine the locations of any
other print stations as well.

Once you have done this, it's time to decide exactly how the cabling will
be done. Basically, there are two choices. You can do the job—by yourself
or with your own employees—or you can hire a contractor to do the job. If
you have more than a half dozen workstations that are in the immediate
vicinity of each other, it's probably a good idea to have a cabling contractor
do it.

If you already have a minicomputer or a mainframe, you probably had
someone to install the terminal wiring. If not, you can find a network
cabling contractor through references from the company who sold you
NetWare. In any case, the installer should be prepared to meet all existing
building and fire codes, and to test the installation and to repair any cable
segments that aren't working properly. The requirement to meet local
codes is very important, since network cable is required to be non-flamma-
ble. Your community may also require a visit from the building inspector.

Once you have selected the installer, either a contractor or your own
staff, go over the floor plan carefully with them. Make sure that everyone
involved understands where the cable is to go in each work area, as well
as where the servers are to go. Any printer installations, gateways to other
computers, or any other requirement for cables should be discussed, and
the installer should be asked to confirm that the installation plan looks
reasonable. Once that is done, ask the installer to prepare a plan with the
intended installation drawn on it.

Before you give the contractor the order to start installation, take one
last look to make sure that the drawing accurately reflects your desires.
You should realize that the initial drawing will likely differ in places from
the actual installation. This is because some characteristics of the building,
including support beams, air conditioning ducts, water lines and the like,
may prevent installation of the cable according to the plan. These changes

will be reflected on the "as built" drawings which you will receive once the cabling is complete.

When the cabling is complete, the installer should perform a continuity test to confirm that the cable segments are connected properly. You should request that the contractor also conduct tests once the file servers are operational, if they are not when cabling is completed. Some contractors will charge extra for this service, but it needs to be done. There are many occasions in which the continuity test is acceptable, but in which the data will not be passed.

You should make sure that the testing takes place with any faceplates, connectors, patch panels, hubs or MAUs in place that will be installed in the actual LAN. These are all part of the cabling plant, and it means nothing to test without them.

Some Ethernet LANs may have repeaters installed, and all LANs may have bridges connecting segments. These items also need to be tested, both for initial operation, and also for proper operation within the network.

Interface Cards

Sometime during the cable installation, probably when it started, you should have placed the order for the interface cards for workstations and servers. These are available from a variety of sources, including Novell. Novell manufactures two varieties of Ethernet cards, the NE-1000 which will fit an 8 bit bus (like a PC/XT) and the NE-2000 which will fit a 16 bit bus (such as the PC/AT). Under normal circumstances, an 8 bit card is adequate for workstation use. For workstations requiring high access speed, such as CAD stations, and for servers, a 16 bit card is recommended.

Normally, it's considered good practice by most LAN installers to stay as much as possible with a single brand of interface card. For the most part, they will all work, but installation becomes much easier if there are fewer types. This is because you can create a single workstation shell, (that's the software that allows the workstation to access the network) and install it on all of the workstations in which the same card has been installed. Installations with different cards will require that a separate workstation shell be created.

In the NetWare installation process, one of the first procedures you'll complete is the creation of the network workstation shell. This is simply a program that loads into your computer's memory and allows access to the network. To function, the software needs to know what network interface card is installed in the workstation, and what version of DOS is being used. Fortunately, versions of cards for each version of DOS are created at the same time. You can simply load all of them into the workstation, and choose which to run according to the version of the operating system the workstation is running.

In some cases, you will find specialized versions of workstation software for NetWare. Usually, this is because you are using a network interface card that is not supported as standard by Novell. An example of this is the Xircom Pocket Ethernet Adapter from Xircom, Inc. In these cases, the manufacturer will supply a version of the driver software to work with NetWare. Generally, the manufacturer will also supply workstation shells that have already been generated.

Server Installation

Once the cabling is in place and tested, the file servers can be attached to the network. You should do this before the workstation installation is complete, because the existence of the server on the network will allow you to confirm operation of each workstation as you connect it to the LAN. Normally, server installation involves installing the NetWare operating system on the server's hard disk, and then connecting the server to the network. It's the software installation that can be tricky.

As long as you're using a disk drive type that is supported by NetWare, installation of version 2.15 is fairly straightforward. You will need to know what sort of drive you have, how many, and how they are attached to the server. NetWare is capable of reading the drive table and determining the details about the size of the drive, including the number of heads and cylinders the drive has.

If you are using a disk drive not normally used by NetWare, you may find that the manufacturer has supplied a drive definition along with the disk drive. You will be given instructions about when to load the drive definition file during the server software installation process. NetWare can be picky about drives, so you may find that the hard disk you picked up for a good price at the computer flea market won't work. It's a better idea to select a hard disk that is labeled as "Novell Certified."

The NetWare server software installation begins using MS-DOS. In fact, you can start it using a computer that isn't intended to be used as the file server. If you do this, select a computer that has a fast hard disk, and you will speed your work.

NetWare gives you several options for the type of available installation. These include the standard (floppy disk) method, the hard disk method, and the network method. You are most likely to use the second, hard disk method. To do this, you find a computer with a hard disk that has some room on it, about 5 megabytes. You then insert the installation disk into drive A:, and type "NETGEN." At this point, you will be prompted to insert disks in turn until they are copied to the computer's hard disk. Then you will be asked to insert any additional disks. This is when you will load any disks provided by manufacturers. Once this is complete, the installation program, Netgen, will busy itself with creating the network operating system. You will be asked a number of questions, but if you are using the default installation (as most new users do) most of the answers will be determined by the software.

Once you have loaded the software onto the hard disk and answered the questions, most of the process will take place automatically. Eventually, it will stop and will ask you if you want to upload the resulting files onto your floppy disks. You do, because these files are the ones that will be used to create NetWare on the file server. Just make sure you use copies, not the original system disks that came from Novell.

If you are using the floppy disk method of NetWare generation, you will go through the same process, except instead of the process taking place automatically, you will be prompted when to change disks. The process is slow, time-consuming, and boring. When you are done, you will have the same files on the same disks as you did with the hard disk method, but it will have taken you significantly longer to do it.

The network method assumes you have a LAN already running, and that the loading process takes place from a server already on the LAN. Normally, this is done by professional LAN installers, but you might want to use it if you already have a network, and simply want to add another server. This is the fastest method of all, since it uses the disk space on the LAN's file server to help in generating the operating system for the new file server.

Once the network generation is complete, you will have the opportunity to load the remainder of the NetWare utilities onto the file server. You will have to do this as the network supervisor from a workstation. Once NetWare is operating on the file server, the server's floppy disk drive is no longer useable. This is a valuable security feature, but it means that you have to have at least one workstation with a floppy disk drive.

Part of the installation process will include telling the server software if you have a hard disk to mirror the primary disk on the server. Novell SFT NetWare supports disk mirroring, either using the same or additional controllers. You have the opportunity to specify the disk channel as a part of the installation. Most PC/AT compatible computers with standard AT disk drives use disk channel 0 during the installation. If you have a Novell Disk Coprocessor Board (or a compatible product) you have the opportunity to choose additional channels. If you choose to have additional disk controllers, the disk mirroring protects you against the chance of failure of the hard disk controller. If they are on the same channel, and sharing the same controller, you protect only against failure of the hard disk. In either case, one disk is used as the primary server disk, while the other is kept as an exact duplicate. If one fails, the other goes into operation automatically. While Novell supports this capability only with SFT NetWare, there are products available that allow disk mirroring with Advanced NetWare.

Utilities

Novell NetWare includes utilities to support the operation and administration of the LAN under normal circumstances. In addition, there are some third-party packages, such as Ontrack Computer System's NetUtils that will allow you to recover data from a server that has gone down. These utilities add to the capabilities of NetWare, but most of the functionality is already included.

Most of the utilities that come with NetWare are for the use of the system supervisor as well as the users. They include utilities such as Syscon, which provides a system console. The supervisor has more choices than do the other users. These items will be covered in Chapters 7 and 9.

Facility Support

Finally, we come to the part of the LAN over which you have the least control—the facility. This means the building that the LAN is in and its related services, including electricity, cooling, and telephone services. Problems with the facility can have a profound effect on your LAN, and you have to take them into account during the design. Unfortunately, you may not be able to control these factors yourself.

The building's electrical supply is usually the first concern you will have. The LAN's file servers, printers and print servers, and support equipment need a clean, reliable source of power if they are to function. If you have a problem with power surges, if you have frequent blackouts or brownouts, or if your electrical system is overloaded, you may lose data and even damage the components of the LAN.

As we mentioned above, an uninterruptable power supply is vital for the file servers. Most people know this. What many forget is that a UPS is just as vital for network bridges, repeaters, print servers, line amplifiers, and other network equipment as it is for the file server. In addition, at least one workstation needs to be protected by a UPS so that the system administrator can direct the saving of files and the shutting down of the system if necessary. Some of these devices can share the UPS with the file servers or with other network support equipment, but they should all be protected.

Cooling is usually taken for granted in a modern office building. Unfortunately, it shouldn't be. There are two reasons for this. The first is that not all LANs are in modern office buildings, and the second is that even the newest building can have a poorly ventilated room or two. Unfortunately, it is often these poorly ventilated rooms that end up with the file server, if for no other reason than that they can't get anyone to work in the room, thereby freeing it for the file server.

Your file server needs to exist within a specified environment, which is described in the specifications for the equipment that the server contains. What these specifications don't tell you is that operating the machinery near the upper end of its range will often shorten its life significantly. It may even cause intermittent and hard-to-fix problems with marginal components. While the file server doesn't need the same kind of cooling as computer rooms for mainframe computers, it does need to be kept at a comfortable, shirt-sleeve temperature.

Then there are the telephone lines. If you plan to have asynchronous communications with your LAN, such as you would use to dial MCI Mail or BIX, you will be using telephone lines. These need to be dedicated to the use of the LAN. You shouldn't have to worry about someone picking up an extension while you're transmitting a FAX image. In addition to being dedicated to the LAN, communications lines that connect to the outside world, including phone lines, should be routed through a surge suppressor. A lightning strike could be fatal to the LAN.

The building and the location of the LAN components within it are your final concern. You not only need to put the components near power and in a cool area, you need to keep them free from excessive moisture (including rain) and from being bumped by people, mail carts, or forklifts. A jar at the wrong time can destroy a hard disk.

Now that you know what you need to buy, requisition, and otherwise obtain, you need to know how to justify it. In the next chapter, we will look at the costs and benefits of your Novell NetWare LAN.

6

The Novell LAN—Costs and Benefits

The decision to install a Novell local area network involves many trade-offs. As with any large project, there are costs involved and benefits to be derived. In this chapter we'll look at the costs you are likely to incur beyond the obvious price of equipment and software. We'll also explore further the benefits of a local area network in general and a Novell LAN in particular.

The Price of a LAN—More Than Iron and Diskettes

Installing a local area network requires a fairly significant commitment both on the part of management and the future network administrator. Before we get into the mechanics of producing a realistic estimate of what your new network will cost, we should examine the process of planning for, costing, proposing and selling the concept of a LAN to higher management.

Many network administrators have found that the success or failure of a new network can rest on the degree to which their management is committed to the project. Often that commitment is a direct reflection of how well the project was presented from the beginning.

We have, over the past few years, talked to many network administrators about how they approached the prospect of a new network. Here is what they told us about the keys to success in the planning stages.

First, do your homework. Many times LANs seem to grow out of an office full of single-user machines. That's all right, administrators feel, if you plan carefully for the conversion. If you have the benefit of proposing a system from scratch, successful administrators are unanimous in their advice—get the largest system you can afford. Because, if you don't, they say, you'll end up replacing it in fairly short order. The old adage about data expanding to fill available space seems to hold true in the network world.

Remember the issues. Size of the LAN in terms of workstations, both today and tomorrow is a critical factor. The number of users affects the size and number of network drives, data rate and, to some extent, the topology and protocol you select.

The need for internetworking is another important issue. Will you need to communicate with external LANs? With wide area networks? With public data networks? With mainframe or minicomputers? And what about the types of applications you'll be running? Do you need large databases? If so, you may need to consider a distributed network with at least one dedicated database server. Does your organization do extensive word processing or desktop publishing? That will dictate the types and number of printers and the possible need for a printer server.

What resources currently exist? Do you have an installed base of stand-alone workstations? What wiring and cable is already installed in your building? How far are the users physically separated? Do you need to support users on more than one floor? In more than one building? Examine your requirements carefully and begin to assign actual costs to your equipment, software and cabling. As we discussed in the previous chapter, a detailed requirements analysis is the key to a smooth and cost-effective installation.

But, how do you assign costs to the various components of a LAN? And, perhaps more importantly, how do you assign costs to the intangibles like training, down time, learning curve, installation time and a host of other hidden expenses?

The cost of the network in terms of work stations is fairly easy to figure. For each workstation you will need a network interface card. The interface card is the printed circuit board that plugs into the workstation and connects it to the LAN. At this writing those cards can vary in cost from around $300 to around $1,000 each with prices coming down almost daily. Depending upon the type of protocol you plan to use, your network interface cards can be slightly more or less expensive.

Network software from Novell comes as a complete kit which includes both the server end and all of the workstation software. When you buy NetWare you get a full network's worth of software for a single price regardless of the number of users (unless the number of users is restricted by the design of the LAN).

Although prices probably will increase during the useful life of this book, here is a representative listing of NetWare prices as of July, 1989.

SFT NetWare	$4,695
Advanced NetWare	$2,695
ELS NetWare, Level I (4 users)	$ 595
ELS NetWare, Level II (8 users)	$1,395

The cost of servers also can vary tremendously depending upon the level of sophistication you require. Your server can be as small as an AT clone for around $3,000 to a sophisticated server from a supplier like Network Connection which specializes in optimized network servers at $6,000 to $10,000 depending upon options.

The final aspect of hard network costs is cable and installation. Cable can cost anything from a few cents per foot for twisted pair cable to more than a dollar a foot for coax or fiber optic cable. Installation costs vary greatly, depending on what area of the country you're in and who you contract to do the physical installation.

If you get the idea that the hard costs of a LAN vary greatly, you're right. You can, to a significant degree, control your hard costs through choice of topology and protocol. But there are many so-called soft costs that are harder to estimate. These include disruption during installation, training and learning curve.

Soft Costs—The Hidden Price of Networking

There are a few hidden costs involved in setting up a LAN that may not be obvious at the start of your network design project. The first you will encounter is the disruption of your normal routine during installation and setup. How serious this cost is will depend upon how well you plan.

Setting Up and Installing

It is possible to limit the disruption of computing by users to a few hours per user plus learning curve. If you set up your server and test it thoroughly from your own workstation before trying to set up the first network user, you'll save yourself a lot of pain. The key is to spend the extra time it will take to properly configure and test the server and one workstation before attempting to set up further stations.

Before you even attempt to begin your installation it's imperative to assess what will be physically involved in running cables and attaching them to the workstations. This tends to be the most disruptive because users lose the use of their computers. They also lose the opportunity to gain any benefit from learning about the network. So, the end result from the user's point of view is that he or she lost valuable work time, got behind their schedule, and has nothing to show for it. Needless to say, your new network won't be about to win any popularity contests at this point.

If, on the other hand, you carefully plan the physical disruptions for periods when workers are not using their machines, you'll save yourself a lot of grief and your staff will lose less work.

Here are some hints for cutting your work disruption to a minimum. First, run cable from the server location to the individual workstations. In some buildings this can be done in two steps. If you have a wiring closet in your building which you plan to use for cable distribution, wire from the server location to the closet and then from the closet to the workstations one at a time.

Some topologies require hubs or bridges. Whenever possible, wire to the hub first, then branch out to the workstations. Since you will want to test each of your cable runs before hooking up the LAN, it is usually easiest and least disruptive to run the cable from the workstation to some intermediate point like a hub, test the line and get out of the user's way. If you are using existing cables within your facility, your job can be even less disruptive. The key point to remember, however, is that you should completely test each piece of the network, separately and together, before you log on the first user. That way you can 'plug and play' each workstation in a very short period of time.

The second hint for limiting disruptions is insure that any hard disks on individual workstations have been backed up before you install the network card and boot the workstation on the LAN. Although it is unlikely, it is possible to damage data on a workstation drive during the process of conversion from a stand-alone computer to a network workstation.

Also, if the workstation has a hard drive, you should put the user's network workstation files in a directory on the workstation fixed drive. A word or two of caution here—don't include passwords. Although it may seem much more convenient to include passwords in the log on files, doing so completely subverts the security inherent in your LAN. With passwords embedded in the log on files of a workstation, any user who wants can log on. You as the supervisor will have no control over your users or how they interact with the network.

Once you have installed the cables up to the workstations, take some time and set up your own workstation for testing. You will need to have two workstations initially. The first is the server console, which really is just the keyboard and screen attached to the server. It's the way you will be interacting with the server during the installation. We'll discuss the installation of the server in Chapter 10. You will also use a separate computer (which could be your own workstation if it has a hard drive) to generate the network operating system. You will use the console to install the server and perform many of your administrator tasks. The second is your own workstation. This may or may not be the console, but using the FCONSOLE virtual console utility there are many tasks you will carry out from it.

Also, you can use it for testing the basic network before connecting the first user. Once wiring is in and you have connected the console and your workstation, you'll be ready to install the server. In Chapter 10 we'll discuss server installation in detail. For now, it's important to realize that you can install the server using the console and test it using your workstation without disrupting the routines of your staff. You can also test the generic boot disk you'll be building a bit later.

Your objective at this point should be to prepare a user's boot disk in advance of trying to set up the user. The only variables left when you begin the individual user's installation should be the cable between the workstation and the server, and the user's learning curve. Our preference in setting up users is to set up and train each user individually and completely, one at a time. The exception to this preference is that it is a good idea to hold some general training with all users to provide basic familiarity with the network before moving individual users to their LAN workstations.

Even if you plan to put the boot information on a workstation's fixed drive, you should make a boot disk as for use as a backup and to speed workstation installation. In most cases the boot disk will be pretty much the same from workstation to workstation. Different computers used as workstations will vary somewhat, of course, but generally speaking you can build a single boot disk including general purpose batch files which you can simply modify for individual cases. Again, it's possible to build this disk from your own workstation without getting in your staff's way.

Your next step is to install the network adapter cards. We suggest that you either log a bit of overtime or work nights while your staff works days. In any event, you'll want to install a workstation while its user doesn't need to use it. That way you'll simply install the card, load and modify the boot files and test the workstation. The next day you can complete the training of the workstation operator.

Training—Keep It Short, But Keep It

This leads us to the second major cause of disruption—training. You can carry out preinstallation training in a variety of ways. But, and this is an important proviso, you should provide it prior to cutting over to the network.

Training takes a couple of forms. The first is familiarization for the network administrators.

What kinds of resources should you commit to training? In the case of basic training, as we will soon see, there is the time spent in formal classroom training and the time spent coaching new users as they become more and more familiar with the new LAN. Basic training is rarely more than a week in length. However, individual coaching time varies based on individual skills and the complexity of the network.

Training of system administrators is another situation entirely. Usually supervisor training, unlike basic-user training, takes place outside of your facility. This requires travel and time away from the office in many cases. Generally, you should plan on at least a week of off-site training for your administrators—longer if they're less experienced. However, unless your administrator is quite experienced, it is a good idea for him to get the formal training if you are installing a medium to large LAN. On-the-job-training for the administrator will usually take the form of working along with the designers and installers of the system.

Often organizations assign several administrators, each with special duties, to a large network. Some of these future network managers will have Novell experience, some will have experience with other networks and some will have only single-user PC backgrounds. They should all be involved with the set-up of the new network from the beginning, including receiving a similar level of training and working along with the installing team if possible. This provides a degree of on-the-job-experience added to the formal training sessions.

There are many organizations that are Novell-certified to train users and administrators on NetWare. Often, if you have hired an outside consultant to install a system, you will find that your installer also provides training classes. At this point the only workers who will have had their routines disrupted for training are the future network administrators. Users have yet to be involved.

Once the network is nearly installed it is a good idea to hold a familiarization session with the users. Each user should be provided with a workstation users guide along with a copy of Novell's "NetWare Basics." Make
sure that the administrators are prepared to answer basic user questions
and perform simple troubleshooting of operator problems.

When the network is ready for connection to the workstations, you can
save a lot of problems by hooking up workstations individually and training the users as you bring their workstations on line. In a small installation
this is not a problem. But in a large installation you may be better off to
install and train workgroup clusters, perhaps in groups of four or five
users.

The final step in the training process actually takes place as the users
become familiar with their new procedures through repeated use. However, you should be certain that administrators are capable of supporting
their users as the users venture further afield. The best way to insure that
your level of administrator support is at its peak is to provide periodic
advanced training. Time spent keeping the skills of network administrators finely honed will pay big dividends in user-efficiency and reduced
frustration. You will also limit the load placed on administrators caused by
constant operator difficulties and the resultant need to recover lost information. We cannot stress the importance of ongoing network administrator training too heavily.

With the availability of preinstallation training and a skilled group of
network administrators to support users on the new LAN, how long does
it take for operators to become proficient with the network? That is largely
dependent on how you install the system.

Remember that most of the application software your users will be running is the same as that they have been using on single-user stations.
True, there are some differences in the operation of a LAN from the user
standpoint, but most of these can be masked behind a competent shell or
menu system. The biggest barrier to proficiency exists within the administrator community. For it is the administrators who will need to go beneath
the surface of a menu to ferret out problems, recover lost or damaged
data, install new users and applications, expand the network and keep the
LAN finely tuned.

The only way to limit the learning curve for administrators is to involve
them from the beginning. Decide who your administrators are to be at the
outset of your network planning and bring them into the development
and installation process as early as possible. If you prepare your administrators properly and provide a simple user interface, you'll limit the users'
learning curves significantly. There is little barrier to smooth operation at

the workstation level if you prepare both the system and the users for their new environments.

Benefits Can Outweigh the Drawbacks

Even though the installation of a local area network is not without its costs, most workgroups who must share data find that the benefits far outshine the costs. There are several specific benefits you will derive from the ability to work from a consistent and sharable base of information. One of the chief benefits is the ability to keep information current. When you are using one database instead of several, or one set of word processing documents or spreadsheets, you can insure that your data remain current and consistent.

In addition to the obvious benefits of using the same data, there are some other benefits that are specific to the way LANs work. For example, if many users are connected to each other on a network, there is the possibility of greatly improved communications. One specific network tool for improving communications is electronic mail (E-Mail). Another tool is coordinated calendaring. Finally, you will achieve material savings in some areas of hardware and virtually all types of software. Of course, there is far less paper to be lost, stored or passed around.

Data Sharing—The First and Most Obvious Area of Savings

The benefits of data sharing tend to be a bit abstract on first examination. The obvious reason is that it is difficult to put a dollar value on improvements in efficiency. However, some of the specific benefits of data sharing are best illustrated by database management applications. DBMS packages offer so much power for today's business users that many organizations are finding that they can create entire office environments out of database systems. Indeed, with powerful database programming languages such as dBASE, Paradox's PAL and R:Base, it is possible to build a set of complete applications and databases customized for your environment. That's the good news. The bad news is that unless your entire workgroup has universal access to these systems, they are of little if any benefit.

Keeping databases up to date when several users need access to them is virtually impossible in a non-networked environment. On a Novell LAN, however, a single copy of the database is available to all those who wish to use it. When one user updates the database, the other users gain access to the most current information. The same benefits accrue to users of word processors and spreadsheets. Word processing documents, especially, lend themselves to workgroup editing.

Word processors such as the network version of WordPerfect allow workgroup editing of documents. When documents are edited, the "red-lined" (edited) version remains with the document. Thus, each subsequent editor can see what went before as well as work from a current version of the document. On a simpler level, a secretary can generate a document, pass it over the network to her boss, who makes changes and passes it up the line to the next level for approval. When the document returns to the secretary for final typing and printing, it has been completely revised and approved. All that remains is for the secretary to reformat and print.

Spreadsheets, like databases, lend themselves to group use. Spreadsheets tend to be produced by a few people and used by many. Also, there is a tendency for several users to perform "what if" analyses on spreadsheets produced by a relatively small group of individuals. The key benefit of the LAN in this case is that universal availability of a spreadsheet insures that all users on the network can work from the same base of information.

Improving Workgroup Communication—E-Mail and Other Tools

Although Novell no longer supplies E-Mail as part of its current NetWare release, there are several competent E-Mail packages available. They operate differently depending upon the package, but, in general, E-Mail is handled like a utility that you invoke for either a command line or a menu shell. We'll show you in Chapter 9 how to use menu shells.

But, improving communications using a LAN is only partly a function of E-Mail. Other tools such as FAX servers, network scheduling packages and bridges to wide area networks enhance inter- and intra-office communications. Novell supports virtually all of these tools, even though most must come from third-party vendors. Because Novell commands the largest market share of any single network provider, however, you will have no trouble finding the Novell-compatible communications tools you need.

Let's examine some of these communications tools in a bit more detail. What should you expect from your E-Mail package? E-Mail packages need to be able to take advantage of the message-routing capabilities of the network. That routing, you'll recall, is a specific function of the network layer of our Open Systems model. It is important that you select a package that allows you to communicate with other networks connected to your LAN. This includes not only other local area networks, but also wide area networks with which you interconnect.

However, there is a relatively new concept called Message Handling Service (MHS) which takes simple network E-Mail a step further. MHS allows other messaging services such as FAX, Telnet and internetwork mail to operate transparently to the user. Networks with MHS installed can communicate directly, as if they were one network. Thus, you can use MHS to send a FAX to any FAX machine in the world if your LAN has a FAX server and the appropriate MHS support.

Probably the most exciting aspect of a MHS system is that it remains virtually transparent to the users. One of the most difficult tasks on a LAN is communication with other networks, both LAN and WAN. Networks using MHS communicate directly through the appropriate layer of the model. Thus the usual physical layer may occasionally be bypassed, achieving greater efficiency and transparency. Current releases of NetWare (from 2.11 on) have abandoned traditional E-Mail for compatibility with MHS.

Other tools for improving workgroup communication are the calendaring and scheduling capabilities present in many network shells. A network shell, in general terms, is a software program that resides in the workstation's memory and stands between the operator and the network. In the case of the NetWare Shell, which we discussed earlier, the Shell actually provides all of the interface between the workstation and the network. However, there are other shells which perform similar functions for the user. For example, instead of sitting between the workstation operating system and the network operating system (NOS) these shells provide a user interface and menu system.

There are many menu systems available that are NetWare compatible, including an excellent version available from Novell. In many regards, the Novell NetWare Menu Utilities is a do-it-yourself approach. The Utilities have two parts. The first is access to several submenus. The submenus each provides specific capabilities such as system configuration, session management, directory and file management, and printer management. You invoke a submenu by typing its name at the DOS prompt.

The second aspect of the menu system is the ability to create your own menu shell. The menu shell you create may be a set of submenus called from a master menu. Each of the submenus can contain choices of yet more submenus or invoke particular applications. Thus, if you wanted calendaring and other efficiency-improving utilities, you would need to have the individual programs and invoke them from a menu you create with the menu-creating utility.

However, you might select a LAN shell which already has several special utilities associated with it if you're dealing with a third-party vendor. Often, one of these utilities is a scheduling program. Network scheduling programs allow workgroup members to send out messages calling other members to a meeting or some other workgroup activity. Once the members receive these "invitations," they have the option of accepting, declining or asking for the activity to be rescheduled to a more convenient time. If any one requests a reschedule, the member calling the meeting can ask the network to find the most universally convenient time and reinvite.

One of the best of the available shell programs is WordPerfect Office. Office is a sophisticated shell that provides a complete menuing system for network users as well as a scheduling package. It even goes so far as to allow users to schedule resources as well as people. Thus, if you held a meeting for five people in Conference Room B with an overhead slide projector, Office would invite the people, request the conference room from the person responsible for assigning it, and request the projector.

Some programs allow users to evaluate their use of time. Some provide facilities for predetermining best schedules based upon the typical workdays of the network users. All are Novell-compatible. All improve workgroup efficiency. Taken with the other benefits of LANs, these shells materially improve the way offices function.

Some Other Network Benefits

There are some benefits of networking that can be measured in dollars and cents, chiefly savings in some types of hardware and virtually all software. Your biggest hardware savings will be due to the reduced number of printers required for a network as opposed to a single user environment. As you analyze the number of printers you need you'll want to look at how you are using the network as well as how many users you have.

For example, if you do a lot of desktop publishing, you'll certainly need a laser printer for finished documents. If several people need lasers in a single user environment, you must have several printers at an average of $2,000 plus each. But on a network, depending upon the number of users, you may only need one. In fact, a few "workhorse" printers will usually be enough on most LANs—which makes quite a contrast with a printer for every workstation.

Another area of savings derives from centralized WAN communication. No longer does each user need a modem and a dedicated phone line. Instead a communication server, modem and dedicated phone line will suffice. Also, don't forget the benefits that come with control of external communications. Scripts can be written for interconnection to wide area networks that limit users to those networks to which they need access. Such communications programs often allow for tracking of users and the amount of time they spend on long distance data calls or access to public data networks such as Tymnet. Public Data Networks, or PDNs, are the data communications equivalent of the long-distance phone system.

Security of Information—The Hidden Network Benefit

There is a final benefit that stems from the way LANs are organized. Data in a network environment is inherently more secure than data on individual PCs. The reason for this is that, although there are many more users within typing distance of the data, there are substantially more controls on how they get at it than in a single-user environment.

Some of these controls are real, others are psychological. The psychological controls have to do with the perception of security as a way of network life. Users with individual stand-alone workstations tend to lapse into an attitude that "the data is mine because it's on my machine." Also, the feeling that their personal machine bears their individuality and, therefore, may not be so easy to get into gives a false sense of security.

But, on a network, all data is protected because "that's the way networks are." Data becomes the property of the group and the network administrator has a more acceptable role than the office manager who is always complaining about papers on the desks or disks left around the office.

Remember that most threats to the security of data come not from malefactors attempting to compromise the company secrets, but from carelessness. Disks get erased, coffee gets spilled in just the wrong place, data gets lost in someone's desk. Single user computers invite computer anarchy and subsequent lost data.

Going hand-in-hand with data security is data convenience. Files on a LAN are (or should be) well organized and accessible to those who need access. LANs have a variety of menu systems available to standardize the access to those files. In Chapter 9 we'll show you some examples of the better menu shells (in addition to WordPerfect Office), but, for now, you should be aware that they can help bring out a network's more sterling qualities.

All of these issues go towards improving workgroup productivity, security of information, efficiency, and the general atmosphere of the workplace. However, while it certainly is true that when you are able to organize the workplace into some semblance of order, things go much more smoothly; it is also true that our industry moves at a lightning clip, with products leapfrogging each other almost daily.

So, here's another helpful hint: if you are new to the networking game, get some familiarity with the products on the market to support your LAN activities. The best place to get that kind of information is from the better trade journals and computer periodicals. These magazines and newspapers come at a variety of levels of sophistication. Some are very technically oriented, while others reflect more of a managerial turn of mind.

In any event, they all contain a rich variety of editorial information, new product announcements—and advertising, which is where you'll find a treasure trove of information. Look for new products that will help you manage your system. Look for information and products to help your installation. Be especially vigilant for case histories and "how-to" stories. All of this information will help you avoid the pitfalls that supposedly accompany your first installation. As you look for products and advice, however, be sure it's appropriate.

We know of one product, for example, that is a superb tool for managing network directory trees. It works only on Novell systems, however. If you happened to have some other network, you'd have a useless piece of software. But most of the developers' advertising conveniently leaves out the Novell information. Keep your eyes open for that sort of oversight.

Can you install a local area network without turning your organization upside down? With the right preplanning, certainly. Will the final costs be more than you anticipated? Probably. So, take a little extra time and care during the planning stages. Finally, will you derive benefits that are worth the costs? If you go about your planning and installation carefully and methodically, you will almost certainly gain the benefits—and they will be very much worth the costs.

Summary

The bottom line for network planners and managers is that, as in all things, the benefits come at a price. The price of network installation goes beyond the equipment and software you'll require for your LAN. If you are to experience a smooth network installation and turn-up you need to understand the so-called "soft" costs and plan for them.

But, in all but the smallest two or three person organizations, the benefits of data sharing, equipment and software cost savings, intrapersonal communications and planning far outweigh any of the costs of installation, training and learning curve.

Now that we've introduced you to the fundamentals of Novell NetWare, LANs, standards and the philosophies involved in the network decision-making process, it's time to roll up our sleeves and get our hands dirty, so to speak. In Part 2 you'll learn the specifics of using Novell NetWare; being a network supervisor or administrator, and selecting, installing and running applications on your new Novell LAN.

In the next chapter, we'll take our first jaunt down Novell Lane and learn first-hand what it's like to use NetWare, what NetWare can do for you, and how to make it work in your computing environment.

Part II
Using Novell
NetWare

Chapter 7

The Novell NetWare Commands and Their Environment

Now that you know something of the theory and design of Novell local area networking, it's time to get your hands on the software. At this point, we're going to assume that your copy of Novell NetWare has already been installed, your workstation attached, and all of the other installation work performed. If you need to refer to how to install your Novell NetWare, see the description in Chapter 10.

As a user, you will be interacting with NetWare from your personal computer. Even when NetWare is actually running on the file server, you will be able to use the utility programs and commands that are available with NetWare. You will do this by telling NetWare that you want to have access to the server, and then by executing commands, just as you would from MS-DOS.

The First Steps

You perform a function called "logging in" to tell NetWare that you want your personal computer (or workstation) attached to the network. There are at least three steps to this process, although there can be (and usually are) more. First, you have to run the workstation software, then you have to tell NetWare who you are.

The workstation software itself consists of two programs.

First, there is a program called IPX.COM which is Novell's hardware driver. This means that it knows what sort of computer you are using and what sort of equipment is attached to the computer. IPX was created when the workstation shell was generated. A separate version of IPX must be created for each type of workstation and each type of network interface card. IPX is very hardware-specific, so that if you change even a small setting on the network interface card, such as the address setting, you will need to generate a new version of IPX.

You run IPX by typing its name. When the program starts up, it will report its existence and tell you what sort of network interface card it's using and the card's address. Once IPX is running, you can then run the workstation shell.

The workstation shell works with COMMAND.COM on your computer to allow you to use the added capabilities of the LAN running NetWare. When the workstation shell is generated during the installation process, there will be one for each major revision of MS-DOS, called NET2, NET3 and NET4. You run the one that conforms to your version of MS-DOS. If you are using MS-DOS 3.3, for example, you would run NET3.COM. When you do this, the program announces its presence, and you're ready to log in.

Up to this point, you have been using the hard disk or floppy disk on your computer. Both IPX and NET3 were in a directory on one of your local drives. Now you will take advantage of the capabilities added by the workstation shell and move to the network drive. Normally this will be drive F: although there may be some differences depending on the way the network is set up.

When you tell the computer to go to drive F: you will see something like this:

```
F:\LOGIN>
```

When you see this prompt, you will need to enter the command, LOGIN. NetWare will prompt you for your name. You will need to give it the name that the system administrator gave you for logging in. Chances are, you won't use all of your real name. Most network systems administrators will use a person's first initial and last name, expressed as a single word. If your name were Jane Doe, for example, you would probably find your login name listed as "JDOE" or possibly as simply "DOE." Exactly what you get will depend on how your system administrator has it set up.

If your network is using passwords, you will then be prompted for your password. Normally, you will choose a password when you use the network the first time, and may change it whenever you wish. Not all system administrators require users to have passwords, but most do, and it's always a good idea to use them, even on small systems.

Once you have entered your password, NetWare will run what is called a login script. This is a series of instructions similar to the AUTOEXEC.BAT file on your MS-DOS disk that tells NetWare how to configure the network for you. It will set up sections of the file server's disk to appear as disk drives to your computer. You might find, for example, that the WordPerfect subdirectory on the file server was listed as drive G:. Again, the details of your login script will depend on your system administrator.

There are two types of login scripts. The first (which we've just discussed) is the system login script. There is also an individual login script, which you can set up yourself to configure the network or perform other functions, such as checking your electronic mail. Once you have finished running the login scripts, you will be using NetWare, either at the command prompt or within a menu. As you will see later, NetWare can offer you either type of user interface. The menus will be discussed in Chapter 9.

The Directories

In its normal configuration, NetWare sets up four subdirectories on the file server's disk. They are SYSTEM, MAIL, PUBLIC, and LOGIN. There will also be subdirectories for applications that the system administrator has set up on the file server.

You've seen how the LOGIN subdirectory is used. The MAIL subdirectory is created by NetWare when it is installed on the file server; it contains the user's personal login script, but otherwise it is empty unless it is used by the electronic mail system on your network. You will, however, have occasion to use the PUBLIC subdirectory frequently. This is where most of the system utility programs are located, as well as additional software including menus and the like. The SYSTEM subdirectory is normally only open to the system administrator.

The programs in the PUBLIC subdirectory include those you need to control system functions, such as printing and passwords, to those that will show you who controls which files, to a multi-user arcade game called Snipes. They are handled in the same way as are any other MS-DOS commands, and, in some cases, they replace commands that won't work with networks, such as CHKDSK.

In short, you have what appears to be MS-DOS, with some enhance-ments. You run programs the same way, you look at directories the same way. You can carry out most MS-DOS operations just as you would on your own personal computer. There are, however, some differences.

The biggest differences are related to security and file protection. The system administrator has the ability to hide files and directories from you, to prevent files from being copied, or to prevent files from being erased. This prevents you from seeing files belonging to other users, or from acci-dentally erasing a data file needed by others. Of course, it also means that other users can't see your data files or other information unless you want them to.

The ability to control who gets access to programs and data files, word processing files, and the like is an important feature of NetWare. It means that people get to share information, while retaining the ability to protect the information they want to keep private. Normally, a system administra-tor will set up a special area of the disk, often within the PUBLIC subdirec-tory, as a place for people to place information that they want to share.

Moving this information to those special areas involves nothing more complicated than the MS-DOS COPY command. You use COPY to move information into a public area just as you would use the same command to make a copy of a word processing file on your own computer. The ability to appear just as if it were MS-DOS is an important feature of Novell NetWare.

The Command Reference

Now that you know that Novell NetWare resembles MS-DOS so closely as far as the user is concerned, it's time to take a look at the commands, how they are used, and who can use them. You should know that there are four types of commands. There are simple commands and utilities, very much like the MS-DOS commands you are already used to. There are also special commands, for use only by the system administrator. There are a few commands that lead to menuing environments, and, finally, there are commands that are used only within the login scripts.

There is one additional class of command that is used at the file server's keyboard. These are called console commands, and they control a few of the basic functions of the server operation, such as shutting the server down or controlling the print queue. Most of the functions of these com-mands are duplicated by commands that the supervisor can execute from a workstation.

The first set of commands will be those that everyone will use. These are the commands that are in the PUBLIC subdirectory or in other public areas, and are available for any user. Each command will be listed, its proper use explained, and examples given. There will be many examples of the results of commands. Just as in the case of MS-DOS commands, the NetWare commands are executed by simply typing their name at the MS-DOS prompt. If the command is within that directory, or is otherwise in the MS-DOS path, then it will be executed.

Each command will be explained in its operation. Where applicable, the command will be followed by any appropriate arguments or other statements. Novell NetWare will usually allow you to enter arguments or not as you desire. If you do not enter them, the software will prompt you for the information.

In this section, there are some conventions that we are using to make the instructions as clear as possible, while still keeping the explanation to a reasonable length. For example, the command's name will be in bold letters. A key on the keyboard will be enclosed in angle brackets. Arguments that follow the command will be enclosed in square brackets. These are the same conventions as those used in the Novell manuals, so you can see the same thing in either place. Otherwise, the instructions are consistent with the MS-DOS manuals in the use of such things has asterisks to represent any character.

ATTACH

Command Format:

ATTACH [server[/user]]

Command Function:

Because NetWare allows you to use multiple file servers in the same network, you need to have a way to use those servers. When you log on to NetWare, you will find yourself using a default server. This could be considered your home server, and it is the one that you will always log onto initially. When you want to use an additional server, you must ATTACH to it. You do this by typing the ATTACH command, followed by the name of the server that you want access to. You can find the names of available servers using the SLIST command, which will be explained later in the section.

There are two ways to use the ATTACH command. If you simply type the word ATTACH, you will be prompted for the server name and your user name. If you give only the server name, you will be prompted for your user name. If you give both, you will be attached without added prompts.

Using ATTACH

If you want to let ATTACH prompt you for answers, simply enter the following:

```
ATTACH
```

You will then receive the following prompt:

```
Enter server name:
```

You will type in the server name and then will receive the following prompt:

```
Enter user name:
```

You will then enter your user name for that server. It may not be the same as the user name that you used before. Normally, user names are kept the same on all servers on a LAN for convenience, but this is not a requirement, and your system administrator may have set it up differently. If you are in doubt, you should check with your system administrator.

Here is how a session would look:

```
F:\LOGIN> ATTACH

        Enter server name: SERVER_ONE

        Enter user name: SJONES

        Enter your password:

        Your station is now attached to server SERVER_ONE

F:\LOGIN>
```

Note that if you don't have a password, you won't be prompted for one. Also, before you can actually do anything with the server you have just become attached to, you must still MAP it to a drive letter. This may be done automatically, or it may have to be done manually. See the MAP command for more information. You may also map the new server to a drive letter through the use of the SESSION utility, which also will be explained later.

If you want to run ATTACH using the command line approach, you simply type in the variables you would enter at prompts. If you type in only the server name, you will be prompted for your user name. This is how the command would appear:

```
F:\LOGIN> ATTACH SERVER_ONE/SJONES

        Your station is now attached to server SERVER_ONE
```

If you use a password, you will be prompted for it as you saw above. If you don't enter your user name, you will be prompted for it, as follows:

```
F:\LOGIN> ATTACH SERVER_ONE
        Enter user name: SJONES
        Enter your password:
        Your station is now attached to server SERVER_ONE
```

You can verify that you are attached to a specific server through the use of the WHOAMI command. Remember that you must map the added server to a drive letter before you can use it. If you do this frequently, you may want to create a batch file to do the attaching for you. If you do it every time you log on, you may want to make it a part of your user login script, which will be explained in the next chapter.

CAPTURE

Command Format:

CAPTURE [Options]

Command Function:

CAPTURE is a command that allows you to redirect a workstation's printing to the network. That means that characters that would normally be sent out of the printer port to a local printer are instead intercepted and sent through the network to a network printer. CAPTURE works with nearly all software destined for a printer. It does not work with plotters. The CAPTURE command may use one or more of the following options:

SHow

Use the SHOW option to see what the current settings of CAPTURE are. It will show you the current server, print queue, and network printer that the local printer port has been redirected to. You must not combine this option with any other option.

Autoendcap

The AUTOENDCAP option makes sure that any information that remains to be printed by your application gets sent to the printer when you enter the application or when you start another one. Otherwise, it works like the ENDCAP option (discussed later) except that the redirection to the network printer remains active.

NoAutoendcap

This is the option that is the opposite function from AUTOENDCAP, above. It prevents data from being sent to the printer when you exit or enter an application.

TImeout=n

This option turns on the TIMEOUT feature of Capture, which automatically sends any data to the printer once the application has stopped sending it for a specific period of time. You replace the letter n with a number from 1 to 1000 to specify the number of seconds that Capture should wait for additional input before sending information to the printer. A good number for this is 2, although some applications, such as dBASE, often require settings of 30 or higher if significant delays are expected in data being sent to the printer.

Local = n

This option tells the printer what LPT port is to be redirected to the network printer. The default is LPT1, but you can use 1 through 3.

Server = server

The SERVER option lets you specify which server on the network will handle your printing. It will default to your default server, but you can specify another server as well. Make sure you substitute the name of a server on your LAN for the word "server" above.

Job = job

You can specify a particular print job configuration, provided your system administrator has defined one using the PRINTCON utility. You will need to check with the supervisor to see what, if any, print job configurations are available, and what they are configured to do.

Printer = n

You use this option to specify which of the server's printers your work will go to. You have a choice of printers numbered 0 through 4. The default is 0. If you choose a printer number that doesn't have a printer physically attached, the print job will be stored in the disk, and printed when a printer is attached. Normally, you would use this option in conjunction with the SERVER option above.

Queue = queue

Information is stored on disk in a print queue until the printer is ready for it. Each print queue has a name, and you can choose to send your print job to a particular queue. To do this, you use this option, replacing "queue" with the name of the print queue you want to use.

Form = form or n

NetWare will let you use predefined forms, which are used as a part of the print job. The system administrator will choose and set up the forms, and you will need to check with the system administrator to see what forms are available, and what they do. You replace "form" or n with the name or number of the form.

Copies = n

You can have NetWare print multiple copies of a document. You do this by using the option, replacing n with the number of copies you need, up to 256.

Tabs = n

If your application does not support print formatting, NetWare will do it for you. You can choose the number of spaces to replace a tab with, and CAPTURE will do it for you. You can choose a number from 0 to 18 to replace n with. Very few applications will need this option.

No Tabs

If you'd rather your print formatting arrive at the printer with tabs intact, use this option, but use it only for applications that don't do their own print formatting. Very few applications will need this option.

NAMe = name

Normally, CAPTURE will print a banner at the beginning of each print job identifying the job and the user ID of the sender. This allows you to see which job on a printer is yours, while allowing you to pick and choose whose document to snoop through. If you want some other name replace "name" with the one you want to use. Normally, the user-ID you logged in with will appear here.

Banner = banner

CAPTURE uses a banner to identify each print job. The banner is a sheet that is printed ahead of the print job that contains the name of the user (see NAME, above) as well as other information. Normally, the acronym LST: appears on the bottom of the banner sheet, but you can choose any 12 characters you want. An example would be something like this:

FRED'S_STUFF

You use the underline to denote a space between words.

No Banner

If you don't want a banner for some reason, you can eliminate it entirely with this option.

Form Feed

If you want your network printer to perform a form feed after a print job, you use this option. This will result in a blank sheet being placed between print jobs, and is sometimes necessary on printers using continuous form paper.

No Form Feed

This option turns off the FORM FEED option, above.

CReate = filename

If you want the print job to go to a file rather than a printer, you use the CREATE option. It creates a file under the name indicated by "filename." The file will be created in your default directory, unless you specify some other path. You can specify a complete path, including the specific file server where you want the file stored.

Keep

This option tells NetWare not to discard information if the process of printing is interrupted. It is especially useful in cases where information may be collected over a long period of time before printing actually occurs. In those circumstances, CAPTURE will tell NetWare to keep the partial print queue file rather than erasing it. That way, if the power fails or your server or workstation is interrupted for some other reason, the information collected for printing to that point will be preserved. If your workstation fails, the file server will print whatever information it did receive after 15 minutes have elapsed. If you do not use KEEP, this information will be discarded.

Using CAPTURE

Not all applications require you to use CAPTURE. Some, including the network version of WordPerfect, handle printing tasks themselves, and will direct print jobs to the appropriate server and printer. Applications that were designed for a single user environment will require it, however, if printing on a network printer is desired.

Normally, you will run CAPTURE using only the TIMEOUT option. This is because the defaults in CAPTURE are set so that they will work properly with most software. You set the timeout option because you rarely want separate documents printed as a single print job, and the TIMEOUT option will assure that they are printed separately. For example, if you were using a stand-alone word processor and sent a series of short letters to the network printer using CAPTURE, the TIMEOUT option would assure that they would appear as separate documents. If you didn't use the TIMEOUT option, they would appear as one long document. This is because the print queue would store the information until you left the application, and then would print all of it.

As we mentioned earlier, you may have to vary the amount of time that TIMEOUT waits before printing. Not all applications will be able to keep the delay between sections of text to less than two seconds. Some database programs may require times in excess of 30 seconds. You will have to find out the correct setting empirically, increasing the time allowed until the printed output arrives properly. You can usually find out the approximate time that you should set the waiting period by trying the application in a stand-alone mode, and seeing how long the printer waits for input.

Normally, though, you will find a two second timeout period to be adequate. To set this, you would enter the following command line:

```
CAPTURE TI=2
```

Capturing your output to a file instead of the printer is just as simple. The difference is that you have to specify the name of a file, and tell CAPTURE to create it. Here is an example:

```
CAPTURE CR=LETTERS.TXT
```

You can put a path description in front of the file name. The path can include the name of the server, as well as the name of the drive (as it's mapped on your system) and any subdirectories. You can add any appropriate options. Here's an example:

```
CAPTURE CR=SERVER_ONE/SYS:WORDPROC\FILES\LETTERS.TXT NA
```

That string of instructions means that you want CAPTURE to create a file named LETTERS.TXT. It will be placed on a server named SERVER_ONE on the SYS: volume, in a subdirectory called WORD-PROC\FILES. The NA at the end means that Autoendcap is disabled.

Finally, there is a way to find out what your CAPTURE configuration is through the use of the SHOW option. Show will list the status of each of your printer ports, whether it is active, and, if so, what it is doing. To use SHOW, you use the following command string:

```
CAPTURE SH
```

CAPTURE is a command that permits nearly all software to handle printing in a network environment. There are exceptions, mainly with software that will use a plotter, but for the most part, CAPTURE is transparent to applications.

CASTOFF

Command Format:

CASTOFF [ALL]

Command Function:

CASTOFF allows you to prevent broadcast messages from reaching your console. When you use it by itself, CASTOFF will restrict only messages from other user workstations. If you include the ALL option, you will also restrict messages from the server console. To use the command, you simply type its name:

```
CASTOFF
```

If you want to keep the system administrator from bothering you, you do the following:

```
CASTOFF A
```

You would do this either because you simply don't want to be bothered or, because you are using an application that objects to the interruption that the broadcast message causes.

CASTON

Command Format:

CASTON

Command Function:

CASTON reverses the effects of CASTOFF, above, and enables your workstation to receive broadcast messages from the server console and from other workstations. You will receive a prompt indicating that you may now receive broadcast messages.

CHKVOL

Command Format:

CHKVOL [PATH]

Command Function:

This is the Novell replacement for the MS-DOS command CHKDSK, which won't work in a network environment. It gives the same basic information about the hard disk (but does not cover system memory as CHKDSK does), except that it is reporting on the disk on the file server. The information will include the name of the file server and volume name (the volume name is the name of the server's hard disk), the total size of the volume, the amount of space used in bytes, the number of files on the disk, the remaining space in bytes, the remaining space available to the user running CHKVOL, and the number of directory entries remaining.

Because NetWare allows the system administrator to limit the amount of space that is available to any one user, the space remaining on the disk and the space remaining to the user may be different.

If you only enter the command, it will report on the default volume, that is, the volume that you are using when you invoke the command. You may, however, find information about other volumes on the same server, and about volumes on other servers. If you like, you can even look at the information for all disks on all servers.

Using CHKVOL

Most of the time, you will simply run the command for the disk you are using at the time, and therefore will simply type in the name of the command, like this:

```
CHKVOL
```

You may, however, follow the name of the command with the path you want to check. You may use wild card characters to specify the path, and/or the volume name. The wild card characters (explained above) are * and ?. You can use either in referring to the name of a path, with * replacing all characters, and ? replacing a single character. Because CHKVOL will accept arguments containing the server name and the volume name in the path description, you can include both. Here are some examples:

CHKVOL *

Will show information for all volumes on the default server.

CHKVOL */*

Will show information for all volumes on all servers.

CHKVOL SERVER_ONE/*

Will show information for all volumes on SERVER-ONE, whether that is your default server or not.

CHKVOL SERVER_ONE/SYS:

Will show information for the SYS: volume on SERVER_ONE.

CHKVOL ????

Will show information for volumes with four-letter names on the default server.

You must be ATTACHed to a file server before CHKVOL will recognize it, but you do not need to have it mapped as a disk drive. If it is mapped as a drive, however, you may use the drive letter designation instead of the volume name. For example, you might type CHKVOL P: to look at the volume that has been mapped as drive P: on your system.

ENDCAP

Command Format:

ENDCAP [OPTION]

Command Function:

The ENDCAP command stops the functioning of the CAPTURE command, discussed above. You may use it alone to simply terminate CAPTURE altogether, or with an option to terminate only a portion of the CAPTURE process. The options allow you to specify which printer port's capture you want to terminate, and whether or not you want any remaining characters to be printed. Here are the options:

Local = n

Ends the capture of a specific LPT port. Replace n with the port number, from 1 to 3. The specific port's capture will be terminated, but the remaining ports will be unaffected.

ALL

Terminates the capture process of all LPT ports in the workstation. You must type the entire option name to make this one work.

Cancel

Terminates the capture process for LPT1, and clears any remaining data without printing it.

CancelLocal = n

Terminates the capture process for a specific LPT port, and clears any remaining data without printing it. Replace n with the LPT port number, from 1 to 3.

Cancel ALL

Terminates the capture process for all LPT numbers, and clears the data without printing it.

You may use more than one option at the same time to follow the ENDCAP command.

Using ENDCAP

ENDCAP is invoked by typing the name at the DOS prompt, followed by an option if needed. Options can be combined, and the result of using ENDCAP can be checked by using CAPTURE SH, explained earlier, which will show the current status of the CAPTURE command. If you want to use a local printer, but to continue using network printers for other purposes, you can do this by using an option that will remove the capture process from one LPT port, but not from the others. Here are some examples:

ENDCAP

Terminates the CAPTURE command, but allows existing data to be printed.

ENDCAP ALL

Terminates the CAPTURE command on all ports, but allows existing data to be printed.

ENDCAP C

Cancels printing on LPT1, and clears any remaining data.

ENDCAP CL = 2

Cancels printing on LPT2, and clears any remaining data. You can also use 1 or 3 to cancel those ports, respectively.

ENDCAP C ALL

Cancels printing on all LPT ports, and clears any remaining data.

ENDCAP L = 1 CL = 2

Terminates CAPTURE on LPT1, but allows remaining data to be printed, while cancelling the CAPTURE on LPT2, and clearing any data there.

FLAG

Command Format:

FLAG [PATH\FILENAME [OPTION]]

Command Function:

NetWare allows you to flag any file with a number of attributes similar to those in MS-DOS. Some of the flags, such as Read Only, are the same as MS-DOS flags. Others, such as Transactional or Indexed, are unique to NetWare. The command will let you set or remove the flags. Normally, you will use flags on files to permit users to share files that require access by more than one user at a time, or to prevent files from being erased accidentally. If you enter the command FLAG by itself, it will show you the current settings of the files in your current directory. If you add a path, it will show you the files at that location instead. You can set the flags by using an option, but you must have Search and Modify rights to the files you are trying to set.

There are four attributes that can be set with FLAG, and a command to set each one in alternating ways. These settings are accomplished through the use of the following options that are used following FLAG:

Sharable

Sets the attribute flag on the file so that it can be shared.

NonSharable

Sets the attribute flag on the file so that the file cannot be shared.

ReadOnly

Sets the attribute flag so that the file cannot be written to. This also means that it cannot be erased.

ReadWrite

Sets the attribute flag so that the file can be written to, and so that it can be erased.

Normal

Sets the attribute flag to NonSharable and Read Write.

Transactional

Sets the attribute flag to indicate that the file is a Transactional file used by the Transaction Tracking System in SFT NetWare.

Indexed

Sets the attribute flag to indicate that the file should be indexed. This means that the file's entry in the file allocation table (FAT) on the hard disk is indexed, which will speed up access on large files.

SUBdirectory

Allows the flag command to affect not only the current directory, but also any subdirectories that it contains. You can use this to view or change attributes in subdirectories.

There are four additional attributes that you cannot set. They are Execute Only, Hidden, System, and Modified. The first three can be set by the system administrator, and the last is set as a part of the archival or backup process.

Using FLAG

You can look at the settings for the flags on a single file, or on many files. To look at a single file, enter the name of the file after you invoke FLAG. You can look at the settings of flags in the current directory by simply typing in the name of FLAG with no other arguments. You can set flags by following with one of the options, provided you have the rights to do the setting. If you do not have the proper rights, FLAG will inform you. Normally, you would only set flags on those files you created and wanted to protect. The system administrator would set flags to programs and data files that would be used system-wide.

Here are some examples of the way FLAG works:

FLAG

Shows the attribute settings of files in the current directory.

FLAG SUB

Shows the attribute settings of files in the current directory and of the subdirectories beneath it.

FLAG LETTERS.TXT S

Flags the file LETTERS.TXT as sharable.

FLAG *.TXT RO

Sets the attribute flags on all files with the .TXT extension as Read Only.

FLAG SERVER_ONE/SYS:LETTERS.TXT S RO

Sets the flag for the file LETTERS.TXT, which is located in the main directory of the SYS: volume on file server SERVER_ONE to Sharable, Read Only.

You must be ATTACHed to a file server to view or change file attributes. You do not need to have the server mapped to a drive letter on your system, although if you do, you may use the drive letter instead of the server name and volume name. File attribute flags may also be set by the FILER program, explained elsewhere in this book.

FLAGDIR

Command Format:

FLAGDIR [PATH[OPTIONS]]

Command Function:

FLAGDIR performs basically the same function for subdirectories as FLAG does for files. With it, you may add attributes to directories to control the way they are used, and to control who may use them. There are four options that control attributes that you may set for a directory. They are:

Normal

This option cancels other attributes that may have been set on the directory. This will allow a directory to be generally available to all users.

Hidden

Setting the directory to Hidden prevents the name of the directory from appearing in a directory listing, but does not prevent its use. A user may change to a hidden directory, if the existence of the directory is known to him or her.

System

This is an option used to indicate that NetWare uses the directory for system functions. It will not show up in a directory listing.

Private

The Private flag prevents users from seeing the contents of a subdirectory unless they have Search rights to it. Users will be able to see the name of the directory from the parent directory only if they have Search rights. They will be able to change to the directory, however, if they know the path.

Using FLAGDIR

You must specify the path of the directory that you change or check, unless it is the one that you are currently using. You can include the name of the server and volume number in the path, as well as any directories that may lead you to the directory that you want FLAGDIR to work on. Here are some examples of how FLAGDIR works:

FLAGDIR

Shows you the attributes of the current directory.

FLAGDIR *

Shows the attributes of the current directory, and all subdirectories within that directory.

FLAGDIR LETTERS

Shows the attributes of the LETTERS subdirectory within your current directory.

FLAGDIR SERVER_ONE/SYS:WORDPROC\LETTERS

Shows the attributes of the LETTERS subdirectory, which is within the WORDPROC directory, in the SYS: volume, on the file server SERVER_ONE.

FLAGDIR LETTERS P

Gives the LETTERS subdirectory the Private attribute.

FLAGDIR SERVER_ONE/SYS:WORDPROC\LETTERS P H

Gives the Private and Hidden attributes to the LETTERS subdirectory, which is within the WORDPROC directory on the SYS: volume of the SERVER_ONE file server.

You can only change directories for which you have Parental and Modify rights. Normally, this will only be your personal HOME subdirectory, and you may not have them even then. Normally, FLAGDIR is used only by the system administrator, but there are circumstances in which it can be available to other users.

HOLDOFF

Command Format:

HOLDOFF

Command Function:

This command reverses the operation of HOLDON, which is explained next. If you have run HOLDON, and no longer need to hold files open against writing by other users, HOLDOFF will accomplish this. You use the command by entering its name at the DOS command line:

```
HOLDOFF
```

HOLDON

Command Format:

HOLDON

Command Function:

The HOLDON command keeps a file you are using open while you work on other files. In some cases, your application will do this for you, but most will not. When you hold the file open, it tells other users' applications that the file is in use, and prevents writing to the file. It does not prevent the file from being read. This keeps your file from being changed while you are working with it. Once a file is open, it will remain open until you run HOLDOFF (see above) or until you reboot your workstation. You run it by typing its name at the DOS command line:

```
HOLDON
```

LISTDIR

Command Format:

LISTDIR [PATH] [OPTION]

Command Function:

The LISTDIR command displays the subdirectories within the specified path or directory. It may also list the rights in each, as well as the date and time that it was created. There are four options available for LISTDIR, but note that, unlike other commands described so far, the options follow the path designation and are delimited by a slash. The four options let you choose what you want to see in addition to the directories:

/Subdirectories

Shows you all subdirectories within the current directory, and all subsequent directories at lower levels.

/Rights

Lets you view the maximum rights in each subdirectory. Individual users may have fewer rights than those indicated.

/Date or /Time

The date or time option lets you see the date and time that the directory was created.

/All

Includes all of the above options.

You can find out the subdirectory information for directories other than your current directory by entering the path information with each inquiry. The path can include the name of the volume and file server. You must be attached to a file server to use LISTDIR, but you do not need to have it mapped to a disk drive letter in your system. However, if you do, you may use the disk drive letter instead of the server and volume name.

Using LISTDIR

Using LISTDIR for your current directory is as simple as typing its name. If you want another directory, you need to enter the path listing, and then any options you want. In this case, it follows the syntax for the MS-DOS DIR command, rather than most NetWare commands. Also like MS-DOS, the options follow a slash. You may find LISTDIR more familiar to you than some of the other NetWare commands.

The most informative way to run LISTDIR is to use the /A option, like this:

LISTDIR /A

Which gives you a full listing of all subdirectories within the current directory, a full listing of the rights, and the creation date. The other options give you a partial listing of this information.

If you add a path designation, you will list the subdirectories in another directory. This directory may be on another server or volume, but you must be ATTACHed to that server in order to use it. An example of LISTDIR with a path follows:

```
LISTDIR SERVER_ONE/SYS:WORDPROC /S /R
```

This would list all of the subdirectories within the WORDPROC directory, and would show the rights to each. In this case, the WORDPROC directory is located on the SYS: volume on the SERVER_ONE file server.

LOGIN

Command Format:

LOGIN [SERVER[USER[OPTION]]]

Command Function:

The LOGIN command gives you access to a file server. It can also start the login script running if you have one. The login script is a series of commands that configure your network session to your needs. It will perform such actions as mapping the server to one or more drive letters, attaching other servers, and starting the NetWare menu system. The commands unique to login scripts are described later in this chapter.

You have the option of letting LOGIN prompt you for your user name, or you can enter it on the command line. You can also specify the name of a file server other than your default server. Once you have logged in, you will be prompted for your password, if you have one. At that point, you will be attached to the file server, a drive letter will be assigned (the first login will usually be to drive F:) and your login script will run. The only option that you can add to the LOGIN command is your user name. You must enter a server name if you are planning to log in to a server other than your default server. Here is an example of the LOGIN command:

```
LOGIN SERVER_ONE/SJONES
```

If you prefer, you can let the LOGIN command prompt you for the user name. This will happen if you don't enter it as above.

Using LOGIN

The vast majority of users perform the login function by simply typing LOGIN, followed by their name. They login to a single server, and they stay there. If they need to use an additional server, they use the ATTACH command. You may have the ATTACH command as a part of your login script. If you do, LOGIN will attach you to each server, check the passwords, and complete the attachment. If your user name is the same on another server, LOGIN will also check the passwords, and, if they are different, it will offer to make them all the same, a process called "synchronizing" the passwords.

If you run LOGIN again from the same workstation, LOGIN will first log you out of the current session, so that the new login can be performed. Normally, this happens when another user logs in using their user name, but on the same workstation. This affects any file server you are attached to at the time.

LOGOUT

Command Format:

LOGOUT [SERVER]

Command Function:

LOGOUT will log you out of a single file server, or all file servers. If you enter the name of a file server, it will only log you out of that one. Otherwise, it will log you out of everything. Here are some examples:

LOGOUT SERVER_ONE

LOGOUT

MAP

Command Format:

MAP [DRIVE]
MAP PATH
MAP DRIVE = [DRIVE:[PATH]]
MAP [INS] DRIVE = [DRIVE:PATH]
MAP DEL DRIVE
MAP REM DRIVE

Command Function:

MAP allows you to assign servers, volumes or paths to a drive letter. MAP will also let you view your current drive assignments, and will let you specify the current order of drive search assignments. MAP is a very flexible command, allowing you to view or change drive mapping in a variety of ways.

Because MAP is so flexible, using it can be a bit complex. You do have to remember what you're trying to do, and make sure that you are entering the command properly. Fortunately, most single-users only use MAP to find out what their current drive mapping is. It normally is only used to change drive mappings as a part of the login script or as a part of a batch file. For that reason, you, as a user, may never be required to perform drive mapping yourself, but in those circumstances where you find yourself having to ATTACH to another server, you will. The reason is that even though you are ATTACHed, you cannot actually use a server until it is also MAPped to a drive letter on your workstation.

Using MAP

MAP can either be used to display current drive mappings, or it can be used to change those mappings. If you simply want to see which drive letters are assigned to your local workstation drives, and which are assigned to the network, you simply enter the name of the program:

MAP

This will result in a message that looks like the following, although the details will vary according to the exact mapping scheme your system administrator is using:

```
Drive A:   maps to a local drive
Drive B:   maps to a local drive
Drive C:   maps to a local drive
Drive D:   maps to a local drive
Drive F: = SERVER_ONE/SYS:HOME/SJONES
Drive G: = SERVER_ONE/SYS:
Drive Y: = SERVER_ONE/SYS:PUBLIC

         --------------
SEARCH1 := Z:. [SERVERONE/SYS:PUBLIC]
SEARCH2 := C:\MS-DOS
SEARCH3 := C:\
SEARCH4 := C:\NORTON
```

You can also see the mapping for a specific drive by entering the drive letter as an argument after the MAP command. Here's an example:

```
MAP Y:
```

The report would come back looking like the following:

```
Drive Y: = SERVER_ONE/SYS:PUBLIC
```

While changing the mapping is not normal procedure for most users, there are times when it can be useful. There are, for example, still a few programs around that can't handle all of the permutations of MS-DOS paths. In other cases, it's simply easier to type a drive letter rather than to have to type in a long path name if that's something you do frequently. In these circumstances, you can add a drive to your list of drives, and have it represent a particular path in the file server. You could, for example, make your E-mail directory so that it is related to a drive letter:

```
MAP Drive H: = SERVER_ONE/SYS:MAIL
```

MAP will confirm the change, and you will be able to view it the next time you look at your drive listings. You can change to the path that is now represented by a drive letter in exactly the same manner as you would move to any other disk drive. In this case, you would move the MAIL subdirectory by typing H:.

Changing your search drives is done in the same way, except that you use the INS option. A search drive allows the workstation to look for an executable file if it can't find it in the current directory. In MS-DOS, the search path is represented in the PATH command in the AUTOEXEC.BAT file. Incidentally, MAP will also work to remap a search drive even if you don't add the letters INS to the option, as long as you enter everything else correctly. Either of the following would result in adding a new search drive:

```
MAP S3:=SERVER_ONE/SYS:HOME
MAP INS S3:=SERVER_ONE/SYS:HOME
```

If you want to remove current mappings from the network or search drives, you use the DEL option. The option DELetes the specific drive mapping you indicate. You can use the drive letter designation, the volume name, or the path. For example:

```
MAP DEL H:
MAP DEL S3:
```

Normally, MAP will proceed to carry out instructions without prompting. However, if you attempt to map a local drive letter to a network drive, MAP will ask for confirmation. Also, you must be ATTACHed to a file server before you can MAP it to a drive letter.

NCOPY

Command Format:

NCOPY FILENAME [TO] [PATH] [FILENAME] [/Verify]

Command Function:

Novell's NCOPY command is the equivalent of the MS-DOS COPY command, and it behaves in the same fashion, using the same syntax. The difference is that NCOPY will also handle Macintosh files that exist on the file server, and it will allow you to include the file server name and volume name in the path listing. In addition, NCOPY will allow you to include the word TO before the name and path of the destination. This has no function other than to make the user feel good.

Using NCOPY

NCOPY will work with either network or local drives, and can be used for day-to-day copying in the same way as the MS-DOS COPY command. For these purposes, it offers no other features. In working with the network drive, however, it will let you copy files to or from volumes to which you are ATTACHed, without their having a drive letter assigned. NCOPY will not copy a file that has the ExecuteOnly attribute set.

NCOPY follows the same syntax as does the MS-DOS copy command. In its simplest form, an NCOPY command would take the form:

```
NCOPY F:LETTERS.TXT G:
```

As in the case of COPY, NCOPY will let you specify that the destination will have a different name from the source. This allows you to create an extra copy of a file in the same directory. You would use a command like this:

```
NCOPY F:LETTERS.TXT G:JUNKMAIL.TXT
```

Otherwise, the only notable difference is that NCOPY allows the use of the server name and volume name in the command. For example:

```
NCOPY LETTERS.TXT SERVER_ONE/SYS:WORDPROC
```

Using the /Verify option will cause NCOPY to check the file as it's written against the original to confirm that the copy was made correctly:

```
NCOPY LETTERS.TXT /V
```

Under normal circumstances, such as when you're not dealing with both Macintosh and PC files, and when you are logged into a server to which you are ATTACHed, you can use the MS-DOS COPY command to the same effect. Remember that you must be ATTACHed to a server for either command to be used in conjunction with the server.

NDIR

Command Format:

NDIR [PATH]
NDIR [FILENAME]
NDIR PATH [OPTION]
NDIR FILENAME [OPTION]

Command Function:

NDIR is a replacement for the MS-DOS DIR command. It operates in much the same way as DIR, but it has some significant enhancements, both in terms of the information it will show, and the options it will accept. In addition to showing the file name and extension, size, and the date and time of creation, NDIR adds the time the file was last accessed or modified, any attribute flags, and the name of the file's owner.

NDIR's enhancements were added to support the greater size and complexity of a network environment. For that reason, the command has a wider variety of display and selection criteria, and it has many more options than does the DOS DIR command. The NDIR command will not, however, work on local disk drives.

The following options are available for use with NDIR:

FILENAME [NOT] = FILE

This option will show you files that match the file name you give. You can use wild card characters if you wish. Adding the [NOT] shows you everything except those matching the file name you give. NDIR is able to show you the name of the owner of a file or directory. This option will allow you to specify that you want to see all files owned by a particular user. Adding the [NOT] will show you all files except those owned by a particular user.

ACCESS [NOT] BEF = MM-DD-YY
ACCESS [NOT] AFT = MM-DD-YY

You can look at files that were last accessed on, before [BEF] or after [AFT] a specific date. Adding the [NOT] means that you want to see those files not accessed on, before or after a certain date.

UPDATE [NOT] BEF = MM-DD-YY
UPDATE [NOT] AFT = MM-DD-YY

You can also look at files that were modified on, before [BEF] or after [AFT] a certain date. Adding the [NOT] means that you will see those files not modified on, before or after a certain date.

CREATE [NOT] BEF = MM-DD-YY
CREATE [NOT] AFT = MM-DD-YY

This will show you files that are created on, before [BEF] or after [AFT] a specific date. Adding the [NOT] shows those that were not created on, before or after a certain specific date.

SIZE [NOT] GR = nnn
SIZE [NOT] LE = nnn

The SIZE option will show you files that are greater [GR] or less [LE] than the size specified. Including the [NOT] will show you files that are not greater than or less than the size specified.

[NOT] SYstem

The SY option will show you all files with the SYstem attribute set. Adding the [NOT] will show you all files except those with the SYstem attribute set.

[NOT] Hidden

Using the H option will show you those files that have the Hidden attribute set. adding the [NOT] will show all files except those with the Hidden attribute set.

[NOT] Modified

A modified file is one that has been changed. The M option will show you those that have the Modified attribute set. Adding the [NOT] will show you all files except those with the Modified attribute set.

[NOT] ExecuteOnly

A file with the ExecuteOnly attribute set can by executed, but it cannot be copied. This option will show you all files with the ExecuteOnly attribute set. Adding the [NOT] will show you all files except those with the ExecuteOnly attribute set.

[NOT] SHAreable

Using the SHA option will show you all files that have the SHAreable attribute set. Adding the [NOT] will show you all files except those with the SHAreable attribute set.

[NOT] ReadOnly

The RO option with show you those files that have the ReadOnly attribute set. Adding the [NOT] will show you all those that don't have the ReadOnly attribute set.

[NOT] ReadWrite

NDIR will show you all files with the ReadWrite attribute set with the RW option. Add the [NOT] to see those that do not have the RW attribute set.

[NOT] Indexed

The I option will show you all files that are Indexed. If you use the [NOT] you will see all files except those that are indexed.

[NOT] Transactional

This will show you the files that have the Transactional attribute set. Using the [NOT] will show you all files except those with the Transactional attribute set.

[REVERSE] SORT FILENAME

The SORT option will let you sort in alphabetical order by file name. Using the REVERSE option will make it sort in reverse alphabetical order.

[REVERSE] SORT ACCESS

This option will let you sort by access date. The REVERSE option will reverse the order.

[REVERSE] SORT UPDATE

The Update option will let you sort by the date the file was last updated. Adding the [REVERSE] sorts it in reverse order.

[REVERSE] SORT CREATE

The Create option lets you sort by the creation date of the file. Adding the [REVERSE] sorts it in reverse order.

[REVERSE] SORT SIZE

The Size option lets you sort by file size. Using the [REVERSE] option sorts in reverse order by size.

FilesOnly

This option shows you only the files in a directory. Subdirectories are not shown.

DirectoriesOnly

This option shows you only the subdirectories in a directory. Files are not shown.

MAC

The MAC option shows Macintosh files and directories only.

SUBdirectories

The SUB option lets you see all subdirectories in a directory, and all subsequent subdirectories within them.

BRief

Displays the directory information, giving only the file size and last update.

BACKUP

Displays directory information with the last modified and last archived dates so you can compare them to see what files have been changed since they were backed up.

WIDE

Shows archiving information in the standard NDIR format.

[NOT] ARCHIVED

Shows files that have been archived. If you use the [NOT] option, it will show you files that have not been archived.

Archived Date BEFore
Archived Date AFTer

Shows you files according to whether they were archived before or after a specific date.

CHANGED

Shows you files that have been modified since the last archive.

[NOT] Archived Bit

This option lets you see those files that have the MS-DOS archive bit set. The MS-DOS archive bit is set by some backup programs, such as MS-DOS BACKUP, to indicate that the file has been archived. Using the [NOT] will show you all files that do not have the archive bit set.

TOUCHED

Shows files changed since the last time the MS-DOS archive bit was set.

HELP

Online help for NDIR, showing the options and syntax. This is a critical feature for this command.

Using NDIR

The syntax for NDIR is similar to that of the MS-DOS DIR command, except that there are many more options that can follow the command. The basic pattern for the command is to type NDIR, followed by the Path and Filename, and then by any options. You can string options together. Words like NOT and REVERSE give you the opposite action from what the option would otherwise give.

Using the command itself is straightforward, despite its many options. You can use standard MS-DOS path names, and then follow with whatever options are appropriate. You can also use the Novell path name, with the name of the server followed by the name of the volume. Here are some examples:

NDIR *.EXE

Will show you complete directory information for all EXE files in the current directory.

NDIR F:

Will show you complete directory information for all files in the directory assigned as drive F:

NDIR SERVER_ONE/SYS:LETTERS.TXT

Will show you complete directory information for the file LETTERS.TXT, which is located in the SYS: volume of SERVER_ONE.

NDIR F: ACCESS BEF 09-15-89

Shows all files in the directory assigned as F: that were accessed before September 15, 1989.

NDIR REVERSE SORT SIZE

Shows the current directory, sorted by size in reverse order.

NDIR NOT RW

Shows all files in the current directory that do not have the ReadWrite attribute.

NDIR SERVER_ONE/SYS: MAC

Shows all Macintosh files in the search path, and all Macintosh subdirectories. The MAC option will show the file names in their long version as created by the Macintosh, rather than in a short DOS format.

NPRINT

Command Format:

NPRINT FILENAME [OPTION]

Command Function:

This is a replacement for the MS-DOS PRINT function. It performs the same purpose for printing, but it has several enhanced functions, and it supports the use of network printers and Novell path names. The options are similar to those used by CAPTURE:

Server = server

This option will let you tell NPRINT what file server the information will be sent to for printing. You can only use a server to which you are ATTACHed. Make sure you use the name of an actual file server instead of "server."

Job = job

This lets you tell NPRINT the configuration name of the print job they want to use. You define print jobs using the PRINTCON utility, described elsewhere in this book.

Printer = n

This tells NPRINT which printer on the server is to get the printing. You replace n with a number from 0 through 4.

Queue = queue

The Queue option specifies which print queue should get the print job. Put the name of the print queue in place of "queue."

Form = form or n

This option tells NPRINT which form you want to use for printing. Replace "form" or n with the name or number of the form you want to use. You will need to check with the system administrator to see what forms are available.

Copies = n

You can tell NPRINT to print multiple copies of a document. Replace n with the number of copies you want, up to 256.

Tabs = n

If your application does not have a print formatting function, this option will expand tabs into spaces. You will need to define the number of spaces by specifying a number from 0 to 18 for n. Most applications have print formatting, and should not use this option.

NoTabs

This causes tabs to arrive at the printer without modification. It should only be used with applications that do not have print formatting.

NAMe

This tells NPRINT what name is to appear on the banner. If you don't enter anything here, NPRINT will use your Novell user name.

Banner = banner

NPRINT uses a banner to identify each print job. The banner is a sheet that is printed ahead of the print job that contains the name of the user (see NAME, above) as well as other information. Normally, the acronym LST: appears on the bottom of the banner sheet, but you can choose any 12 characters you want. An example would be something like this:

```
FRED'S_STUFF
```

You use the underline to denote a space between words.

No Banner

If for some reason you don't want a banner, you can eliminate it entirely with this option.

Form Feed

If you want your network printer to perform a form feed after a print job, you use this option. This will result in a blank sheet being placed between print jobs, and is sometimes necessary on printers using continuous form paper.

No Form Feed

This option turns off the FORM FEED option, above.

Delete

This option will tell NPRINT to erase the file being printed automatically once it is printed.

Using NPRINT

Despite the number of options, NPRINT is easy to use. Essentially, you enter NPRINT on the DOS command line, followed by the file you want to print, followed by any options. The file name can be a full path to the file, including the server and volume name. Here are a few examples:

NPRINT F:\WORDPROC\LETTER.TXT

This will print a file called LETTER.TXT, located in the WORDPROC directory on drive F:

NPRINT MONTHLY.RPT B=MONTHLY_RPT

This command will print the file MONTHLY.RPT, and include a banner with the words "MONTHLY RPT" on the lower half.

NPRINT SERVER_ONE/SYS:WORDPROC\LETTER.TXT C=2

This will print two copies of the file LETTER.TXT, which is located on the server SERVER_ONE, in volume SYS: and is contained in the WORDPROC directory.

You must be ATTACHed to a file server before you can print a file located there, or send a file there to be printed. You don't need an assigned drive letter. However, if a drive letter has been assigned to you through the use of the MAP utility, you may use the drive letter instead of the path listing.

NSNIPES
NCSNIPES

Command Format:

NSNIPES [OPTION]
NCSNIPES [OPTION]

Command Function:

SNIPES is a network based multiuser arcade game for up to five players. You use the NSNIPES version if you have a monochrome monitor, and the NCSNIPES version if you have a color monitor. The option is a number from 1 through 10, which represents your skill level.

Your character moves through a maze populated by other players' characters and by maze denizens, all of which are out to get you. You move it using your arrow keys, and you shoot the others with the AWSD keys. A = left, D = right, W = up and S = down. You can file diagonally by pressing two keys at the same time.

If more than one player will be enjoying the game, one player is assigned to enter the command with an option representing the skill level. The others begin by entering the command, NSNIPES or NCSNIPES, without specifying the option. The player assigned to enter the option number enters last. You can exit the game by pressing <CTRL> <BREAK>.

You can only play SNIPES in a directory where you have Read, Write, Open, Create and Delete rights. Most likely, this will be in your home directory.

NVER

Command Format:

NVER

Command Function:

NVER will tell you the version number of all network-related software running on the file server and on the workstation. This allows you to confirm that all of your software has been updated properly. A report is generated for each server as well as for the workstation software. Multiple servers will result in a listing for each one. This is an example of a typical listing for NVER:

```
NetBIOS:   V1.0

IPX Version: 2.12
SPX Version: 2.12

LAN Driver: Micom-Interlan NI5010 V2.30EC (880513) V2.30
           IRQ = 3, IO Address = 300h, No DMA
Shell:     V2.12 Rev. B
DOS:       MS-DOS V3.30 on IBM_PC

FileServer: SERVER_ONE

Novell  SFT NetWare 286 TTS V2.15 Rev. A  12/11/88
```

PSTAT

Command Format:

PSTAT [OPTION]

Command Function:

The PSTAT command allows you to view information about printers attached to a server. You can check a specific printer, or you can check the printers on a specific server. Entering the command PSTAT without options will give you the status of all printers attached to your default server. If you follow the command with an optional printer number or server name, you will be shown information about that printer or server. The options are used as follows:

Server = server

Using this option will show you the status information for a specific server. Use the name of the server instead of the word "server."

Printer = printer

Using this option will show you the status information for a particular printer. Use the printer number instead of the word "printer."

Using PSTAT:

Invoking the command PSTAT will produce a report on your screen of the status of the printers on your default server. Following it with either or both options will produce reports about a specific server, a specific printer, or a specific printer on a specific server. The report will include the name of the server, the printer number, whether the printer is on line of off line, whether the printer is active, and the type of paper, if known.

Following is an example of such a report, generated by PSTAT:

```
Server SERVER_ONE: Network Printer Information
Printer  Ready    Status  Form: number, name
------   ------   ------   ----------------------------
    0    On-Line  Active   0, unknown name
    1    On-Line  Active   0, unknown name
    2    On-Line  Active   0, unknown name
```

If you specify a particular server, you will get that server instead of the default server. If you specify a particular printer, you will get only that printer. For example, entering the following:

```
PSTAT S=SERVER_TWO
```

will give you the printer status of all printers attached to the file server named SERVER_TWO. Likewise, entering the following:

```
PSTAT P=1
```

will give you only the information for printer number 1. If you enter both, like this:

```
PSTAT S=SERVER_TWO P=1
```

you will get the status of printer 1 on the server SERVER_TWO.

PSTAT doesn't actually test to see if a printer is on line or not. It leaves that up to the application. This means that if you have told NetWare that there are three printers attached to the server, and then only attach one, NetWare will report all three as being on line and active. This will only change when someone tries to use the printer. The failure to access the printer will cause NetWare, and then PSTAT, to change the status to off line.

PURGE

Command Format:

PURGE

Command Function:

The PURGE command removes an erased entry from the file server's disk. When a file is erased, it's not actually removed, rather the file's directory entry is changed to show that the file is erased. With MS-DOS, this means that the disk space and directory entry are available for reuse. Novell NetWare doesn't do this. Instead, the directory entry and the disk space are reserved so that the file can be restored if need be.

Because there are a limited number of directory entries and space available on a file server's disk, eventually this space needs to be returned to use. The PURGE command does this by actually removing the erased file's directory entry. Once PURGE is run, a file cannot be recovered, either by NetWare's SALVAGE utility or by third party data recovery packages. Issuing the command removes all previously erased entries from the file server's disk.

RENDIR

Command Format:

RENDIR olddir [TO] newdir

Command Function:

The RENDIR command allows you to change the name of a directory. You can rename any directory to which you have modify rights. The command allows you to change the name of the directory, but it does not affect trustee rights, so users or groups who have trustee rights before the directory was renamed will still have those rights.

The RENDIR function operates the same way as does the REN or RENAME function in MS-DOS. Briefly, you invoke the command followed by the complete name (including the path) of the directory to be renamed, which is then followed by the new name of the directory. You can use the word TO in the command line if it helps you keep it all straight, but this isn't required. In other words, the following two command lines are exactly the same:

```
RENDIR SERVER_ONE/SYS:HOME\MJONES MSMITH
RENDIR SERVER_ONE/SYS:HOME\MJONES TO MSMITH
```

Both of the above would change a directory named MJONES to one named MSMITH. The word TO is not necessary but can be used. In addition, if a path has been mapped to a drive letter, then you can use it instead of the path. If the directory you want to name is the default directory, you can use the period (.) as in MS-DOS to represent it. You can rename a directory on another server, although you must be ATTACHed to that server first.

Using RENDIR

As explained above, RENDIR uses the same syntax as the RENAME command in MS-DOS. The most noticeable difference between the two is that you may need to list the entire directory path for the directory that is being renamed. It isn't always necessary, though. If the directory's path is mapped to a drive letter, or if it is the default directory, there are shorter ways. Here are some examples:

```
RENDIR SERVER_ONE/SYS:TEMP TO PROGS
```

This will rename the directory TEMP on volume SYS: to PROGS.

```
RENDIR . PROGS
```

This will rename the default directory to PROGS.

```
RENDIR Y: TEMP
```

This will rename the directory that has been mapped to drive Y: to TEMP from whatever it was. Note that you should check to make sure that you are really renaming the intended directory, or you could have some trouble finding things.

RIGHTS

Command Format:

RIGHTS [path]

Command Function:

The RIGHTS command will show you what your rights are for a particular directory. (See Chapter 8 for a discussion of rights). The RIGHTS command will then show you what your rights are for that directory. Following is an example of the RIGHTS report for a supervisor:

```
SERVER_ONE/SYS:

Your Effective Rights are [RWOCDPSM]:
      You may Read from Files.                    (R)
      You may Write to Files                      (W)
      You may Open existing Files.                (O)
      You may Create new Files.                   (C)
      You may Make new Subdirectories.            (C)
      You may Delete existing Files.              (D)
      You may Erase existing Subdirectories.      (D)
      You may Change Users' Directory Rights.     (P)
      You may Search the Directory.               (S)
      You may Modify File Status Flags.           (M)

      You have ALL RIGHTS to this directory area.
```

Normal users, on the other hand, have rights that are much more restricted. In some cases, they will have no rights to a directory at all. In others, there may be only a few rights. Here is an example of a typical users rights:

```
SERVER_ONE/SYS:PUBLIC

Your Effective Rights are [R O  S ]:
      You may Read from Files.                    (R)
      You may Open existing Files.                (O)
      You may Search the Directory.               (S)
```

As you can see, this user doesn't even have the ability to write to a file or to create a file in this directory. They would probably have a directory, such as their HOME directory, where they would have substantially more rights than they do in the PUBLIC area, which is open for use by everyone.

To use RIGHTS, you simply invoke it, and it will tell you the rights you have in the default directory. If you want to find out about your rights in another directory, you must include the path. You could, for example, type this:

```
RIGHTS SERVER_ONE/SYS:PUBLIC
```

to get the same display as above. You must be attached to a server to find out your rights to an area within it. If the path you wish to use is mapped to a drive letter, you can use that instead. You can, for example, type this:

```
RIGHTS Y:
```

to find your rights to the area mapped to drive Y:.

SALVAGE

Command Format:

SALVAGE [path]

Command Function:

The SALVAGE command will recover files that you have erased, provided you are careful not to write over the file, and provided you haven't logged out of the system. If you have run the PURGE command, you cannot recover an erased file. There are utilities that will recover files even if you have logged out of the server, but SALVAGE isn't one of them.

SALVAGE is fairly non-specific. You only have to specify what volume you want a file salvaged on, and the utility will recover whatever was the last file erased on that volume from your workstation. There is no need to specify the complete path or file name. SALVAGE will only work with the last file that you erased. Once a new file is created or another file erased, SALVAGE will no longer recover it. This means that you need to run SAL-VAGE as soon as possible after you realize that you erased a file by mistake. If you're lucky, and you didn't do much in the interim, SALVAGE will recover your files.

If you erase several files using the same command (say if you do an ERASE *.*) the SALVAGE will recover all of them. In general, though, SALVAGE will only recover the last file erased, and only then if you didn't do much else before you discovered the erasure. SALVAGE will not work if you try to log in from another work station. It requires that the user and the workstation doing the erasure make the recovery.

You can run SALVAGE on a server other than your default server by invoking it with the name of the server and volume where the recovery is to take place. More detailed information isn't necessary, since SALVAGE works on the entire volume.

An example of how to use SALVAGE follows:

```
SALVAGE SERVER_ONE/SYS:
```

This is all the information that's necessary.

SEND

Command Format:

SEND "text" [TO] [USER] [server/]user(s)
SEND "text" [TO] [USER] [server/]group(s)
SEND "text" [TO] [USER] [server/]users(s) [GROUP]
[server/]group(s)

Command Function:

The SEND command lets you transmit a message to other users and/or groups on the network. The total message, including your user name, can only be 45 characters long, though, so the message needs to be brief. An example of such a message would be a note to a coworker that said something like "Want to do lunch?"

The SEND facility is really only useful for casual communications. For anything more complicated, you'll need to use an electronic mail system. Obviously one reason for this is that it's difficult to say a lot in 45 characters or fewer. Another reason is that if you send to a group, you won't know which members of the group received the message, and who missed it. At least with electronic mail, the message will wait until they read it, and will encourage an answer.

When you send a message with the SEND command, the bottom line on the recipient's screen is replaced with the message in reverse video. They are alerted by a beep, and they must press CTRL-ENTER to clear their screen and return to work. This doesn't fail to get their attention.

You can SEND messages to one or more users, to one or more groups, or to some of each. They may be on your default server, or on any other server to which they are ATTACHed. To do this, you use the SEND command, followed by the message in quotation marks, followed by the names for the users or groups who will get it. You can use the words TO, USER and GROUP if you like as a way to make things clearer, but they are not required.

Using SEND:

To SEND a message to another user, you simply invoke the SEND command, follow it with the message, and say who you want to receive the message. Remember that you only have 45 characters available, including your user name, so messages have to be brief. Here is a typical message from one user to another:

```
SEND "How about lunch today?" MSMITH
```

If you want to use the words TO and USER to help you keep things straight, you can, but they are not required. The message above could also be worded as follows:

```
SEND "How about lunch today?" TO USER MSMITH
```

Sending a message to a group works exactly the same way:

```
SEND "Free beer in the conference room!" TO EVERYONE
```

This command will send the same message to every user that's logged on to the network at the time. You can also send the message to another server by changing the message slightly:

```
SEND "Free beer in the conference room!" TO  SERVER_TWO/EVERYONE
```

Note that adding the name of the server then sends the message to everyone on SERVER_TWO. You can also combine users and groups. The following command will send a message to a user named Sam, and to the programming staff:

```
SEND "Free Jolt Cola in lounge!" SAM PROGRAMMERS
```

Note again that the word TO can appear if you like, but it is not required. Once you send a message to an individual user, you will get confirmation from NetWare that the message was sent. You will not get such a confirmation if you send to a group.

SETPASS

Command Format:

SETPASS [server]

Command Function:

The SETPASS function allows you to change your password whenever you wish. You can either change it on your default server, or, by adding the name of another server, change your password on another server. SETPASS works to set your password for the first time, and to change your password once you have one.

Once you have a password, SETPASS will ask your old password before it gives you a new one. This prevents someone else from locking you out of your account by changing your password.

While it is possible to set up a Novell network so that users don't have to have passwords, it is always possible for an individual to set up a password for their own account.

When you are setting up a password for the first time, SETPASS will still ask for your old password, but since you don't have one, you simply press the ENTER key. Here is an example of how SETPASS works:

```
SETPASS

Enter your old password:    (You would enter your old password
                            here, if you had one, or you would
                            simply press ENTER).

Enter your new password:    (You would type in your new password
                            here).

Retype your new password:   (You would type your new password
                            again. This assures SETPASS that you
                            typed it correctly).

Your password has been changed.
```

That's all there is to it. The only difference would be when you want to have SETPASS change your password on another server to which you have access. Then you would follow the command with the name of the other server, like this:

```
SETPASS SERVER_TWO
```

The dialogue with the SETPASS software would be the same, regardless of whether this is the first time for setting a password, and regardless of whether the server is your default server or another server. You should change your password frequently (every month or two) so that no one can learn it and use your account without your permission. It is possible for the system supervisor to require password changes at regular intervals, and to require that you use a fresh password each time.

SETTTS

Command Format:

SETTTS [logical level[physical level]]

Command Function:

SETTTS is a command that is required only rarely, and should never be used unless it is required. It exists to tell the Transaction Tracking System, used by some database and accounting software, to ignore some logical or physical record locks before it begins tracking a transaction. Currently, the only widely used commercial software package that requires the use of SETTTS is Ashton-Tate's dBASE III+ version 1.0, which requires it because of the copy protection scheme used. More recent versions do not require SETTTS.

If SETTTS should be required by software other than dBASE III+ version 1.0, the software vendor would tell you. Normally, your system supervisor will also tell you this when the software is installed. If you are not told to use SETTTS, you shouldn't use it, because it will then cause the Transaction Tracking System to ignore some transactions. If this were to happen, those transactions would have the potential for creating corrupted data. Normally, the Transaction Tracking System helps enable the record locking that prevents data corruption in transactional or shared files.

You can only use SETTTS if you are using SFT NetWare with TTS enabled. In addition, you must have shared files that are flagged as transactional (see FLAG in this chapter, p. 203) and your software must require its use.

Using SETTTS

To find out the current settings of the Transaction Tracking System, you simply invoke the command by typing the following:

SETTTS

You will then be shown a listing such as:

```
Transaction Tracking Record Lock Threshold

        Logical Level:       2
        Physical Level:      2
```

This would tell you that the Transaction Tracking System will ignore two logical record locks and two physical record locks before it begins tracking. You can change this setting by invoking the command, followed by the new settings:

```
SETTTS 3 3
```

This would change the logical and physical record lock thresholds to three apiece. Again, you should check with your software vendor and with your system supervisor before changing the Transaction Tracking threshold with SETTTS.

SLIST

Command Format:

SLIST [server] [/C]

Command Function:

You can view the list of servers attached to your network by using the SLIST command. If you follow the command with the name of a particular server, you can confirm that the server is attached to the network and is operational. If the list is longer than a single screen, the scrolling will stop until you press a key, and then continue for another screenful, and so on. The /C switch following the command will tell SLIST to display the list of servers in a continuous stream.

SLIST will take the name of a server as an argument, and you can use wild cards in specifying the name. That way, if you can't remember the exact name of a server, but can remember what it started with, you can see only a list of servers starting with that letter or group of letters. Here is an example of ways to use SLIST:

SLIST	This will give you a list of all servers on the network.
SLIST SERVER_ONE	This will tell you whether SERVER_ONE is attached to the network.
SLIST SE*	This will give you a list of all servers that start with the letters SE. It would include SERVER_ONE.
SLIST /C	This will give you a list of all servers in a continuous listing, without stopping after every screen.

SLIST will show you the name of the server, the network number of the server, and the node address of Network A on the server. File servers on the same network will have the same network address. File servers on the same internetwork but on different networks will have different network addresses. The node address is determined by a unique ID in the network interface card installed in the server.

SMODE

Command Format:

SMODE [path] [option]
SMODE [filename] [option]

Command Function:

Many executable files (meaning they have the COM or EXE extensions) require the use of data files for their operation. Exactly what these data files are used for depends on the specific application, but frequently they are used for such things as screen settings, user preferences, and the like. The application looks for this data file when it begins operation or needs to carry out some function, and it needs to know where to find it.

Because most applications were never designed with network operations in mind, they have no provision for locating their data files on the network. As a result, they need a way for a search path to be defined to tell them where to find those data files. SMODE defines that path.

You can use SMODE to define a search path for a specific application, or for all applications in a specific directory. The path that is defined depends on the numeric option that follows the name of the path or the application when SMODE is invoked. Here are the meanings of the eight available options:

SMODE[path]0

This option tells the application to follow the instructions in the SHELL.CFG file, which would then have a command SEARCH MODE = n. The n would be replaced by a number from 1 through 7. This is the default setting for executable files.

SMODE[path]1

The executable file will follow whatever search instructions it contains internally. If there aren't any, it will search the default directory and all search drives.

SMODE[path]2

The executable file will search the default directory and no others. This is a useful choice when the application is located in a directory that is normally in the search path, but where you want each user to have their own data file for the application rather than a shared one.

SMODE[path]3

The executable file will follow whatever search instructions it contains internally. If there aren't any, and if the file opens files flagged ReadOnly, it will search the default directory and all search drives.

SMODE[path]4

Reserved

SMODE[path]5

The executable file will be forced to search the default directory and the search drives, regardless of its internal instructions.

SMODE[path]6

Reserved

SMODE[path]7

If the executable file opens files flagged ReadOnly, it will be forced to search the default directory and the search drives, regardless of its internal instructions.

If you include an option with SMODE, you must also include either a path or a file name (including the path to the file) as a part of the command line. You can specify either a file name or you can specify a path, but you cannot specify both at the same time.

Using SMODE

If you invoke SMODE by itself, you will be shown the current settings for all executable files in your default directory. If you want to see only the settings for a specific file, you should follow SMODE with the name of that file. Here is an example of what such a command would look like:

```
SMODE ADVENT.EXE
```

SMODE would then return the following answer:

```
ADVENT.EXE mode = 5, search on all opens
```

If you wanted to change the setting for the program from what it was to mode 5, you will issue the following command:

```
SMODE ADVENT.EXE 5
```

SMODE would make the change and return the same answer as above. If ADVENT.EXE were in some directory other than the default directory, you would have to precede the name of the application with the path leading to it. You can also set the applications in a specific directory:

```
SMODE SERVER_ONE/SYS:UTILS 5
```

This will change the executable files in the UTILS directory to mode 5. If you have mapped UTILS to a drive letter, you can substitute that for the path listing. Remember that if you are changing the settings for all of the executable files in your default directory, you should use the period (.) to represent the default directory in the SMODE command line.

SYSTIME

Command Format:

SYSTIME [server]

Command Function:

The SYSTIME command allows you to check the current time and date settings for any file server on the network, and to synchronize your workstation to those settings. If you simply enter the SYSTIME command, you will see the setting for the default server. If you follow SYSTIME with the name of a server, you will be shown the current settings for that server, and your system time on your workstation will be reset. This is a useful feature for work-stations that do not contain an internal clock, since SYSTIME can be used as a part of a batch file to set the workstation clock.

Using SYSTIME

To view the current time and date settings of the default server, enter the following:

```
SYSTIME
```

You will receive a response like this:

```
Current System Time: Sunday September 17,
1989 8:40 pm
```

To view the time on a specific server, and set your workstation time accordingly, you enter SYSTIME followed by the name of the server:

```
SYSTIME SERVER_ONE
```

You will receive the same response as above, but your workstation's time will be reset to match that of the server you chose.

TLIST

Command Format:

TLIST [path[USERS]]
TLIST [path[GROUPS]]

Command Function:

The TLIST command allows you to see the trustee assignments for a particular directory. If you specify USERS, you will see only the users with trustee rights. If you specify GROUPS, you will see only groups. If you want to view the trustee rights for a directory other than the default directory, you must enter the name of the path. The trustee list shows the name of the trustee, whether they are users or groups, and what rights each has for that directory.

Using TLIST

Simply typing TLIST at the command line will give you the list of trustees for the default directory. You enter the following:

```
TLIST
```

The TLIST command would then give you a list such as the following:

```
User Trustees:
     MSMITH   [RWOCDSPM]    (Mary Smith)
     LJONES   [R O S ]      (Larry Jones)


     -------


Group Trustees:
     PROGRAMMERS [R O S ] (Programmers)
```

If you enter TLIST, followed by a path, you will get a similar report for that directory. If the path is mapped to a drive letter, you can use that instead. Here is an example of using a path:

```
TLIST SERVER_ONE/SYS:UTILS
```

This would give you the trustee list for the UTILS directory on the server SERVER_ONE, volume SYS:. If you follow a TLIST command with the word USERS or the word GROUPS, you will get only users or only groups.

USERLIST

Command Format:

USERLIST [server/] [user] [/All]

Command Function:

The USERLIST command is normally used to show you who is logged on to the network at a given time. The standard display will show you the connection number, the user name, and the time that they logged into the network. If you only want to see if a specific person is on the network, you can follow the USERLIST command with their user name. You can check your default server with USERLIST, or if you specify another server, you can see who is on that one. If you use the /A switch, you can find out the user's network address and node address. The network address shows which network they are on, and the node address shows the unique identifier of their network interface card.

The most common use for USERLIST is to check to see if another user is logged on to the network prior to sending them a message (see SEND) or sending them electronic mail. The system supervisor will have a need to check a user's network and node address from time to time as a part of running diagnostic routines.

Using USERLIST

Normally, you will use USERLIST from your default server. To do this, you need only type the name of the command itself:

```
USERLIST
```

The command will respond with a list of users, their connection number, and when they logged on:

```
Connection      User Name        Login Time
     1          MSMITH           9-17-1989 9:22 pm
     2          LJONES           9-17-1989 8:30 pm
     3          SUPERVISOR       9-17-1989 9:15 pm
     4          RNOORDA          9-17-1989 7:02 am
```

The list will be in order by connection number.

If you are only checking for a particular individual, you can enter their user name, like this:

```
USERLIST MSMITH
```

This will result in a report like that above, but with a single line for the user name you requested. If that person is on another server, you would include the name of the server also:

```
USERLIST SERVER_TWO/MSMITH
```

The use of the /All option will give you a listing of the network and node numbers. Here is how that would work:

```
USERLIST /A
```

The report on your screen would look like this:

[[NOTE: this will have to wait till the server gets fixed or replaced]]

You can, of course, string all of this together:

```
USERLIST SERVER_TWO/MSMITH /A
```

And you will get the following:

```
[[NOTE: This will have to wait for the server
also]]
```

WHOAMI

Command Format:

WHOAMI [server] [option(s)]

Command Function:

The WHOAMI command tells you what user name you are using, which server you are attached to, and what your rights are. With the proper selection of options, you can see your rights in every directory on every server in the entire network. Normally, you wouldn't want all of this information, but with the use of the options it is available.

If you only invoke the command without options, you will simply be told the user name you have on each server to which you are attached. It can be different for different servers. If you need more information, you can use one of the following options:

/Groups

This option tells you which groups you are a member of on the file servers you specify.

/Security

This option shows you your security equivalence for each file server you specify.

/Rights

This option tells you the rights you have in each directory on the file server you specify.

/All

This option combines the information of the three options above. If you simply type WHOAMI /A you will see everything you can for all servers you are attached to on the network.

Using WHOAMI

If you simply run the WHOAMI command, you will get the basic information you need regarding the servers you are attached to. Here is an example:

```
WHOAMI
```

The response will be something like this:

```
You are user MSMITH attached to server SERVER_ONE connection 2
Login Time: Sunday September 17, 1989 9:33 pm

You are user SMITH attached to server SERVER_TWO connection 6
Login Time: Sunday September 17, 1989 9:34 pm
```

If you use the options, you will get a more complete report. In addition, you can specify a particular server, and receive information only on that server. If you are doing the /A option on a large network, this might be a good idea, because otherwise you might be inundated by the listing. Here are some examples of how the options will make the report appear:

```
WHOAMI SERVER_TWO

You are user SMITH attached to server SERVER_TWO connection 6
Login Time: Sunday September 17, 1989 9:34 pm
```

To look at the groups you belong to:

```
WHOAMI SERVER_ONE /G

You are user MSMITH attached to server SERVER_ONE connection 2
Login Time: Sunday September 17, 1989 9:33 pm
You are a member of the following Groups:
EVERYONE (group)
```

To look at your security equivalences:

```
WHOAMI SERVER_ONE /S
You are user MSMITH attached to server SERVER_ONE connection 2
Login Time: Sunday September 17, 1989 9:33 pm
You are security equivalent to the following:
EVERYONE (group)
```

To look at your rights in each directory of a file server:

```
WHOAMI SERVER_ONE /R
```

If you don't list the specific file server, you will get information on all file servers to which you are attached.

The following chapters will discuss those commands that are unique to the system supervisor, and those commands that are menu-based. The commands for the system supervisor include commands for granting and removing rights, creating users, setting up security, and archiving the information on the file server's disks. The menu-based utilities have a variety of functions, some of which are restricted to supervisors, and some of which are available to any user.

8

Being the Network Supervisor

What's involved in being a supervisor or network administrator on a NetWare LAN? What tools do you have? What do you need to know? What are your responsibilities? In this chapter, we'll answer these and several other questions. We'll describe the supervisor's role in managing the network and assigning and maintaining network security through user privilege levels. We'll take a detailed look at the special capabilities supervisors have on the LAN. We'll discuss the use of the network console and describe the differences between the supervisor and a sort of minisupervisor called a console operator. We'll show you how to customize the NetWare environment using supervisory tools that affect the entire network. And we'll describe the various supervisor commands and utilities. That's a lot to cover in a single chapter, so let's get started.

What is a Network Supervisor?

Before we dig into the specifics of doing the supervisor's job on a Novell LAN, a bit of philosophy is in order. Network supervisors have one and only one responsibility. They must maintain order on their network. Now, the good news is that it's easy to write a job description like that. The bad news is that accomplishing that objective is no trivial task.

The various duties of a network supervisor break down into a few specific categories. The first of these categories is network organization. Network organization first rears its head when you install the network for the first time. We'll discuss the details of network configuration in Chapter 10, but here it's enough to say that you will be preparing the network drives when you first set up the LAN. Preparing the drives involves assigning various volumes to various general tasks. However, over the life of the network, you'll make changes, deletions and additions to your original network scheme. The continuing growth of the LAN will dictate your needs. You may add other volumes, subdirectories or even new network drives.

The second duty of the supervisor is security maintenance. This is one of the most important tasks you will perform. Good network security has little, usually, to do with cloak-and-dagger intrusions. Most often it simply means keeping users in the areas where they need to be. That's a two-edged sword, by the way. On one hand you want to limit users to their legitimate areas. On the other hand you want to make certain that they are not *excluded* from their necessary areas. We strive to keep users where they belong for many reasons. For example, in some cases application software has limits on the number of users that can log on at any given time. Extraneous users could take up needed user spaces unnecessarily.

Another reason is that it is often desirable to restrict access to private information, such as payroll records, to those who, in government jargon, have a need to know. We also want to prevent users with no training on an application from attempting to use it. This could result in lost or damaged data. All of these are security considerations.

Another task is an accounting one. Supervisors manage the charge-out rates on LANs that charge users or departments for use. They manage other basic bookkeeping functions such as when and for how long a user may be on the LAN.

Supervisors determine who may use the LAN and to which other LANs their network will connect. As part of their security functions they regulate who has access to the LAN from external locations and, if charges are levied, what those charges are.

Finally, supervisors manage the day-to-day activities on the network. This includes monitoring network activity to insure that the LAN has adequate resources to run smoothly under normal loads. It also includes responding to trouble or user difficulties and installing and supporting application software.

If you get the idea that many of these functions could be more than a full-time job on a large network, you're exactly right. So good supervisors appoint subsupervisors and console operators. In these cases, the subsupervisors have supervisory privileges within a narrow range of activities. Perhaps there is a subsupervisor responsible for E-Mail. Or, in a large LAN with many workgroup clusters, each cluster might have its own supervisor. The cluster supervisors would be responsible for supporting the applications his or her workgroup uses. He or she would, perhaps, regulate who the users in the workgroup are and what their privileges are. This level of supervisor would not have the ability to make global changes in the network or its users.

Although these are possible scenarios, there are many other ways to divide the supervisor's workload on large LANs. These methods are not embedded in the operating system, rather, they are created by the network supervisor by the judicious use of privileges.

A console operator generally has very limited supervisory capabilities. Console operators can access the server through the FCONSOLE command. The level to which the console operator can make changes on the server is somewhat less than the ability of the network supervisor. Console operators, depending upon their privileges, can manipulate the server using many of the FCONSOLE commands. We'll discuss those commands later in this chapter along with other supervisor commands and utilities. Console operators, unlike the rather nebulous category of subsupervisors, are a genuine class of NetWare users. They are assigned by the network supervisor and are locatable as console operators by some of the supervisor's tools such as SYSCON. We show you how when we discuss commands.

Setting Up Users and Assigning Privileges

One of the ongoing tasks of the supervisor or administrator (two names for the same person) is maintaining user levels. That means that supervisors must add, delete and modify users and their privileges on a regular basis. So, since this is such an important part of being a network administrator, that's where we'll start.

User Privileges and Trusteeships

We regulate who can and can't use our LAN through a process which maintains network security. Part of this process includes assigning new users to the network, determining what their privileges are and what areas are open or closed to them. Implied as well are changes to user privilege levels and deletions of users from the LAN. A discussion of user privileges, therefore, is inextricably wound up in a discussion of network security. We'll start our discussion by introducing you to NetWare's four types of network security and how each interrelates with users.

The first type of security is at the boundary of the network. We regulate who can or can't log on to the LAN by assigning passwords. There are several levels of password security on a NetWare LAN. Various passwords are required to log on to the LAN, to use various files and to perform various tasks. At the simplest level, password security provides a door to the LAN for which a prospective user must have the key (password). This applies to anyone who wants to use the LAN. Login security has two parts: a user name and a password. As the supervisor you have a unique user name: SUPERVISOR.

You not only regulate the users who can log onto the LAN, you regulate how long and when they may log on, what workstations they are allowed to use and how many stations they can log into at the same time. All of these restrictions are optional, of course. As well, if you have a small LAN or workgroup, you can opt not to require a password. For example, Mary Jones may gain access to the network simply by typing her user name, perhaps maryj. If you opt for passwords, you may even go so far as to require specific lengths and allow passwords for limited periods before they must be changed. Passwords and user names are not case sensitive.

The second type of network security is Trustee Security. Trustee rights belong to a particular user and dictate which directories he or she may access. Trustee rights do more than allow access to a directory, though. They dictate the *type* of access the user is allowed. These types are Read, Write, Open, Create, Delete, Search, Modify and Parental. Figure 8-1 shows what these rights mean.

There is a shortcut to assigning Trustee rights to individuals called Security Equivalence. What this means is that you can assign trustee-like rights to a user by giving him or her the Security Equivalence of another user. You can also grant the Security Equivalence of a group. So, instead of assigning Trustee rights individually to all the members of a workgroup, you can assign Trustee rights to the group, and give the members a Security Equivalence of that group. The end result will be the same as if you assigned rights individually.

Let's keep track of how we've regulated users so far. First, we regulated their log in to the network. Then, by assigning Trustee rights, we gave them rights in one or more particular directories. Now, we want to have some measure of additional control over directories on a directory-by-directory basis. We can assign a Maximum Rights Mask to each directory at the time we create it. The Maximum Rights Mask has the same categories as Trustee rights. It allows us to place maximum limits upon what we will allow any user in that directory to do. The supervisor is, of course, excepted.

TRUSTEE RIGHT	CODE	DESCRIPTION
Read	R	Read data from an already open file
Write	W	Write data to an already open file
Open	O	Open an existing file
Create	C	Create a new file
Delete	D	Delete a file
Search	S	Search the directory
Modify	M	Change file attributes
Parental	P	Completely manage a directory, including assigning rights to it and its subdirectories, creating and deleting subdirectories and modifying file attributes

Figure 8-1   Trustee Rights

Here's how we might use the combination of the Trustee rights and the directory's Maximum Rights Mask. Suppose we want to limit the rights in a directory to a maximum of R, W, O, C, and S (Read, Write, Open, Create and Search). But we want to allow only a group supervisor (remember we alluded to subsupervisors above?) to actually create a file or subdirectory. So, we assign a Maximum Rights Mask to the directory of RWOCS, but we assign no Trustee rights to any member of the group allowed to access the directory to RWOS. Now, we add C to the subsupervisor's Trustee rights and we have only one user allowed to create files or subdirectories. All users except the subsupervisor are said to have **Effective Rights** of RWOS while the one person we are giving the unofficial title of subsupervisor has Effective Rights of RWOCS.

Now we have one last level of security. This type is on the file or directory level. It determines what may or may not be done to files individually. There are only two attributes which we can assign to files with this type of security. They are Read-Write or Read Only, and Sharable or Non-sharable. In other words, we can restrict individual files from being written to or being used by more than one user at a time.

We have similar attributes for directories. In the case of directories they may be designated as Normal, Hidden, System or Private. Normal directories have no attributes and are available to any users with Trustee rights that at least equal the directory's Maximum Rights mask. In other words, users with effective rights that allow access to the directory.

Hidden directories are not visible to any user in a directory listing, but may be accessed by any user with effective rights that allow access. They are sort of like unlisted phone numbers. You can't find out what the number is from the directory or the operator, but, if you know it, you can dial it.

System directories are exactly what the name implies—directories of system files. They are hidden from directory searches. Finally, there are Private directories. Private directories appear in directory listings but the contents are hidden unless the user's effective rights include Search. These file and directory attributes are "senior" to user's effective rights and a directory's Maximum Rights Mask. In other words if a file is Read-Only, no amount of effective rights will allow a user (other than the Network Supervisor) to write to it. Later in this chapter we'll show you how to use some of the supervisory utilities to set up new users.

Some Special Supervisor Capabilities

Later on, in Chapter 9 we'll be discussing some of the menu utilities. And, in Chapter 7, we told you about the command line utilities. Some of those utilities have special capabilities that only supervisors may access. In order to avoid confusion these capabilities are not even displayed to users without supervisor or supervisor-equivalent status. The menu utilities affected are SYSCON, FILER, PRINTDEF, PRINTCON and PCONSOLE. The MAKE-USER utility is only available to supervisors or their equivalents. And FCON-SOLE, while not strictly a supervisor utility, is used often by supervisors.

In addition there are several command line utilities used only by supervisors. These are ATOTAL, BINDFIX, BINDREST, HIDEFILE, MAKE-USER (used with the MAKEUSER menu utility), PAUDIT, SECURITY and SHOWFILE.

Basically, these special command line and menu utilities are divided into two types. The first includes extensions to the same utility used by regular users. The second includes special utilities for supervisors only. The specific purposes for these utilities varies with the utility or command. But, broadly speaking, they all provide the supervisor with tools to monitor network activity, manage network resources and control network access and security.

Because it is a basic part of maintaining the network, we'll start out our discussion of supervisory utilities with a brief discussion of the console. The console device is, as we have said earlier, a sort of master workstation for the server. In other words it is the screen and keyboard that control the server. Only through the console or through the FCONSOLE utility can a supervisor or console operator issue commands to the server. FCONSOLE

```
┌──────────────────────────────────────────────────────────────────────┐
│ NetWare File Server Console  V2.01       Monday  January 29, 1990  11:54 am │
│           User GAMAL On File Server PRUFROCK Connection 4              │
└──────────────────────────────────────────────────────────────────────┘
```

```
┌────────────────────────────────┐
│       Available Options         │
├────────────────────────────────┤
│ Broadcast Console Message       │
│ Change Current File Server      │
│ Connection Information          │
│ Down File Server                │
│ File/Lock Activity              │
│ LAN Driver Information          │
│ Purge All Salvageable Files     │
│ Statistics                      │
│ Status                          │
│ Version Information             │
└────────────────────────────────┘
```

Figure 8-2   Main FCONSOLE Menu

is a special utility that allows authorized users to access the server from a workstation as if the workstation were, in fact, the console. The utility makes any workstation a console device. When you type FCONSOLE at the network prompt you'll see (if you are logged in as the supervisor, console operator, or equivalent) the menu in Figure 8-2.

You'll notice that there are several broad categories of available options. These options are:

Broadcast Console Message
Change Current File Server
Connection Information
Down File Server
File/Lock Activity
LAN Driver Information
Purge all Salvagable Files
Statistics
Status
Version Information

Each of these menu options either invokes additional menus or performs its stated function. We'll explain, briefly, each of the FCONSOLE choices.

Broadcast Console Message

This option allows the supervisor or console operator to send a message to every user on the server. This is useful if you plan to down the server for maintenance, or, if you simply want to send a general bulletin to all your users.

Change Current File Server

At any given time the network has a default file server. If your LAN has only one server, this command won't be much use to you. This is one of the few options that lets both users and supervisors affect the network server. At any time you wish, you can use this choice to designate a different server as the default. It doesn't make the new server the default for all the users on the network. Rather, it makes a different server the default for the user who selected it.

Connection Information

This choice shows all of the logical connections to a given server. Supervisors and console operators can view a variety of information about these connections. Not only can you view information such as record locks in place, open files and usage statistics, but you can clear a current connection. Once you clear a user's connection, that user must log out and log back in again to reestablish the server connection.

Down File Server

This choice allows you to bring down the server. You'll be warned of open files and you should never down the server while files are open if you can avoid it. To do so could result in lost or damaged data. We suggest that you send a broadcast message prior to downing the server and wait until all files are closed and users have logged off the LAN. Theoretically the server should close all open files and roll back incomplete transactions. But it is always better to orchestrate an orderly shutdown if you can manage it. It's certainly good supervisor-etiquette to warn network users in plenty of time for them to complete their transactions.

File/Lock Activity

This choice simply displays information about the files in use on your LAN. It examines the locking, semaphores and transaction status on your files.

LAN Driver Information

This one displays the information about all of the LAN drivers on a particular server. The display includes the addresses (network and workstation), the board type (Arcnet, Ethernet, etc), the configuration and the hardware options such as interrupt request and I/O address.

Purge All Salvageable Files

On the Macintosh this would be called Empty Trash. As you may know, in a DOS environment files don't really get deleted when you delete them. Their FAT and directory entries are altered and they disappear from the directory listing. This is why file-recover utilities such as Norton's Utilities can salvage a deleted file as long as the disk sectors have not been overwritten.

NetWare takes this one step further. It deliberately protects deleted files until you say to purge them. This is the computer equivalent of dumping paper files in a trash basket, but not emptying the trash. If you find you need something you threw away in error you can still root it out of the trash.

Statistics

This is another treasure trove of information about how your LAN is performing. From this choice you can get cache and channel statistics, Disk mapping information, disk statistics, file system statistics, LAN I/O statistics and information about your network volumes and transaction tracking.

Status and Version Information

These two are simple information screens that tell you what the server's status is and what version of NetWare is running on it. Status refers to the server's time and date settings, the ability of the server to accept new logins and the status of transaction tracking, if available on your server.

The Network Environment and the Supervisor

Over the course of your supervisor tenure, you'll alter the network environment on two occasions. The first of these, which we discuss in detail in Chapter 10, is when you install the server. You may have to install one or more servers, or you may modify a current server installation.

The second time is when you are called upon to make adjustments to the network drives and directories, printer configurations or user login scripts. We will discuss the server in Chapter 10 and the various supervisor command line and menu utilities later in this chapter. Now, however, we'll go into some detail regarding user scripts.

User Logon Scripts

When you build a user's boot disk, you probably will place two things on it. The first of these is the IPX configuration which you'll set up in Chapter 10. You set up that portion of the workstation environment when you use SHGEN to generate a network shell.

The second piece of the login disk is the login script. The purpose of the login script is to customize your workstation/network/server environment for your personal use. Such functions as drive mappings or greetings set the path to the command interpreter and, generally, personalize your computing environment. You create login scripts for yourself or, if you are the supervisor, for other users, with the SYSCON utility. SYSCON has its own text editor. There is a default login script, shown in Figure 8-3, that takes over if you don't have a custom script. We'll show it here, courtesy of Novell, as it is a good example of what a login script looks like. Then we'll get into the script language commands.

The Script Commands

When you write your script using SYSCON, you will have use of the SYSCON editor. You will also be prompted. There are only two rules for scripts. First, no line can exceed 150 characters and, second, you may put only one command on a line. A login script ends up looking a lot like a DOS batch file. Now to the script commands. Remember to follow each command line with [ENTER].

```
WRITE "Good %GREETING_TIME, %LOGIN_NAME."
MAP DISPLAY OFF
MAP ERRORS OFF
Remark: Set 1st drive to most appropriate directory.
MAP *1:=SYS:; *1:=SYS:%LOGIN_NAME
IF "%1"="Supervisor" THEN MAP *1:=SYS:SYSTEM
Remark: Set search drives (S2 machine-OS dependent)
MAP S1:=SYS:PUBLIC; S2:=S1:%MACHINE/%OS /%OS_VERSION
Remark: Now display all the current drive settings
MAP DISPLAY ON
MAP
```

Figure 8-3   Default Login Script

ATTACH
ATTACH [file server[/username[;password]]]

ATTACH connects servers other than the default server to your work-station. If you do not specify the server, username or password, you will be prompted for them

BREAK
BREAK ON | OFF

BREAK is used to execute a nonconditional exit from your script. For example, if you are using the IF. . . THEN construct, you might want to make the consequence of an event an exit from the script. In this case you would use BREAK ON or OFF. BREAK does not in itself interrupt the script execution. Instead it allows the user to execute and [Ctrl] C to exe-cute. If the BREAK is ON, typeahead keyboard buffer contents will not be saved. If it is OFF, they will be.

COMSPEC
COMPSEC = *n:[/]filename | drive:[\]filename | Sn:[\]filename

COMSPEC designates the name and location of the command inter-preter, usually Command.com. The location could be *n: which refers to the nth network drive, drive: which refers to a named driver (d:, e:, f:, etc) or Sn: which means the nth Search Drive.

[F]DISPLAY
[F]DISPLAY [directory/]filename

FDISPLAY displays the contents of a text file with word processor con-trol codes filtered out of the display. DISPLAY performs the same task without filtering out the commands. You can use these commands to bring up the contents of a text file during login.

DOS BREAK
DOS BREAK ON | OFF

Performs the same function as BREAK for DOS files instead of script files.

[DOS]SET
[DOS]SET name = "value"

[DOS]SET allows you to set the various command line variables as specified in your DOS manual. The [DOS] part of the command is optional and the command works just like its DOS SET companion. For example, you could use the SET command to set the prompt to something other than the drive letter by using SET prompt = "PG" to get the directory and > sign. Don't forget the quote marks (" ").

DOS VERIFY
DOS VERIFY ON | OFF

Insures that files copied are copied correctly when DOS VERIFY is ON.

DRIVE
DRIVE n: | *n:

Specifies a default drive for your workstation different than the network default. The drive will be the nth (a number) if you select the *n: option or will have a specific designation if you select the n: option.

EXIT
EXIT "filename"

Exits (quits) the script and executes a program named "filename." Filename may not exceed 14 characters and must be a .COM, .EXE or .BAT file.

#
#[directory/]filename parameter line

The # command lets you execute any executable program along with its command line parameters and return to the script. If there is not enough memory to run the external program or if it cannot be found, you will return to the script. Don't use this command with a memory resident program. Use EXIT instead.

FIRE PHASERS
FIRE PHASERS n TIMES

This is not a joke. The FIRE PHASERS command, strange as it may seem, is really a sound effect command that can be helpful and less irritating than the persistent BEEP whenever you make an entry error. Use this one to give an aural acknowledgment after the execution of some other command.

IF. . . THEN
IF condition(s) THEN command

IF. . .THEN constructs are among the most useful of programming commands. They allow you to specify a pair of alternatives and issue instructions for execution in either event. For example, you could say
IF something happens THEN do this

THAT
What that means is, if something happens, execute the "this" command. If it doesn't, execute the "that" command. Your program has a choice of two commands depending upon whether or not "something" happens.

INCLUDE
INCLUDE [directory\]filename

This command allows you to include subscripts in your scripts. You can nest subscripts up to ten levels deep and they, unlike the master script, can be created as a standard ASCII text file with a text editor.

MACHINE NAME
MACHINE NAME = "name" (or MACHINE = "name")

This is required by some PC DOS systems to identify the station with a unique name.

MAP
MAP Displays the current drive mappings for the server
MAP drive: Displays only the mappings for the designated drive
MAP drive:=directory Maps the drive to the specified directory
MAP directory Maps the default drive to the designated directory
MAP drive:= Maps the specified drive to the same directory as the default drive.
MAP drive:=directory; drive:=directory . . . Maps multiple drives to multiple directories
MAP INSERT search drive:=directory Inserts a new search drive designated by the next available drive letter
MAP DEL drive: Deletes a drive mapping
MAP REM drive: Is the same as MAP DEL

PAUSE (or WAIT)
PAUSE
WAIT

Temporarily halts script execution. Pause includes the familiar "Strike a key when ready . . ." message

[PC]COMPATIBLE
[PC]COMPATIBLE

This is pretty obscure. However, if you plan to use PC compatible files on a computer that is not 100% compatible with an IBM PC you'll need it. One area where this could occur is, if you show your workstation as something other than IBM PC in your SHELL.CFG (shell configuration) file, your programs won't run without it. For example, you might want to do this on a Compaq or Zenith computer to access those manufacturers' DOS systems.

REMARK, REM, * or ;
REMARK [text], REM [text], * [text] or ; [text]

Lets you add remarks for the purpose of documenting your script.

WRITE
WRITE [text string; . . .identifier;]

WRITE lets you make your script write a message to the screen as it executes. The message could be a text string or any of several specific identifiers in Figure 8-4. Enclose text strings in quotes (" ") and use \r for a carriage return, \n for a new line and \7 to sound a beep. To use several strings and identifiers in the same message separate them with semicolons (;). An example of the WRITE command in the default script is

```
WRITE "Good %GREETING_TIME, %LOGIN_NAME."
```

Using the script commands, you as the supervisor can create custom login scripts for your users that will let them work in an environment defined specifically for them.

Supervisor Menu Utilities

As we have pointed out, there are two sets of tools available to supervisors. They are the menu utilities and the command line utilities. In a few cases these tools overlap the same tools available to regular users with the exception that there are some additional menu choices or command line options available to supervisors. When this overlap occurs, the basic function of the command or menu doesn't change, it simply gets expanded for the supervisor. We'll look at the menu utilities first.

The Filer Utility

You will use the Filer utility to deal with files and directories. As a supervisor you can change the owner, creation date, and time of files, directories and subdirectories. There are a number of user options as well which we have discussed elsewhere. When you invoke Filer by typing FILER at the prompt you will see a menu like that in Figure 8-5.

In order to change the creation date simply select the Current Directory Information. The Filer program will prompt you for new creation date and time information. The selections you should make from the drop down menu are Creation Date followed by Creation Time if you wish to change both. To change the owner, select Owner instead and press [Ins]ert. You will then see a list of valid potential owners. Select one and your job is finished.

IDENTIFIER VARIABLES	SCREEN DISPLAY
HOUR	Hour of Day or Night (1-12)
HOUR24	Hour on a 24 Hour Clock (00-23)
MINUTE	Minutes (00-59)
SECOND	Seconds (00-59)
AM_PM	Day or Night
MONTH	Month Number (01-12)
MONTH_NAME	Month Name (July, etc)
DAY	Day Number (1-31)
NDAY_OF_WEEK	Weekday Number (1-7, Sunday is 1)
YEAR	4 Digit Year (1990)
SHORT_YEAR	2 Digit Year (85, 90, etc)
DAY_OF_WEEK	Day of Week (Monday, etc)
LOGIN_NAME	User's Login
FULL_NAME	User's Full Name from SYSCON
STATION	Workstation Number
P_STATION	Physical Station (12 HEX Digits)
GREETING_TIME	Morning, Afternoon, Evening
NEW_MAIL	YES or NO - Automatic on Login
OS	Workstation Operating System
OS_VERSION	Workstation OS Version
MACHINE	Full Name of Machine for Script
SMACHINE	Short Name of Machine for Script
ERROR_LEVEL	A Value Indicating Errors

Figure 8-4   Identifiers Used with the WRITE Command (Courtesy Novell)

```
NetWare File Maintenance  V3.00          Monday  January 29, 1990  11:58 am
                         PRUFROCK\SYS:HOME\GAMAL
```

```
            Available Topics
   Current Directory Information
   Directory Contents
   Select Current Directory
   Set Filer Options
   Volume Information
```

Figure 8-5   Filer Main Choices

The Makeuser Utility

There are two times when you need to add or delete users from your network. The first is when you set up your LAN and second is in day-to-day operations. You can create and delete users in two ways as well. The first is with the SYSCON utility. The Second is with the MAKEUSER utility. SYSCON is used when you configure the system. Although you can use it any time, Makeuser is more convenient for routine use. There is a difference, though. Syscon creates users directly as part of the system configuration. Makeuser creates special files with the extension .USR containing user information. .USR files are recognized by SYSCON, but system defaults set by SYSCON do not apply to .USR files. When you type MAKEUSER the menu shown in Figure 8-6 will appear.

```
NetWare Make User  V2.00            Monday   January 29, 1990  11:59 am
File Server: PRUFROCK
```

```
        Available Options
   Create New USR File
   Edit USR File
   Process USR file
```

Figure 8-6   MAKEUSER Main Menu

MAKEUSER is really a sort of special text editor. In fact, you can create .USR files using a regular ASCII text editor. However, you must use MAKEUSER to process the new .USR file before your entries are valid. The format for a .USR file is similar to a script. It contains a series of keywords which define the environment for the particular user. Here are the keywords and their meanings.

ACCOUNT EXPIRATION   Specifies the expiration date of the user's account

  SYNTAX: ACCOUNT_EXPIRATION date

ACCOUNTING   Allows the user access to certain accounting services and defines them

  SYNTAX: ACCOUNTING balance, Low Limit

CLEAR or RESET   A programming step which allows you to start a new set of keywords in the same .USR file

  SYNTAX: #CLEAR or #RESET

CONNECTIONS   Maximum number of concurrent connections

  SYNTAX: #CONNECTIONS Number

  NOTE: This command must appear before the CREATE keyword and affects all of the users created from that point until a CLEAR or RESET

CREATE   Creates the users

  SYNTAX: CREATE Username; Fullname; Password; Group [,Group];
Trusteedirectory [Rights]
[,Trusteedirectory [Rights]]

  NOTE: Be sure to include the semicolon (;) between fields and place a plus (+) sign after a field to continue to the next line if the instruction is too long for a single line. You must have an entry for every option in the command, but where you don't want an entry you can simply replace it with two semicolons. If you want to terminate the line without further options you may use a caret (^) at the end of the line.

DELETE   Deletes users

SYNTAX: DELETE Username [;Username]

GROUPS   Specifies the groups to which the user belongs

SYNTAX: #GROUPS Group [;Group]

HOME DIRECTORY   Creates the user's home directory

SYNTAX: #HOME_DIRECTORY directory path

LOGIN SCRIPT   Assigns a login script

SYNTAX: #LOGIN_SCRIPT filespec

MAX DISK SPACE   Limits the amount of disk space available to the user

SYNTAX: #MAX_DISK_SPACE number

NOTE: Number specifies the number of Kb

PASSWORD LENGTH   Lets you specify a password's length

SYNTAX: #PASSWORD_LENGTH length

NOTE: Length in characters

PASSWORD PERIOD   Lets you force periodic change of password

SYNTAX: #PASSWORD_PERIOD days

PASSWORD REQUIRED   Lets you force the use of a password

SYNTAX: #PASSWORD_REQUIRED

PURGE USER DIRECTORY	Deletes the user's directories

SYNTAX: #PURGE_USER_DIRECTORY

REM	Remarks—lets you comment on the file

SYNTAX: #REM or REM

RESTRICTED TIME	Specifies when the user may not login

SYNTAX: #RESTRICTED_TIME Day, Start, End [;Day, Start, End]

NOTE: Use normal day of week and times. Day can be everyday

STATIONS	Specifies what workstations are available to the user

SYNTAX: #STATIONS network, station [,station]
         [;network, station[,station]]

NOTE: Stations are the hexadecimal addresses of the stations and the networks on which the user may log in. Without this, he or she may use any station.

UNIQUE PASSWORD	Allows you to force a unique password

SYNTAX: #UNIQUE_PASSWORD

You must use at least the CREATE or DELETE keywords. Anything else is up to you. Once you have completed your .USR file, using either the MAKEUSER utility or your text editor, you must process the file. From the MAKEUSER menu, simply highlight the Process USR File choice and follow the prompts.

Printdef, Printcon, and Pconsole Printing Utilities

These three utilities have both user and supervisor functions. Here, we'll discuss the supervisor functions. We're covering the three utilities together because they all have to do with the network printers. The PRINTDEF utility allows you to set up your network printers by defining

```
Printer Definition Utility  V1.04         Monday  January 29, 1990  11:59 am
              User GAMAL On File Server PRUFROCK Connection 4
```

```
           PrintDef Options

           Print Devices
           Forms
```

Figure 8-7   PRINTCON Edit Print Job Configuration Menu

the devices and forms they'll use. PRINTCON lets you set print job configurations and PCONSOLE actually sets up the print queues and gets the printing done. If that sounds like so much jargon to you, hang on . . . we'll explain the details starting with PRINTDEF.

Basically, a NetWare print job has two parts: a device and a form. The device is the printer and its associated driver that you will use to print the job. The form is the kind of paper on which you will print it. To define a standard job, the user selects a device and a form and prints his or her project. You as the supervisor will define the valid device and forms possibilities using the supervisor capabilities of the PRINTDEF utility.

Forms are the types or sizes of paper you will use to print jobs. For example, you may use 8 1/2" x 11" bond paper for your LaserJet and wide paper for the printer your accounting department uses to print financial reports. To set up the forms you will use, select the Forms choice on the PRINTDEF Options menu and follow the prompts.

Once you have completed the printer and form definition, you can use the supervisor options in the PRINTCON utility to create reusable print job configurations. The difference between using PRINTCON and PCONSOLE is that PCONSOLE is basically a manual utility that uses the default print job configurations. However, using PRINTCON you can create the default configuration users will get if they use PCONSOLE. You can also create custom configurations and copy existing configurations from user to user.

A print job configuration is a combination of special formatting, device selection and form selection. When you type PRINTCON followed by Edit Print Job Configuration you will see the menu in Figure 8-7.

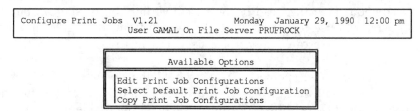

```
Configure Print Jobs  V1.21            Monday  January 29, 1990  12:00 pm
              User GAMAL On File Server PRUFROCK
```

```
                    Available Options

     Edit Print Job Configurations
     Select Default Print Job Configuration
     Copy Print Job Configurations
```

Figure 8-8   PRINTDEF Main Menu

All you need to do is fill in the blanks and name the configuration and you'll have a custom printer setup for your users. To use it they will simply select the configuration by name when they print.

For simplicity, NetWare provides at least 30 printer definitions. These predefined devices cover a very wide spectrum of common printers and more are added frequently. You use PRINTDEF to define the devices you will use in one of three ways. You can use the device drivers (files that end in a .PDF extension) provided with NetWare, you can create your own, or you can transfer them from another server. Simply type PRINTDEF at the prompt and the menu in Figure 8-8 will appear. Select Print Devices and you can Import Print Devices into your PRINTDEF database.

If you need to create a new printer definition select the Edit Print Devices and use the New Device Name box. Enter the name of the device you want to add and, when the Edit Device Options menu is displayed, highlight Device Functions. Type the escape sequences for your printer (you'll find them in the printer's manual) and enter [Esc]ape to quit. When you have defined a printer's functions (escape codes) you can also define what Novell calls modes. A mode is simply an expansion of the escape functions peculiar to a particular print job. It's a bit like customizing the printer driver for a single job on a single device instead of the general device itself. Use the Device Modes choice on the Edit Device Options menu. You'll be prompted for each step.

Finally, you can create and rename print queues, assign users to the queues and assign queue operators using the supervisor options in the PCONSOLE utility. The default action of the server is to assign one print queue to each printer. When you create additional queues for a printer you must also map a spooler for the queue. A queue is a group of jobs that hold something in common. For example, you might want to create a special queue for the finance department so that when someone needs a financial report they won't have to wait for a large number of word processing documents ahead of them to print.

Print queues are a bit like having several lines at the company copier. There is a long line for normal users and a smaller line for executives. If someone is at the head of the executive line, he or she can be the next person to use the copier after the person from the regular line finishes. The executive can't interrupt a user, but has priority when that user is finished.

Queues need spoolers. Spoolers hold the document to be printed in memory until its turn comes up in the queue. All of the functions of PCONSOLE are shown on the Available Options menu when you type PCONSOLE. To create a queue select New Print Queue Name from the

Print Queue Information selection. Likewise you can rename and delete print queues.

You will use the Queue Users choice to add and delete users and the Queue Operators choice to do the same with operators. Basically, this utility lets you create the queues and the users can use them with the default configuration.

Supervisor Command Line Utilities

There are eight command line utilities that are reserved for supervisors or have special supervisor capabilities. A few of these mimic the menu utilities of the same name. These utilities, like MAKEUSER, function precisely the same as a menu or command line utility. The difference is that as a menu utility you typed MAKEUSER alone at the command line prompt and waited for the menu. As a command line utility you will add command line options instead of going step-by-step through the menus.

In some cases, the options you will have as a command line utility are fewer than as a menu utility. Again using MAKEUSER as an example, as a menu utility we can create the .USR file and then process it. The MAKEUSER command line utility only allows you to process a .USR file created with the MAKEUSER menu utility. We'll describe the command line utilities and show you the command line syntax. Where a command line utility duplicates a menu utility, rather than re-explaining the utility, we'll simply give you the command line syntax.

ATOTAL	Summarizes the contents of a PAUDIT file (See also PAUDIT)
SYNTAX:	ATOTAL
USE:	The ATOTAL utility summarizes the information in a PAUDIT file. The PAUDIT file is created by the system when accounting functions are installed. The difference between ATOTAL and PAUDIT is that ATOTAL only provides a summary of Total Blocks Read and Written; Total Connect Time, Total Service Requests; and Total Disk Storage in Blocks/Day. PAUDIT provides the details.
BINDFIX	Bindfix is a utility you can use to repair the bindery. The bindery consists of two hidden files that are actually databases of users, user groups, queues and

charge rates. You will know that you need to run BINDFIX if you can't change a password, username, user rights or you get an "unknown server" error during spooling even when on the default server.

SYNTAX: BINDFIX

BINDREST   You will run the BINDREST utility when you wish to restore a previous version of the bindery after running the BINDFIX utility. When you run BINDFIX, you create new bindery files. The old files get renamed with a file name extension of .OLD. BINDREST restores the .OLD files to the active bindery.

SYNTAX: BINDREST

HIDEFILE   Hidefile is used to hide one or more files in a directory. After you run HIDEFILE you cannot delete or copy over the files and they will not show up in a DOS directory search. To view files hidden by HIDEFILE, use the SHOWFILE utility.

SYNTAX: HIDEFILE [drive:] [directory/] filename

MAKEUSER   The command line utility that goes with the MAKEUSER menu utility. After you have created .USR files with the MAKEUSER menu utility, you can use the MAKEUSER command line utility to process the file.

SYNTAX: MAKEUSER filename

PAUDIT   PAUDIT shows the details of the PAUDIT file summarized by ATOTAL

SYNTAX: PAUDIT

SECURITY   The SECURITY utility allows you to evaluate the security of your network. The utility automatically examines the bindery for objects without password or with easy-to-guess passwords, objects with supervisor security equivalence, objects that have root directory privileges, objects without a login script and objects with rights that are excessive in the main system directories (SYS:SYSTEM, SYS:PUBLIC. SYS:LOGIN and SYS:MAIL).

SYNTAX: SECURITY

NOTE: You can redirect the information to a file by typing
               SECURITY › filename then you can print it with
               NPRINT filename.

SHOWFILE   Used to show files hidden with HIDEFILE

SYNTAX: SHOWFILE [drive:] [directory/] filename

Summary

These are the commands and menus you as a supervisor can use to control
and monitor the activity on your NetWare LAN. As supervisor you have
access to a variety of tools as we have seen. In this chapter we showed you
the various command line and menu utilities for the supervisor. We discussed the art of being the network supervisor or administrator and we
showed you how to build user scripts.

In the next chapter we'll tie it all together with the reason for using computers in the first place: applications. In Chapter 9 we'll look at how to set
up the various types of applications you'll want on your LAN. We'll cover
databases, word processing, spreadsheets and menu shells. We'll show
you how to use some other utilities that come with NetWare to produce a
very useful menu shell for users on your network. Finally, we'll explore
some of the various network services you can use to make your NetWare
computing easier and more efficient.

9

Applications on Novell LANs

Once you install your Novell LAN, the next step is to install the various applications you will use. Often, these applications are the same as those you used on single-user computers before you installed your LAN. In this chapter, we will discuss the various types of applications you can expect to run on a network and how the LAN versions differ from the stand-alone versions. We will learn about the quirks of various database, spreadsheet and word processing programs in a network environment. Finally, we will explore in detail groupware and the menu facility supplied with your Novell LAN.

Some Beginning Words for Beginning Administrators

Before we go into the various applications, let's be sure we understand the basics of a multiuser environment. There are a few things that happen when more than one user tries to get at files and programs at the same time. We have touched on these in earlier chapters, but we're going to go into a bit more detail now. These issues apply to any multiuser system and the applications running on it. It doesn't matter if the application is a database, spreadsheet or word processor.

First, be sure that you are only using network versions of your software if more than one user will have access to the programs. If you are going to place an application program in a private directory for the use of only one person, you can usually use the single-user version from a stand-alone computer. But, if more than one person has access to the program, you are not only violating the program's license, you will get very unpredictable results when you try to use it.

There is one case where a single-user application simply won't work on a LAN. Some cheaper or older programs are not designed to allow use of disks above a certain level. This level is often as low as the D: drive. Attempts to load the program on drives with a higher designation result in failure. In these instances, unless you have a compelling reason for keeping the offending program, it's just as well to find a substitute that's a bit better designed.

Now, on to the basics of multiuser applications. First, don't forget that when any two (or more) users try to write at the same time to a data file of any kind, you must have a way to prevent it. This applies equally to all types of files which hold data as opposed to program files. There is, however, a way to prevent simultaneous updates.

Start out by insuring that you are using a network version of a program that prevents such updates. In most cases, serious programs like dBASE III Plus and dBASE IV, WordPerfect and its ilk, and Lotus 1-2-3 take simultaneous writes into consideration in their network versions.

Occasionally, you will have several copies of an application which you'll want to give individual users for their private directories. The only reasons we can see for doing this are that you don't want to spend the money for the network version of the program, or a network version simply doesn't exist. In these instances, once you're sure that you've complied with the developer's license requirements, you'll need a way to install the applications in such a manner as to protect data.

The best bet is to install both program and data files in private directories, preventing users from having access to each other's data files. If users must have access to each other's data, however, the only way to insure data integrity, while avoiding locking other users out of a directory is to do the following.

Place all program and data files in individual private directories. Create a public directory to be used as a "holding tank" for completed data files. When a user finishes with a file, he or she moves a copy to the holding tank.

This is dangerous, however, because it leaves you with little control over when a file is moved. For example, Joe and Mary may both be working on a word processing document. Joe moves his revision into the holding tank and, a few minutes later, so does Mary. She just overwrote Joe's changes with her own. Joe's are now lost. The solution is to have a system of file naming that prevents revisions from landing on top of each other.

In the case of database files, this method of file sharing is all but impossible. The best bet with databases is to use only a solid networkable DBMS product. Otherwise you're inviting serious trouble and badly corrupted data. In general, there are no really good methods of safely sharing data from single-user programs used in a multiuser environment. If data or documents must be shared, move to a LAN version of the application and install it per the manufacturer's instructions.

Databases on a LAN—The Epitome of Complexity

There are two ways to install a database management system on a LAN. The simplest is the file server approach. The most powerful, however, is the database server. There are real differences between the two. Many of those differences lie in their relative complexities.

File Servers—The Typical DBMS Case

We'll start with the file server for several reasons. First, the file server is the simplest configuration. Second, whether it's been obvious or not, we've been dealing with file servers so far throughout this book. Finally, today, probably 80% of all LAN DBMS installations are file servers. Although we'll use some specific example programs, we are by no means endorsing the ones we choose. We base our choices on the relative popularity of the products and their usefulness as typical examples of their genre.

The file server configuration means just what the term has meant up to now. The server is nothing more than a repository of data and program files. Its intelligence is limited to managing the network. It has no ability to manipulate data or locate databases on other servers. It simply serves up files like any single-user fixed disk. However, what distinguishes a file server from a database server is not the server itself, but the DBMS software program running on it.

In a database installation, the file server provides a set of network drives for storing data and applications. When you invoke the database program from your workstation, the server sends you the appropriate files just as your workstation hard drive would do in a stand-alone system. All the action then takes place in your workstation's memory. When you update a data file, you send the update to the server where the data file is modified. As long as only one user is involved, there is no significant difference between a single and multiuser system.

When two or more users are involved, however, there are a number of new issues. Chief among these are data integrity and security. Data integrity refers to the ability to maintain accurate data as several users update records. Here is an example of what we mean.

In a particular database installation several users share the same data file. When User A calls a record from that file for updating, no other user must be allowed to access that record until User A is finished. Then User B may access the same record with User A's changes intact. Should User A decide to perform an indexing routine on the data file, the entire file must be locked to prevent any other user from changing, adding or deleting records while the indexing is in progress.

There are consequences to two users updating the same record at the same time. The first is that the second update would overwrite the first. Earlier information would be lost. This is limited to single record updates. Batch updates pose a second issue. In a batch process such as indexing or sorting, the number and content of records must not change during the process. If either number of records or content of fields changes, data integrity will be lost. In extreme cases you will no longer be able to get at the data in corrupted records. Some records may be lost or damaged beyond repair.

In the case of indexing the problem can be especially severe. An index is a file that tells the database program where to look for records based upon the contents of one or more specified fields. These special fields are called keys or key fields. If you alter the contents of those fields or change the number of records in the database, the entries in the index file no longer match the actual records in the database. Any attempt to use the index to locate a record will fail. This, of course, is critical. Virtually all well-designed database applications depend upon indexes for rapid record retrieval.

dBASE III Plus—A Common DBMS

Although there are newer generations of the dBASE series of DBMS products, we'll use dBASE III Plus as an example of a file server database. dBASE III Plus is a database workhorse with over one million copies in use worldwide. It is also typical of an entire generation of database products in use on both single- and multiuser systems.

dBASE III Plus has implicit record and file locking in the single-user version. This locking is also in place in the multiuser version. However, the locking is uncontrollable without some additional help from a program called the Administrator. Without the Administrator, no more than one user at a time can access the dBASE program or data files. The Administrator provides the ability for several users to access the program. It also allows developers of dBASE applications to designate record and file locks and unlocks in their program code.

The Administrator also enables a specific number of network users. Once the user count reaches the number designated by the Administrator, no more users can access the dBASE program files. Some other DBMS programs enable all of the users on a single file server. Once the network version of the database is loaded, any user can gain access.

There are specific ways to load these programs on your Novell LAN. Generally speaking, all program and application files are in public directories with READ, SEARCH and OPEN privileges. Data files may be in public or private directories with READ, WRITE, CREATE and MODIFY FILENAME privileges. Whether they are in public or private directories depends upon who must use them.

If a database file is accessible only to a few users, it is a good idea to create a private directory accessible only to those users. In that directory you would place the data files, index files and program files for that application. You would also include any form and label files the application needs.

Be sure that you have included the DOS PATH to the DBMS program files so that the application will have no trouble finding them. It is also a good idea in most DBMS programs to include the specific PATH to the DBMS files in the application code. Don't count on Novell's MAP commands to get you to the files you need. But always make sure that the PATH command and the PATHs designated in your program code match the network drives you map to your directories.

Paradox—A Case Study

Another typical DBMS product is Paradox from Borland. Paradox is one of the DBMS types that count the number of users on the network at any given time. A single executable file, the kernel of the DBMS, resides in a public directory. Other files may reside on workstations to improve performance. A special file called Paradox.net coordinates sharing of resources and keeps track of users. All users must have access to the same copy of Paradox.net in order to be able to share the files it controls.

When you install Paradox on your Novell LAN, you go through a series of steps that are pretty typical of installations of many popular DBMS products. So, in order to provide you with a specific example of DBMS setup on a Novell LAN, we'll go through the installation of Paradox. You will perform five specific tasks when you install Paradox. You will

- Create a Paradox system software directory for the program files.
- Create Paradox shared data directories for shared Paradox data tables.
- Run an install routine.
- Make Paradox available to users, and
- Create a configuration file.

The System Files

The Paradox system files will go into their own shared applications directory. It is best to make this a subdirectory of the network shared application directory but it may be a first level directory if you prefer. We recommend that you create the subdirectory. This makes it easier to keep track of your applications files since they are all in the same location.

You will also need to set the maximum rights mask to S (search for files), O (open files) and R (read files). In effect, you are creating a directory which permits users to find and read files only. Finally, you will designate the users whose trustee rights allow them to access the subdirectory containing the Paradox system files.

To accomplish these first three tasks you log in as the network supervisor and start the filer utility by typing Filer at the prompt. Set the Current Directory to the server's shared applications directory and select Subdirectory Information from the Filer menu. You are going to create a new subdirectory for the Paradox files. You do this by pressing [Ins] and typing the name of the subdirectory you wish to create in the New Subdirectory Name box. You may now [Esc]ape and return to the main Filer menu. Add the name of the subdirectory you just created to the Current Directory box and edit the maximum rights mask to S, O, and R.

Finally, you will need to set the trustees who can access your new subdirectory. If you want to make the subdirectory truly public, simply assign the trustee group Everyone to the subdirectory.

If, on the other hand, you wish to limit access you will need to assign trustee rights to individual users. There are two ways to do this. First, you can name individuals assigned as trustees for your Paradox subdirectory. The other way is to create a new group and assign group trustee rights.

Your next task is to create the shared data directory in almost the same way you created the system files subdirectory. There are a couple of differences, however. First, this directory should be a first level directory. If you wish to have additional subdirectories with specific database tables in them you can do that as well. The second difference is that the maximum rights mask must be set to Read, Write, Create Files and Modify Filenames. In addition to the shared data files you will store here, you need to have a copy of the Paradox.net file we discussed earlier.

Your next step is to perform the Paradox install routines per the Paradox manual. You can either change directories to the subdirectory you designated as the Paradox system files directory or you can map the directory to one of your logical drives and go to that drive.

Your final step is to make Paradox available to users. The maximum number of files and buffers in the workstation Config.sys file must be set to 20. This is lower than many applications require and it's a good idea to have at least this configuration anyway.

Most Novell configurations provide individual users with a private home directory and subdirectories. Paradox needs these private home directories to store what it calls temporary objects. This private directory is also a good place to put the Paradox configuration file peculiar to each user.

We have to be careful here, though. The Novell operating system is not able to search local hard drives as part of its Search path. So the solution of placing the configuration file in the users' individual home directories on the LAN is safe only if no other configuration files are in the user's PATH.

Since there is a default configuration (.CFG) file in the Paradox system file directory, you will need to remove it before bringing users on line. This will avoid confusing Paradox when it looks for the user's individual configuration.

Also, you should use the DOS PATH command instead of the Novell MAP commands to set up the individual user search paths. You can map the Paradox directories to specific drives in the user's login script if the person uses Paradox frequently. Otherwise, include the mapping commands in a Paradox batch file.

This file contains all the necessary commands to set up Paradox on the LAN whenever the user wishes. It does not keep the individual directories mapped to network drives all the time though. For infrequent use this is the best approach. At the end of the batch file you should be sure to use MAP DEL commands to unmap the Paradox directories from network drives and return the drives to general availability.

These two DBMS products typify the file server approach to database management on a LAN. Virtually all such products install on your Novell

LAN in a similar manner. Understanding the way that DBMS system and shared data files reside in their respective directories is important no matter what product you use.

The basic philosophy is simple—system files should be shared, data files should be in separate directories with applications. Sharing of these directories is optional. Access to the DBMS is usually through a batch file in the user's home directory that maps network drives to the DBMS directories. At the completion of the DBMS session be sure to unmap the drives using MAP DEL [d:].

Database Servers—Industrial Strength DBMS Power

The other type of database management system is referred to in several ways. Although there are some important technical differences, these DBMS programs are variously called distributed, cooperative or client-server systems. All have one thing in common. They all use a technology called the database server.

The database server differs considerably from the file server. In the file server, you recall, the server is simply a repository for files. All database processing takes place at the workstation. Results are returned to the server for storage. A database server, in contrast, does some of the work. It has intelligence. How much of the work it does varies from system to system.

In a distributed database system, the application resides on the workstation. The database resides on the database server. There is a subtle difference between the same terms on a file server and database server. For example, we know that the term "server" has very different meanings. But another term, database, also takes on a different meaning when used in the context of database servers.

Since most distributed databases use SQL as the query language, the SQL terminology of "Table" is substituted for the older term "database." In fact, database, correctly used, refers to the tables that make up the various data files and the software that resides on the database server. This software is also sometimes called the database "engine" or, simply, the "backend."

The software on the workstation is called the application or "frontend." In a client-server arrangement it is the client. Client-server systems are also called cooperative processing systems. They are slightly different from distributed systems. In fact, the client-server DBMS is actually a superset of the simple distributed database.

Distributed and cooperative processing systems are different from file server systems in two major ways. First, as we have pointed out, the workstation and the server both carry out intelligent processing of data. Second, the user and the application do not need to know where on the network the data they seek resides. Since data may be distributed among several tables on several servers there needs to be a way of finding it. These systems usually contain a specialized program that keeps track of the locations of various database servers and the data residing on them.

A distributed system is a bit dumber than a cooperative system. In a distributed system, the application can reside on the database server. The application receives instructions from the workstation and either carries them out or passes them to the server. Most of the procedural instructions are carried out by the application. Most data manipulation is carried out by the server. The results are reported to the user and the data is updated wherever it resides by the server.

Cooperative, or client-server systems always use the workstation for application processing. The workstation issues orders to the server which carries them out. These orders only relate to data processing and searching. Once the data has been found the results are sent to the client. The client uses the data and issues further orders. The orders are carried out by the server and the results reported to the client user.

Let's simplify that a bit more. In a client-server system the database server, or backend, manages all data manipulation, security and data integrity. The client, or frontend, contains the application which uses the data managed by the backend. The client can contain almost any application capable of issuing instructions to the backend. The standard language for issuing these instructions is SQL or Structured Query Language.

A big advantage of cooperative processing is that a variety of frontends can communicate with a variety of backends over a network. It means that, in addition to handling data on your Novell LAN, you can use the communications facilities that Novell provides to communicate with the outside world. Now, data on mini and mainframe computers is accessible to users on the LAN.

There are several database server products on the market today. One of the most comprehensive is SQLBase from Gupta Technologies. SQLBase is a true cooperative processing system. It can run in either a DOS or an OS/2 environment. And it is typical of client-server products for local area networks. We won't go as deeply into the installation of SQLBase as we did earlier with Paradox. But, we will show you a bit about how SQLBase works and how to set up a client-server environment.

SQLBase—Client-Server Technology for the Masses

To simplify the installation of SQLBase, let's assume a two node network. One node we'll set up as the server and the other as the workstation or client. Once we've set up the Novell server software, we need to install the server side of SQLBase. Like most database server products, SQLBase installation consists of four steps. They are

- Install the database software on the server,
- Initialize a database,
- Initialize the database server, and
- Install client software on the workstation.

In some regards the database server installation is easier than file server database installation. To install the database on the server we first create a public directory for the database software. We do this in exactly the same way as we did on the file server for Paradox.

There is one difference, however. Unlike the file server database, we will need to allow WRITEs to the database files. This is important because at least one data table will reside in the database's directory. So, we set up the database server directory the same way we set up the shared data directory for Paradox.

The files you will put in this directory are Dbserver.exe, Dbserver.cfg, Start.dbs, Error.sql and init.bat. Dbserver reads the .cfg file at startup time. From the .cfg file it obtains all data on the system's parameters. Typical parameters are the names of all data files on the LAN, the directories and drives for data files, the number of clients allowed to access the database at any one time and the size of the cache used to buffer database pages in memory.

Notice that there are no restrictions on where we can place data tables. We must, however, put their locations and names in the .cfg file.

Now it is necessary to initialize a database on the server. This database, Start.dbs, contains additional information SQLBase needs to function. Some database server products refer to this database as the kernel. Oracle is such a product. You initialize Start.dbs with the Init.bat file.

Once you have initialized the database kernel, you start the database server with the DBSERVER command. Finally, you start each client node with Dbrouter.exe. Dbrouter.exe is a file which, when invoked, remains in the workstation's memory. It remembers the location of the database servers and must be invoked before you can run any applications from the workstation.

Although this is a much simplified procedure, you can see that, unlike the file server, the database server contains software (Dbserver) that manipulates the various database tables on the server and software (Dbrouter) that issues instructions and executes applications from the workstation.

In contrast, the file server DBMS simply contains the database's executable file, or system file, that resides at the file server. When you invoke the system file, the server downloads it to your workstation memory like any executable program on any single-user hard disk.

The file server database program depends upon locking methods in its single system file to allow users access to the program while controlling access to database records. The database server allows the client to execute whatever applications it wishes, providing only those data file records the application needs. It prevents user collision on a record-by-record basis and it controls data integrity from the server without regard for the actions of the client.

The bottom line is that the client-server arrangement is faster, more efficient, allows access to a variety of database backends, provides better security and insures data integrity. It is in all ways superior to file server systems. But, it is more complex to manage, takes up more memory and disk space and, generally, is far more expensive than file server products.

The next type of application which we shall confront is the word processor. Not only more common than database management systems, word processors are also somewhat less complex.

Network Word Processors—Sharing Documents Efficiently

The secret to successful document sharing on a LAN goes beyond simply making text available to several users in an orderly manner. Today's powerful word processors approach desktop publishing in their ability to create sophisticated documents. They allow group writing and editing. And they control access on a network. As examples of how network-oriented word processors work, we'll show you two influential products and how they relate to your Novell LAN.

There are several issues that confront users of word processors in a network. The first is data integrity. We've used that term before, of course, in our discussion of DBMS programs. Here it has exactly the same meaning. We need to be sure that updates don't occur which overwrite earlier changes.

In the context of group word processing simultaneous updates are a real possibility. So, competent network word processors provide document locking in much the same way as databases provide record locking. When a document is in use by one writer, no other writer can save changes to it.

There is one difference here between word processors and DBMS programs. In the DBMS we do allow several users to READ a record simultaneously. We do not allow simultaneous WRITEs. In a network word processor, we do not allow simultaneous saves to a document in any manner at all.

Once a user on the LAN has selected a document for editing, that document is only available to other users for reading. If subsequent users make changes while the document is being edited, most word processors will not allow saves. A few will not even allow multiple access of any kind. The document becomes available again only after the current writer has released it.

Thus, you can see that it is very important to use a real network version of word processing systems on your LAN. It is possible to use single-user text editors and word processors. It is, however, dangerous to allow documents to reside in a shared directory without the ability to properly lock out simultaneous users.

If you have users who require a special type of text editor, and have no need to share it, here is how you can handle it on your LAN. First, create a private directory for the user with READ, OPEN and SEARCH privileges. Next, place the text editor or word processor in this directory. Then, create a subdirectory for documents that also allows writing, creating and changing file names.

If your writer is using a DOS text editor to edit lines of program code, be sure that the code is in a similar private directory. Remember that one of the advantages of a LAN is the ability to send a file to another user on the network. The key to success here is never to allow more than one user in the document directory at a time.

A second issue that confronts word processor users on a LAN is group editing. Group editing is a technique where several authors and editors edit and "redline" a document. Competent network word processors allow such redlining. Here's how group editing works.

First the document's originator writes the document. He or she notifies the first editor that the text is ready for edits. The editor loads the document and edits using redlining. Redlining simply allows the editor to cross out unwanted sections and add changes or additions.

All the redlined copy remains in the document for others to see until the document is complete. Then a finished copy can be printed incorporating the redlined changes. The advantage is that all changes are visible throughout the editing process. Each editing pass produces additional changes until the edits are complete. Only one writer has control of the document at a time, so changes are never made on top of each other.

Another important facet of network word processing is backup. Most modern word processors periodically write a backup copy of the document being processed in a temporary file. On a network this is extremely important. Should the network server fail while you are working on a text, it would be possible to write on without realizing that the server has failed. The reason this is possible is that the word processor, like any application, has been loaded onto the workstation. The only time the server becomes involved is when you attempt to save your work to the server's drive. If the server goes down, you may find that a lot of work doesn't get saved because the word processor locks when it doesn't see the server at save time.

The solution in a good network word processor is to allow frequent automatic saves to a temporary file. That way, if the server fails, you'll have lost little work. Although it causes frequent brief pauses which can be irritating, we recommend that you set the autosave interval to a fairly short time. We also recommend that you save to your local drive as well if possible. That way, if you lose the drive on the network, your document is still safe.

Finally, a network word processor usually has individual configuration files for users. Again, in this respect they resemble the network DBMS programs we discussed earlier. It is very important to place these individualized configuration files in the users' home directories. Also, it is important to place a path to the user's home directory in the word processor's global configuration file. The best approach is to map the same drive to each user's home directory. Doing so will allow the global configuration file to point to a consistent directory and assure that each user's configuration is recognized.

Today's breed of word processor allows group document processing and provides for document locking. Advanced word processors often contain features which approximate desktop publishing. One of these is WordPerfect from WordPerfect Corp.

WordPerfect—Power, Versatility, Popularity in a Network Word Processor

Among today's most popular word processors, WordPerfect is perhaps the star. Not only does the latest release of this best-seller carry virtually all of the features users want, it is very well-behaved on a network.

WordPerfect addresses all the issues important to a good network word processor. The best way to see what this powerful product is all about is to detail its network installation. One of the features that distinguishes

WordPerfect from the other word processor we'll discuss is that WordPerfect contains many features often found on desktop publishing systems.

Starting the WordPerfect Installation

Like our database program, WordPerfect requires files and buffers to be set to 20 in each workstation's Config.sys file. When you start WordPerfect, it must know who you are, what network you are using, and where various files reside. There are three options you may use to give WordPerfect this information.

The easiest method is the individual configuration file we mentioned earlier. WordPerfect calls this file an Environment file. It is simply a text file with a series of parameter switches on separate lines. The second method is to use DOS environment commands in a batch file used to start WordPerfect. The disadvantage of this method is that the Environment is set when you start the word processor and doesn't reset unless you reset it or reboot the workstation.

The final method is to invoke the parameter switches on the DOS command line when you invoke WordPerfect. This is the most awkward. The benefit, however, is that the DOS command line overrides any other settings you may have. This includes the Environment file and the DOS SET commands in a startup batch. If you need to start WordPerfect in some other manner than you have specified in an automated startup sequence, use the DOS command line.

There are three switches that must be set when WordPerfect starts. They tell the program what network is in operation, who the user is, and where the user's directory is. There is also a master setup file which contains default printers, screen colors and other options. Once a user has been established for the word processor, a custom setup file for that user can be created using a utility supplied with the program.

If the user's name and network type are not located in the startup file for each individual, the word processor will ask for them each time the system is started. The user is identified by a three character name. The network is identified by a 1-digit code. We recommend that you create a startup batch file that contains specific startup instructions.

This batch file can contain a variation on the usually awkward use of the DOS command line for starting WordPerfect. Simply create a DOS command line with the proper settings and place it in the batch file along with specific paths to the directory or mapped drive containing the

WordPerfect program files. Since the DOS command line is now contained in the startup batch file, there is no awkward command line to remember.

WordPerfect files are, generally, placed in a shared directory which permits only READs, OPENs and SEARCHes. Some dictionary files require caution, however. If you place the dictionary file in a directory that does not permit WRITEs, you must have a second directory that does to contain supplementary dictionaries. Users have the ability to add words to the supplementary dictionaries, so WRITing must be allowed. Your best bet is to put all dictionaries in a directory that allows WRITEs and show the path to that directory to all users.

If you have template files for various standard documents, you should place them in a directory that does not permit WRITEs. Users can fetch a copy of the template and use it in their own documents, but they cannot alter the original.

There is an exception to the general rule that two users cannot retrieve the same file at once. This exception allows users to circumvent the inconvenience of being locked out of reading a document while someone else is editing it. If two WordPerfect users access the same document only the first user can save it. All other users may read and update the document, but they must save it under a different filename. In this regard, WordPerfect offers a useful alternative to the inability of several users to see the same document at once typical of some network word processors.

In general, the steps to installing WordPerfect on your LAN are

- Create a directory for WordPerfect files,
- Copy the contents of the WordPerfect disks to this directory,
- Create the Environment file,
- Select network printers,
- Define default settings,
- Assign file attributes to program files, and
- Place the dictionaries in user paths.

Here are the specifics. Your first step is to create a WordPerfect directory in much the same way as we did for the DBMS installation. The directory should be a subdirectory of the network apps directory. You may choose to map either a search drive to the directory in the user's logon script or a specific drive to the directory in the WordPerfect startup batch file.

Next, copy all of the WordPerfect files except those on the Learning disk. On the Learning disk, you'll want to copy the .exe and .com files as well. To create the Environment file you'll use WordPerfect itself. You will build a new file called Wp{wp}.env which will reside in the shared directory you just created.

Now it's time to select the network printers. Since no spool or capture commands are required by NetWare, simply start WordPerfect logging on as user {wp. You will be presented with several questions to answer regarding your network printers. When you are asked for the printer port, type the response that lets you select a device name and enter the number of the logical printer to which you wish to print.

Your next task is defining initial WordPerfect settings. Again, you do this as user {wp. These settings include default printers, fonts, colors, monitors, keyboards and paths. After you complete this part of the setup, you can exit WordPerfect.

Now you return to the network to set file attributes. This can be a bit tricky since some of the files in the WordPerfect directory need a mask of READ, OPEN and SEARCH and some need to accept WRITEs as well. In general, all the files except the auxiliary dictionaries require an R, O, S mask, while the user dictionaries get Write, Create and Change Filename attributes as well.

One way to accommodate these differences is to use the FLAG command. Set the file privileges independently on a file-by-file basis. Another way is to remove the user dictionaries and place them in another sharable directory with its own rights mask. This method allows a different global rights mask for each of the directories. Watch out, though, that you set user paths to recognize the additional subdirectory with the user dictionaries.

Your final installation tasks are to add the paths to each user's Autoexec.bat file and insure that the startup batch file for each user is in their home directory.

If we summarize the above, we find that installing a word processor consists of placing shared files in shared directories and building a method of getting to them for users on the network. We want to insure that all but user dictionaries are protected from WRITEs and other changes. We want user dictionaries to be WRITEable by all users. There should only be a single set of user dictionaries, by the way. It is not a good idea to give each user an individual dictionary.

Finally, we can set up both public and private directories for documents. This will depend upon who needs access to the documents. The holding tank method is a good one here. Set up private document directories for each user and put the directory in the user's path. Then set up a shared directory as a holding tank. When a writer completes a document he or she places it in the holding tank where other users can access it for approval or editing. A second shared directory might be appropriate for use as an archive. Old documents reside here and the archive can be purged periodically of very old files.

Now we'll take a look at another word processor with some additional network features and a somewhat different installation procedure.

XyWrite—a Powerful Text Producer

Where WordPerfect is a solid word processor with many desktop publishing capabilities, XyWrite from XyQuest is a text processing workhorse. Many users, such as journalists and authors who produce volumes of text, like XyWrite and its speedy text entry features.

The network version of XyWrite is well thought out and contains some additional features such as individual password security. It also installs a bit differently than WordPerfect. Thus, XyWrite represents another method of using and configuring a network word processor.

The major difference between the two word processors is that while WordPerfect requires a single shared directory (unless you choose to separate user dictionaries), XyWrite requires separate directories for the system files and the user files. But, there is more to the XyWrite program than system files and a user batch to locate the system. The second difference is that most of the XyWrite installation is automated.

Start your XyWrite installation by creating a shared directory for the system files and one (or more) for the user files. The user files can be accommodated in two ways. If all users are to have the same startup settings, you can create a single-user or login directory.

Usually, however, different users will have different settings at startup, which means you will need to create a directory for each user. In this case it is important to give the directory the same name for each user. These directories are not shareable. We suggest that you place the login directory as a subdirectory of the user's home directory. Make sure it is in the user's startup path and map the two directories to network drives using the SYSCON utility.

At the same time, assign trustees to the various directories and create a rights mask of R, O, W, C, S (read, open, write, create and search) for both user and system directories. For simplicity we will refer to the two types of directories as the XyWrite directory (system files) and the login directory (user login files).

Once you have created the two directories, leave the SYSCON utility and enter the XyWrite directory. Copy all of the XyWrite files to this directory. Once the files are copied you can start XyWrite and start the installation procedure. The automated installation creates the user login files in the proper directory.

When you have finished the installation procedure, you will find that, in order to use XyWrite you will need to enter a password at each startup. This is analogous to the three user characters you entered in WordPerfect. The purpose of these entries is to insure that you are credited with the document on which you are working at any given time. Without this tag, another user could gain access to your document and the result could be corrupted text. The user entry is the key to document locking in both systems.

Both of these powerful network word processors install in manners typical of other, similar, products. The system files are usually sharable. They are separate from the user files, if any. They are always separate from the document files. Document files may always be set up as we described earlier. However, there is an important caution for XyWrite and most other network word processors. If you don't specify where the program is to store and search for the document files, it will automatically do so in its own system (default) directory.

WordPerfect has no way of designating an alternative directory to its own for default on a global basis. However, you can use the List Files command to set a new default search path for each individual session. XyWrite allows a default directory other than the DOS default.

Next we will explore another important category of network application, the spreadsheet. We will use the popular Lotus 1-2-3 as the example here.

Spreadsheets—Second Cousins to DBMS Programs

In many regards, spreadsheet programs are similar to database programs. They consist of tables of values which must be shared by many users. Often, a few users create the data in spreadsheets while many use or manipulate it. So, you must pay careful attention to the method of storing worksheets.

One method is a variation on the holding tank we discussed for word processors. The difference is that this holding tank does not allow writing to the spreadsheets stored there. To use a spreadsheet, the user must copy it to his or her own worksheet directory and the results must be saved under a different file name from the original. This allows you to preserve data integrity on the original sheet if necessary.

There is another aspect to the use of spreadsheets that is similar to databases. Often, spreadsheets are financially oriented. Thus, they are often considered confidential. Putting these worksheets in private directories helps insure that only those who must can gain access to them.

There are several popular spreadsheet programs available today. They all install on a Novell LAN in a similar manner. Some are more complex than others. But this usually means that the complex ones have a bit larger complement of files for graphics displays, fonts, printers and other presentation-oriented tasks. A few of the new breed of three dimensional spreadsheets have some extra files to facilitate their additional power. But, as a rule, they all work in much the same way from the standpoint of the network.

We have selected the leading spreadsheet, Lotus 1-2-3 release 2.01 Network Version as a model for a couple of reasons. First, it has the largest installed base of any spreadsheet program. Second, since Lotus removed copy protection, its network configuration is typical of most other spreadsheet programs.

Loading Lotus—Simple as 1-2-3?. . .Well, Not Exactly

The difficulty with loading Lotus 1-2-3 Networker is that, while it's typical of most network spreadsheet programs, it requires a fair number of directories to be effective. While that factor complicates the installation somewhat, it turns out to allow excellent versatility.

Once more, your first task is to create the directories. You will need three sharable directories which should be set up as subdirectories of your network apps directory. These three are the 1-2-3 system files, shared 1-2-3 data files and shared 1-2-3 template files. Notice that we are using the holding tank philosophy for shared data files.

The rights mask for these three subdirectories is as follows. The subdirectory for 1-2-3 system files should be read, search and open (R, S, and O). The same rights mask should be used for the template subdirectory. With the shared data directory you have a choice. You can allow Writes or you can give it the same mask as the template directory.

The individual user directories may be set up as subdirectories of the user's home directories. They should allow read, write, create, and change filename for the user that owns them. If you set them up in this manner, you can also place the users' configuration files here. This is, really, not the best way to set up the user files, though. Here is a better alternative.

Place the users' configuration files in the user's home directory. Then create a subdirectory called /users. There is no data in this subdirectory (a subdirectory of the apps directory). However, there are private subdirectories under it for each user's data. The benefit of this scheme is that it becomes easy to find all of the subdirectories associated with your spreadsheet program because they are located together. Also, placing the configuration files in the user's home directory keeps all such files in the same place. The home directories of all users can be mapped to the same drive designator simplifying installation.

Lotus 1-2-3 Networker allows five network users per copy. It is a type of program that counts the number of users accessing it at any given time and locks out users after the counter is full. Setting and resetting the counter is done with the Administrator's Utility. However, setting up users is done with the Newuser Utility. Here's your next step after creating the appropriate directories and assigning rights and trustees.

Initialize the 1-2-3 system disk and then copy all the files to the subdirectory you created for that purpose. Also, copy the contents of the other four disks that accompany the system disk. After you copy the 1-2-3 files onto the server, run the first time installation.

Once you have installed 1-2-3 Networker you have to set the user counter so that users (including you) can log into the program. You do this by running the Administrator's Utility and following the prompts. Once you have set up the system it's time to make users. Now we need to be very careful with paths.

What we are going to do at this point is to copy and rename some global configuration files. These files reside in the 1-2-3 system subdirectory. Newuser copies those files into the individual user directories and changes their names to avoid confusion with the global files. 1-2-3 Networker must know how to access these user configuration files. Be sure that the path to the user's home directory (or wherever the files reside) is in the user's Autoexec.bat file. Also, be sure that if you map a network drive to the directory, the drive is in the path correctly.

Using 1-2-3 Networker, or any spreadsheet program, simply requires that you pay careful attention to the rights masks, trustee privileges and paths. In this respect it's no different than any other application program.

Next, we'll look at a special type of application called groupware and we'll explore a network management tool called a menu shell.

Groupware—Sharing Resources in an Orderly Manner

Groupware is a special type of application peculiar to LANs. A simple description of groupware would be that it is an application that allows users on the network to share information in an orderly manner.

Groupware provides several levels of usefulness. How many of those levels you use depends upon many factors. How closely do the users on your network need to work? Do they share much data? Do they need to coordinate schedules? All of these factors will affect your decision to use a groupware program. They will also dictate the extent to which you use the program should you decide to install one.

Groupware is, in some respects, a superset of another type of application, the menu shell. The major difference between the two is that while a menu shell is only a device for managing the files on a network at the user level, groupware contains specific modules which help network users work closer together. Competent groupware programs also contain a menu shell.

We will explore a typical, and very well constructed groupware product. As we investigate it we will see how the application fits users together as a work unit. We will see the usefulness of the menu shell. And, we will see how such a program installs on your Novell LAN.

WordPerfect Office—An Excellent Groupware Program

For our groupware example, we have selected WordPerfect Office. Office has many of the features you will want if you are going to make the best use of a groupware product. First, it has a menu shell that permits virtually seamless access to other programs on the LAN. This is an important part of any network menu shell.

Later, we will see that groupware products, especially the good ones, are distinguished from menu shell programs by the simplicity of their menus. Menu shell programs, on the other hand, tend to have lots of features that help you manage the programs on the network.

Each is an example of a product doing what it does best. Menu shells don't provide the useful workgroup tools you'll find in groupware products and groupware products don't provide the sophisticated manipulation of other applications you find in top drawer menu shells. Also, you'll find that groupware products generally allow very limited manipulation of the menus themselves.

Our groupware example, Office, contains nine separate modules. These modules are: the shell, a scheduler, electronic mail, a calendar, the notebook, a file manager, a calculator, a macro editor and a program editor. Some of the modules are self-explanatory. Some are unique to groupware applications.

For example, the scheduler allows users on the network to schedule events that use resources (things and places) and people. It allows users and owners of resources to interact until a mutually acceptable time for the event is reached. The scheduler provides such sophisticated planning that it can scan the schedules of all the people and resources involved in an event and suggest the time with the fewest conflicts. It then provides automatic notification to the parties involved.

The macro editor is a special text editor used to edit WordPerfect macros. These macros, for a variety of WordPerfect Corp. programs, require a special editor since they are not ASCII text. But, if you prefer to edit an ASCII text file, such as programming code, you can use Office's Program Editor.

The notebook is a sort of simple database program for managing lists, while file manager helps you manage the files in your directories and sub-directories. For users of Novell NetWare without electronic mail included (releases 2.15 and above), Office has an excellent E-Mail facility. Finally, the calculator performs math, scientific, financial, statistical and programming calculations.

These features are typical of most good groupware programs. They depend upon the fact that their files are available to all users on the network for their strength.

Installing Office in Your Office

Office is very simple to install. In most regards it installs exactly like WordPerfect's word processor. Your first task is to set up a sharable public directory and copy all the Office files into it except for five. These five files go into another directory accessible by the system manager only. Of course, there are two ways to do this on your Novell network.

The first method is to create separate directories for the two sets of files with different rights masks and groups assigned trustee privileges. The other is to put them all in the same directory and assign rights and trustee privileges separately. Of the two methods, the first is the safest.

Create a directory for the public files and give it a rights mask of read, open and search. Assign trustee rights to the group Everyone. Create a second directory for the administrator's files and give it the rights mask read, write, create and change file name. Assign trustee privileges to the administrator only. Copy the appropriate files into their respective directories. You will also want to map a network drive to the public directory on a permanent basis.

Your next step is to install the users using the Userid program in the administrator's directory. Finally, you update the shell menu and install the E-Mail and Scheduler programs. Make sure that users' Autoexec.bat files or network login files end by invoking the shell from the public directory. Now each user has a network menu from which he or she can invoke network applications and groupware utilities. There are a variety of administrative tools for maintaining user lists and updating group files and lists.

Menu Shells—The Alternative

Menu shells have a slightly different focus from groupware applications. Chief among these are small management utilities that tend to make the lives of users a bit easier. They also provide utilities for the administrator that, while usually not redundant with the LAN utilities supplied with NetWare, address issues that crop up because a LAN is in use. In other words, most third party shells are less concerned with NetWare-specific utilities and more with utilities to manage generic LAN functions.

For example, one very good menu shell, Saber from Saber Software, provides a utility for metering the use of software on the LAN. Meter can limit the number of users accessing a particular application as well as monitor who is logged onto the application and for how long.

In general, Saber is typical of most menu shells in that it is largely concerned with providing a slick interface between user and network. You load Saber, like most shells, in a public subdirectory which is sharable and has a rights mask of read, write, create and change file name. You add the commands to invoke Saber to the user's login script file and the menu is automatically invoked on login. From the menu, the user can select any of the applications you choose to make available through the user menus. Like other menu shells, Saber provides some password security.

There are very few reasons to use a third party menu shell, however. We will see, next, that if all you need is a menu shell, you can create a very good one using the menu utilities supplied as part of NetWare. While you may enjoy the graphics of many menu shells, they are usually not worth the extra money. Stick to the NetWare menu utilities, a good groupware product such as Office, or, at best, a combination of the two.

Next we will explore the NetWare menu utilities and see how a combination of these utilities and a menu shell we can create builds an excellent environment for users on our LAN.

NetWare Menu Utilities—Power to the User . . . Simplified

Taken by themselves, the NetWare menu utilities provide a set of utilities that are menu driven. You invoke the utilities separately from the command line, much like the command line utilities we discussed in Chapter 7. The difference is that the menu utilities are really suites of commands behind easy-to-use menus. The menu utilities are divided into three groups. These groups—network environment utilities, printing utilities and a menu-creating utility—contain most of the power network users need in their day to day activities on the LAN. Some of the utilities are really more suited to the network administrator.

In this section, we'll explore each of the NetWare menu utilities and finish by creating a user menu shell that takes advantage of the power behind the other utilities.

The Environment Utilities—Syscon, Session, Filer and Volinfo

You invoke any of the menu utilities by typing its name at the DOS Prompt. When you invoke one of the utilities, its menu pops up and you are then able to select from the choices displayed. In some cases your response will summon a list of entries from which you can often make a further selection or modify with additions and deletions. Some responses result in a form in which you make entries. Some, such as requests to exit, result in a confirmation box for you to use to assert that you were serious about your selection or to change your mind.

Syscon—Configuring and Querying the Network

Some of the Syscon (SYStem CONfiguration) options require that you have supervisor's rights to access them. But some are useful for day-to-day users. Users who are not supervisors can see accounting charge rates, select the file servers to which they wish attachment, look up user data, view their own user profile, and modify their own password and login script.

The accounting choices on the Syscon menu are useful when the network you are on charges for its services. Using this choice users can determine which servers on a multiserver network are charging for their services. Using the Blocks Read Charge Rates selection, they can view a table of charge rates for data read from a network drive.

The Blocks Written Charge Rates table shows the rates for writing data to a network drive, and Connect Time Charge Rates show charges on networks that charge based on connect time. Disk Storage Charge Rates present a table of rates being charged for storing data on a network drive and

Service Request Charge Rates shows the cost, if any, for requests sent to the server.

Users can connect to an additional server or change the server to which they are connected using the Syscon Change Current Server selection. They can also change user names and log off of additional servers. The Syscon File Server Information selection displays the following information about a selected server:

- Server Name
- NetWare Version
- System Fault Tolerance (for SFT NetWare)
- Transaction Tracking with the NetWare Transaction Tracking System on versions after 2.1
- Maximum number of users that can be connected at once
- Number of connections in use
- Maximum number of disk volumes that the server can handle
- The network address
- The node address

Users can also view information about groups of users on the LAN including: their names, the group name and ID number, and any trustee assignments to the group and its members. These options are part of the Group Information topic.

With the various User Information options, you can view information about your account and other users on the LAN. This information includes your privilege levels, user-ID, trustee assignments, account balance if accounting is enabled on any of your servers, and additional choices that lead to information about other users on the LAN.

Finally, you can use Syscon to change both your password and your login script. If you are a supervisor there are several choices that are unique to you. First, virtually all of the above choices have additional supervisory tasks which are not visible to users without a supervisor's privileges. For example, in the accounting selection users can view information about charge rates for various services. The supervisor, however, can establish those rates through additional choices visible only to him or her.

With the User Information choice, supervisors not only view information about network users, they set the account restrictions for individual users. One of the choices visible to supervisors is the Supervisor Options selection. This allows supervisors to create or modify the system login script, plus several other options.

Supervisors can also assign or change user passwords, copy scripts from one user to another, change a user's security equivalence, and assign directory trustee rights. Finally, supervisors, using the Syscon utility, can make and delete users, groups and servers.

It is also from Syscon that many of the network's security tools are invoked. Chief among these tools is intruder detection and lockout. Intruder detection and lockout sets a limit on the number of login attempts in a supervisor-specified period for however long the supervisor wishes.

Session—Managing and Interacting with Network Drives

The Session utility allows users to interact with the various drive mappings on the network. Users can add and delete server connections, change their individual drive mappings, select their default drive, message other server users, and view information about current server users. Access to the Session utility is universal whether you are a supervisor or not.

Probably the major use of the Session utility is drive mapping. The use of this utility greatly simplifies connection of various directories to network drives, especially mapping search drives.

Another use for the Session utility is broadcast messaging. Using a broadcast message, you can send messages to everyone, to one or more groups, or to individuals on your server. In general, anything that has to do with the normal housekeeping in a network session is handled by the Session utility except for invoking particular applications. But you will use the Session utility to make and break the application connections.

Filer—Manipulating Your Files and Directories

Just as the Session utility controlled various network connections, the Filer utility controls the directories and files involved in those connections. Users can employ Filer to:

- View directory information,
- List files, much like the DOS DIR command,
- Manage files (Delete, rename and copy),
- Change attributes,
- Choose a directory PATH,
- Set options for the Utility itself,
- Manipulate subdirectories, and
- Manipulate network volumes.

If you are a supervisor there are some other tasks Filer will let you perform. These include: manipulating the creation dates, owners and last accessed and/or modified dates of files, directories and subdirectories. Supervisors also can assign file attributes.

With the Filer utility, users can modify the maximum rights mask in any directory to which they have parental rights. You have parental rights to a directory or subdirectory if you are listed as the directory's owner or as the owner of the subdirectory's parent directory.

If you are the parent of a directory you can also add and delete trustees from your directory or its subdirectories using the Filer utility. If you have modify rights to a file you can also use Filer to change file attributes. Supervisors are assumed to have all security and trustee rights to all directories, subdirectories and files. Thus, they can make any of the changes we have discussed without regard to other security assignments.

In general, Filer allows you to treat files for which you have adequate rights as if they were your files on a single-user DOS PC. You can add, delete, rename, move, copy, change attributes and any other normal DOS file management function. In addition, you can manipulate those directories and subdirectories to which you possess parental rights. Finally, you can control the users of directories and files to which you have the correct level of access rights.

Printdef—Printer Devices and Forms Management

Most of the Printdef utility is restricted to the supervisor. However as a user you can list the printers and nodes defined for the network, view the special codes such as printer escape codes for each mode and list and view the forms that have been defined for printing on the LAN along with their definitions.

Forms and modes are defined by the supervisor, using the Printdef utility. The supervisor also uses Printdef to define the printers that are acceptable on the network. These definitions reside in the printdef database. This database is available only to the supervisor.

There are definitions already in NetWare for thirty different printers. In addition, the supervisor creates the definitions for different modes of printing such as draft and final and different forms such as wide or narrow, legal or other unique formats.

Once the supervisor has used Printdef to build a set of definitions and devices, users may access the utility to view these configurations. However, both users and supervisors will use the Printcon utility to set up specific configurations for print jobs and the Pconsole utility to actually print the job. Printdef is used only for defining forms, modes and devices on the LAN.

Printcon—Configuring Print Jobs for Convenience

Once the print definitions are in place, users can use the Printcon utility to set up standard print job configurations. Most of these configurations could be set up globally by the supervisor. However, users can also set up specific configurations for their own repetitive jobs. For example, if you regularly print a particular type of document using a predefined network printer, form and mode, you may want to define the configuration for future use.

It is not necessary to use the utility to print. You can also print directly from the Pconsole utility. The difference is roughly analogous to the difference between entering a complex command at the DOS prompt and using a batch file to do the same thing.

Some of the parameters you can specify with Printcon are the number of copies you want, tabs, the predefined form, banners and the device you want to use. You can also name, rename, add and delete configurations for future use. In short, Printcon allows you to automate the job of printing common or repetitive jobs.

Pconsole—Getting the (Print) Job Done

Once you have decided whether or not to set up a standard print job configuration, it's time to print. First, we need to put our job in line to be printed, known as putting the job in the print queue. These print queues are controlled by the Pconsole utility. Print queues are necessary, especially on large LANs because several jobs are likely to reach the printer at the same time. A print queue is simply a memory buffer that holds the jobs as they come in and feeds them to the printer one at a time.

On a Novell LAN the print queue also invokes the appropriate print configuration for each job. The print queue receives a job from the server exactly as if it were a printer. It holds the job and its configuration in memory until its turn and then prints it. Pconsole also allows printing across more than one server.

Of course you must be attached to a server in order to print from it, but Pconsole allows you to attach if you aren't already. It also allows you to list the jobs in the queue and set up jobs manually. Setting up jobs manually means that you aren't going to use a predefined configuration. So Pconsole allows you to select files, directories, volumes, devices, forms and modes from the Pconsole menu. All of the parameters which you can define with Printcon, you can also define with Pconsole.

One brief note about the method NetWare uses to print. You have two basic choices for file contents. They are Text and Byte Stream. Text forces NetWare to interpret and print any special control codes in the document. But some word processors create a complete package of codes that the printer itself can read directly. In this case you select Byte Stream. One of the word processors we discussed earlier in this chapter, WordPerfect, is an example. One of the reasons that WordPerfect macros must be edited using a special editor is that all word perfect document files are constructed in a manner similar to binary files. In other words, they are not, for the most part, simply ASCII text surrounded by control characters.

Fconsole—For Experienced Users Only

The Fconsole utility is designed for experienced NetWare users and supervisors. The purpose of Fconsole is to allow a user, supervisor or console operator to use a workstation as if it were the system console. In NetWare this is similar to logging on to other types of networks as the server user.

Depending upon your security level, you can use Fconsole to change servers and view a variety of connect information both on the user and server level. Supervisors and console operators use Fconsole for some other tasks. They can: broadcast messages, purge files, view the details of user and network activity, and control the server. Fconsole operates for the supervisor just like the server console. The difference is that it can be operated from any workstation on the LAN.

Experienced programmers can also use some of the choices on the Fconsole menu to learn about how their application is behaving on the network. For example, programmers can use Fconsole to view semaphore activity on the network in connection with their application. Semaphores are similar to flags. Each time a user logs into an application the programmer may choose to open a semaphore. A routine in the application counts the number of semaphores and determines if the maximum number of legal users allowed by the application has been reached.

Another programmer function is the ability to view the tasks being performed by an application. In this regard it functions like a log of the application's network activity. Fconsole also tracks file and record locking on the LAN as well as any network drivers which may be active. In short, Fconsole allows a look inside the workings of the LAN in general and the server in particular. How deep that look goes is dependent upon your security level.

All of this ability to snoop on network activity is especially valuable when you are expanding your network. By measuring activity on the LAN you can see where bottlenecks occur, what the typical and peak activity levels are, and what parts of the LAN are inadequate. Armed with this information, you can either fine tune your installation or add resources as they become necessary.

Fconsole is an extraordinarily complex and powerful utility. We could produce an entire book on its intricacies. Suffice it to state that once you have mastered the day-to-day operation of NetWare, you can tackle the many bits and pieces of information about your network available with Fconsole. Once you become proficient with it, you can use it to manage your LAN at peak efficiency. Fconsole is a course in network management wrapped up in a network management utility.

Volinfo—Viewing Fixed Drive Information

Volinfo is not designed to view activity on the server's fixed drives. Rather, it is designed to view the information about the drives themselves. Throughout this book we have referred to volumes and network drives. The difference between the two is that a volume is a physical partition on the fixed drive while a network drive may be a virtual designation for a mapped drive or directory. Network drives do not physically exist. They are designations used to simplify keeping track of the complex directory system on a large LAN.

From time to time we need to find out such things as how much disk space we have left, what servers we are attached to and what is the status of the fixed drives on other servers. Volinfo is a rarely used utility but it is useful to have as we plan network resources.

Building Your Own Menus with the Menu Utility

The NetWare Menu utility serves two purposes. First, it provides a means of running network menus, including the NetWare Main Menu. Second, you can build your own customized menu shell using the Menu Utility.

The NetWare Main Menu is a menu that allows you to run all of the other menu utilities from a single menu. You can access the Main Menu from your login script, or you can build you own set of menus, one of which could access the NetWare Main Menu.

Menus are important to smooth operation of the LAN. Many network users are either inexperienced or have no interest in becoming computer gurus. For example, a secretary on the LAN may simply want to have quick and easy access to the applications she uses on a daily basis. Such easy access makes her daily tasks proceed more smoothly and lets her concentrate on her job, not her computer.

Even experienced power users can benefit by the uniformity offered by a consistent, well-designed menu system. In many cases applications and utilities go unused for extended periods of time. Without some form of menu system, those unused programs are often forgotten. You waste time looking for them and recalling how to invoke them.

The key, of course, with power users is to offer an exit to DOS when necessary. One of the objections often voiced by experienced users of the Apple Macintosh is that it is nearly impossible to bypass the desktop menu system. While a good menu shell can be a boon to most users, an escape must be available for use by experienced operators when required. The Menu utility offers just such compromises.

Building Menus—Getting Started

Before you can start building your own menus, you need to load some files into the SYS:PUBLIC directory. These seven files run NetWare Menus and the Menu utility. You will also need to update your Config.sys file to accommodate 20 buffers and 30 files.

Menus are actually scripts. Scripts are ASCII files similar in nature to your Autoexec.bat file. You use an ASCII text editor to create these scripts. The commands you have available are simple and quite limited. Basically they consist of alpha-numeric characters, the % sign, the @ symbol and the names of the applications or utilities you will want to invoke. If you need additional commands you will notice that we are using the command line commands as discussed in Chapter 7. Menu reads the script and does the rest. Here's an example of a menu script.

Let's start our script by naming our main menu "Network Menu." We use the % symbol in front of the name to indicate that a menu title follows. All titles and menu entries must be flush with the left margin. We indent several spaces or one tab to indicate a command or file name we wish to invoke. So our main menu title will show on our script as

```
%Network Menu
```

Next we must tell the Menu utility where to place our first menu. We do that by adding a set of coordinates to the menu title that indicates the screen position. We separate these two numbers with a comma. The first number represents the vertical displacement of the center of your menu from the top of the screen. The second represents the horizontal displacement of the center of your menu from the left screen edge.

There is a third number which refers to the color for the menu from the color palette. For the moment we will leave it at 0, indicating the default color. We're going to place our menu at coordinates 10,15. That means that the center of our menu is ten rows down from the top and fifteen columns over from the left of the screen. The command is now:

```
%Network Menu,10,15,0
```

Next, we add the choices that will appear on our menu. We start with the first choice. Let's make the first choice another menu. We'll select the NetWare Main Menu. But instead of calling it Main Menu, which could be confusing to users, we'll call it NetWare Utilities. Let's add the choice to our script:

```
%Network Menu,10,15,0
NetWare Utilities
```

Next, we must tell our menu what to do if we make that choice. What we want is for the network to invoke the next level menu which will contain the utilities present in the NetWare Main Menu. We don't really want to invoke the Main Menu itself. So what we will do is create our own version of the Main Menu which we will call NetWare Utilities. Actually, when we make this choice, Menu will look down the script until it sees a menu entry called %NetWare Utilities and invoke it. So here's what our menu script looks like so far:

```
%Network Menu,10,15,0
NetWare Utilities
        %Netware Utilities
```

Notice that we have indented the command so that Menu can tell the difference between it and the menu choice text. Next, we want to add some applications to our menu. We would like a separate submenu for our applications so we add the following entries in our script:

```
%Network Menu,10,15,0
```

```
NetWare Utilities
      %Netware Utilities
Applications
      %Applications
```

Finally, we may wish to log off the server. So we add the !logout command, thus:

```
%Network Menu,10,15,0
NetWare Utilities
      %Netware Utilities
Applications
      %Applications
Log Off Server
      !logout
```

We should remind you at this point that even though we have centered these commands here for legibility, they are flush against the left margin in your script, with the exception of the indented commands.

Now that we have built our main menu, it's time to build the submenus. We add the submenus to the script in the order they appear on the main menu. Since the first choice is the NetWare Utilities, that's the first submenu we will create. Submenus are exactly like their parent menus in construction. So, if the utilities we wanted in our submenu happened to be Fconsole and Syscon, we might give them the descriptive entries, Access Console and System Configuration. Our script now looks like this:

```
%Network Menu,10,15,0
NetWare Utilities
      %Netware Utilities
Applications
      %Applications
Log Off Server
      !logout
%NetWare Utilities
Access Console
      fconsole
System Configuration
      syscon
```

In the same way, we can add some applications.

```
%Network Menu,10,15,0
NetWare Utilities
     %Netware Utilities
Applications
     %Applications
Log Off Server
     !logout
%NetWare Utilities
Access Console
     fconsole
System Configuration
     syscon
%Applications
Word Processor
     wp
Spreadsheet
     123
```

The only thing missing is the coordinates of the two submenus. If we leave them as they are, with no coordinates, they will be placed in the default location—the center of the screen. But we might wish to stagger them as they are called from the main menu. The main menu, you will note, is located at 10,15. So, lets move our submenus down and right a bit, perhaps to 13,18. Now we have

```
%Network Menu,10,15,0
NetWare Utilities
     %Netware Utilities
Applications
     %Applications
Log Off Server
     !logout
%NetWare Utilities,13,18,0
Access Console
     fconsole
System Configuration
     syscon
%Applications,13,18,0
Word Processor
     wp
Spreadsheet
     123
```

The only thing left to do is to save the menu file to the public directory. We can give it any eight character DOS file name we want as long as the extension is .mnu. To use our menu, which we have named netmenu.mnu, we simply type:

```
Menu netmenu <Enter>
```

If we had given it any filename extension besides .mnu, we would have had to include the extension in our command. When you make a selection from your menu, you will invoke that selection. When the selection has completed running, you will be returned to the menu that called it. To go directly to your menu on startup, place the MENU command last in your login script.

Summary

In this chapter we have learned how to load and use several types of applications on a Novell LAN—and that there is a pattern of directory usage that is reasonably consistent from application to application.

Application system files generally reside in public, sharable directories. Data files may reside in either public or private directories, depending upon the requirements of the network users.

We have seen how we may use groupware and menu shells to simplify user interaction with the LAN, its applications and utilities. Finally, we explored the NetWare Menu Utilities and built our own menu shell using the Menu utility.

In the next chapter, we will show you how to configure a very powerful file server from the ground up. Since Novell no longer supplies file server hardware, Chapter 10 will be very useful to you.

10

Installing Your SFT NetWare Server and Workstations

We've taken you through the theory of Novell Netware. We've discussed what being the supervisor involves. And we've shown you the tools and commands you'll have available to you on a Novell local area network. Now it's time to actually install the server and workstations. For our example, we've chosen Advanced Netware 286, the most advanced and complex of the Netware offerings with the exception of SFT NetWare.

Advanced Netware 286 is a superset of all of the other levels of Novell NetWare except SFT. So, if you understand its installation, you'll have little trouble understanding the lower level offerings. The only differences you'll experience when installing SFT NetWare have to do with the special redundancy features of the product.

Also, since we've touched on many of the aspects of this installation in earlier chapters, you'll find that you're pretty well prepared to get your new network rolling. Remember, the screen illustrations you'll see in this chapter come from Advanced NetWare 286. Some of them will become familiar to you, even with other members of the NetWare family.

Finally, we are selecting the simplest of the installation procedures, the Standard Floppy Disk method. This is very straightforward and many of the aspects of other, more specialized, methods of installation follow it closely. It is necessary to perform the installation the first time this way since many of the final hard disk setup functions cannot be done from the hard disk. Virtually the entire operating system installation is accomplished with the Novell NETGEN Utility. You will be prompted through the whole process by NETGEN.

Getting Started—Site Preparation

We've discussed many of the aspects of preparation for network installation in Chapters 5 and 6. Let's go into a bit more detail here. First, we want to be sure that the server is in an area separate from other workstations. The server console is accessible only by network supervisors and server operators, so keep it away from normal traffic. Additionally, if security is an issue, the server should be physically secured in a room or office prepared for that purpose.

We discussed power protection briefly. Network servers should (in some cases must) have an uninterruptable power supply dedicated to them. At the very least, the server should have its own power source. That power source should be an incoming power line with no other connections to it. Of course, all power connections should be properly grounded.

All add on peripherals, such as extra disk drives, optical drives or tape backup units should be on a separate power line, unless you are using a UPS. In that case, all of the server peripherals as well as the server can be on the same UPS. Insure that the UPS has the power handling capacity for your equipment.

To determine if your UPS can handle your power requirements, add up the power requirements of each of the pieces of equipment which you will attach to the UPS. The figures are on tags on each piece of equipment. Your UPS should be able to handle double the power your equipment will draw. If wattages are not posted on the equipment tags, you can get an approximation by multiplying the amps the unit draws times the AC current, usually 120 volts. That result is called volt-amperes, and is usually pretty close to the wattage consumed by the unit.

Preparing the Server

You can use any 80286 or 80386 machine as a server. Your machine can be an IBM AT or compatible of one of the IBM PS series computers. In any event, you will want the largest fixed drive you can afford. We recommend that you install a minimum size of 150 MB. 300 MB is better and 650 MB and higher is best. In any event, you'll need at least 2MB of server RAM.

There are some aspects that make a better server. If you install them now, you'll find that your system will perform better from the start. And you won't be faced with reinstalling your server later with a lot of data already on your fixed drive.

When you receive your NetWare software, you'll find several forms included in the technical manuals. You should fill out these forms with the hardware configurations you'll be installing. As you install the operating system you'll find that the entries you make will be needed. This is especially important if you are a first time Novell installer. The first of these forms is the NetWare Hard Disk/Volumes Worksheet. On it you'll record such information as the drive's channel and controller and the name of the volumes on the drive. Remember that we defined a volume as a physical partition on the fixed drive.

Before you can load NetWare, you'll need to prepare the hard disk by formatting it, setting your partitions (volumes) and creating a DOS bootable partition. All of these functions will vary depending upon the version of DOS you are using, the hard drive installed and the computer you select for your server. At this point you are not doing anything that is directly involved with NetWare except preparing the server and recording your equipment.

If you have not purchased a Novell-prepared hard drive with your network server hardware, you will eventually be required to perform a specialized formatting and prep operation called COMPSURF. Don't worry about that now, though. You'll need to boot from a floppy DOS disk during the preliminary NETGEN steps ahead.

Next you need to insure that you have installed the network interface card. You will find a NetWare Installation Parameters Worksheet with your manual set. Be sure to fill it in as you install your various hardware options. You'll need the information later on.

Installing the Interface Card

The network interface card is a board that allows the server or workstation to communicate on the network. It is the physical link between the workstation or server and the cables that connect the network components. Before you can start your software configuration you must install the interface card. The installation on the workstations and server are identical. We'll describe the installation here using Novell's NE2000 Ethernet card as an example—so you can install your workstations and server at the same time. Of course, there are many other network interface cards you can use, so if you are not using the NE2000, you should follow the instruc-

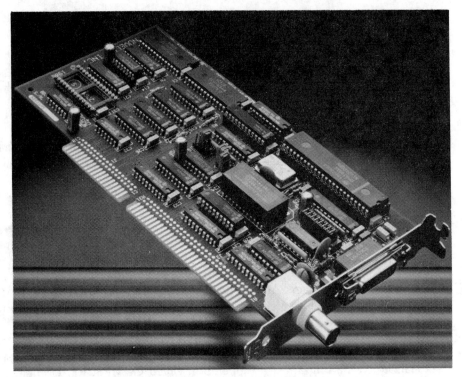

Figure 10-1   The NE2000 Ethernet Interface Card

tions for your type of card. Once you have installed the interface cards, you'll be ready to configure and test your LAN.

There are three options on the NE2000 that you must select. They are the Ethernet Jumper Block, the Interrupt Line and the Base Memory and Base I/O setting. You make these three selections from three sets of jumper blocks on the interface card, which is shown in Figure 10-1.

The Ethernet Jumper Block is a large block containing three rows of eight pins each. There is a single jumper bar that connects the middle row to one of the rows on either side. Start by selecting the type of connector you will use. There are two on the interface card. One is a standard DIX connector (a multi-pin connector) and the other is a BNC connector used by coaxial cable. Most Ethernet installations will use the BNC coaxial connector. Select the BNC by jumpering the middle and bottom rows. Select the DIX connector by jumpering the middle and top rows.

The remaining two blocks allow you to set the interrupt line and the base I/O address as well as make provision for remote reset if you have that option installed. The Interrupt line can be set to allow interrupt requests (IRQ) at IRQ2, IRQ3, IRQ4 or IRQ5. The default is IRQ3. The base I/O can be set to an address of 300h, 320h, 340h or 360h. The default is 300h. The combination of 300h base I/O and IRQ3 interrupt request is configuration option 0. If you don't change these settings, you'll need to record option 0 on the Installation Parameters Worksheet for later use.

In order to understand why we might change from the factory default, let's take a look at IRQs and Base I/Os. When you add peripherals such as disk drives, communications ports, printers, Ethernet cards or any other add on device to a PC, the computer needs to know, first, how to find the device and, second, how to tell if a program wants to use it.

The "how-to-find-it" part is the Base I/O address and the "how-to-direct-a-program-to-it" is the interrupt request or IRQ. Yes, we know that's an oversimplification, but for our purposes it will do. It will do because we simply need to make sure that no two peripherals share the same I/O and IRQ settings.

If you are installing the server from scratch and you have no exotic peripherals, you can keep the factory default setting of 0. If you are adding some additional peripherals, beyond the usual hard disks, printer board, screen drivers and communication port, you may have a conflict. Check the owner's manuals on the other peripherals to determine what IRQ and base I/O they need. Just make sure you don't try to talk to two peripherals with the same settings. You can get an idea of what these switches are and the settings that go with them by looking at Figure 10-2.

Installing the Workstation Shell

Installing the workstation shell has many of the same types of procedures you'll see later on as you build the network operating system on the server. As we will on the server, we'll select the Standard Floppy Disk installation method. This is the best method for beginners and by using it here we'll create a master shell that we can modify if necessary for other workstations.

Although we won't mention it again, you should take time now to make working copies of all of your NetWare diskettes. Then, from now on when we refer to a particular disk, we'll be referring to your copy of it. Never use the DOS COPY command to make these copies, by the way. Whenever you make working copies of diskettes you should use the DISKCOPY command. This makes a bit-by-bit copy of the entire source diskette including directories, subdirectories and volume labels. Some programs won't execute from copies made with the DOS COPY command.

CONFIG. OPTION NUMBER	BASE I/O ADDRESS	INTERRUPT LINE
0	For 300h Jumper W9 and W10	For IRQ3 Jumper W13
1	For 320h Jumper W10 Only	For IRQ2 Jumper W12
2	For 340h Jumper W9 Only	For IRQ4 Jumper W14
3	For 360h No Jumpers	For IRQ5 Jumper W15
4	For 300h Jumper W9 and W10	For IRQ2 Jumper W12
5	For 320h Jumper W10 Only	For IRQ3 Jumper W13
6	For 340h Jumper W9 Only	For IRQ5 Jumper W15
7	For 360h No Jumpers	For IRQ4 Jumper W14
8	For 300h Jumper W9 and W10	For IRQ4 Jumper W14
9	For 320h Jumper W10 Only	For IRQ5 Jumper W15
10	For 340h Jumper W9 Only	For IRQ2 Jumper W12
11	For 360h No Jumpers	For IRQ3 Jumper W13

Figure 10-2   NE200 jumper setting options

Our next step is to format and prepare a blank disk which we will use later as the master shell disk. We are going to use the default configuration in our example. There are two other settings, though. The intermediate setting is the one to use if you had to make any changes on your network interface cards. The custom level is for advanced NetWare installers and systems that use a more exotic driver set than the ones normally installed.

Using SHGEN to Generate Your Workstation Shell

Insert your SHGEN disk into drive A: on any computer with 640 KB of memory and one (or, preferably two) floppy drives. The SHGEN command has the following syntax:

```
SHGEN [-[N] [D | I | C] [S]] ‹Enter›
```

The [N] option means that you are generating a new shell, the [D | I | C] options (choose one) indicate a default, intermediate or custom shell configuration and the [S] selects the standard floppy disk option. Type

```
A:SHGEN —NDS
```

to start a new shell using default configuration and the standard floppy disk installation. You will see a menu as in Figure 10-3 with Available LAN drivers.

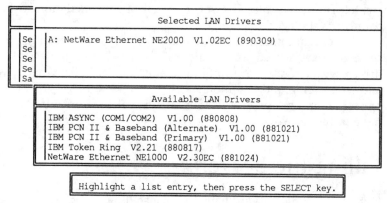

```
                        Selected LAN Drivers
 Se │ A: NetWare Ethernet NE2000  V1.02EC (890309)
 Se │
 Se │
 Se │
 Sa │
```

```
                        Available LAN Drivers
 IBM ASYNC (COM1/COM2)  V1.00 (880808)
 IBM PCN II & Baseband (Alternate)  V1.00 (881021)
 IBM PCN II & Baseband (Primary)  V1.00 (881021)
 IBM Token Ring V2.21 (880817)
 NetWare Ethernet NE1000  V2.30EC (881024)
```

```
 Highlight a list entry, then press the SELECT key.
```

Figure 10-3   Available LAN Drivers Menu

We will install the Novell NE2000 Ethernet board as our example here, so you would make that selection and press ‹Enter›. You will then be asked if you wish to continue using the selected configurations. Since we are using the defaults, we should check the configuration list carefully, and, if we don't want to make changes, answer Yes. If you want to alter a selection, you should answer NO and you will return to a choice that will let you start over. Moving back one step simply requires [Esc]ape.

Before you answer Yes to the question, fill out the NetWare Workstation Configuration worksheet and then select Yes and ‹Enter›. At this point you will be prompted to place your SHGEN-2 disk in the floppy drive. SHGEN will now link and configure IPX.com and create a valid shell. We must now copy the configured shell files to our master shell disk.

Simply copy the following files from the SHGEN-2 disk to your master shell disk (the one you prepared earlier):

```
IPX.COM          The file you just created

NET4.COM         NetWare Redirector for DOS 4.X

NET3.COM         NetWare Redirector for DOS 3.X

NET2.COM         NetWare Redirector for DOS 2.X
```

```
NETBIOS.EXE    NetWare NETBIOS Emulator
INT2F.COM      File Required by NETBIOS.EXE
```

You now have a valid master shell disk. You will not use all of the files on the master disk for every shell. You will, however, use the IPX.COM and one of the NETX.COM files along with any logon script you might create. These two files, however, enable the workstation to access and connect to the LAN.

One point of caution. Since this, like the network operating system we'll soon generate, is a custom configuration based upon a particular network driver, we should be sure and indicate on the disk label what driver it's for and what configuration option was selected. Be sure to generate a separate master shell disk for every different type of network interface card you have in the network.

Installing the Server

Installing the file server begins with installing the peripherals and other included hardware you'll need for your network. We'll begin with a brief discussion of this part of the installation.

Installing the Network Printers

Advanced NetWare 286 supports up to five printers. Two of the printers can be serial (using the COM: ports) and three can be parallel (using the LPT ports). These printers are available for use by any users on the network. Typically, you'll install at least one printer on the LPT1 port. This is the easiest to install since parallel printer connections rarely need any special configuration.

The serial printer, often a laser printer, requires that you set a number of communications parameters. NetWare provides a default set of parameters that will match most serial printers. These parameters are a speed of 9600 baud, 8 bit words, one stop bit and no parity. Often, if your serial printer allows setup, it is easier to match the printer to the defaults than the other way around. But, in most cases, you won't have to adjust anything. The defaults will work.

As before, record the printer information on the Installation parameters worksheet. Leave out the entry in the Printer Number Column, though. That will be assigned during installation. Figures 10-4 and 10-5 show the Installation worksheet and Hard Disk/Volumes worksheet.

NetWare File Server Configuration Worksheet
FOR USE WITH SFT AND ADVANCED NETWARE 286 (v2.15)

■ FILE SERVER NAME _____ INSTALLER _____

OS OPTION: ❏ SFT Level II   ❏ SFT Level II with TTS   SYSTEM SUPERVISOR _____
      ❏ Advanced Dedicated   ❏ Advanced Nondedicated

■ FILE SERVER HARDWARE INFORMATION
    ❏ Novell File Server _____
    ❏ IBM PC AT or Compatible _____
    ❏ IBM Personal System/2 Model _____
    ❏ Other _____

MEMORY: Base _____ Extended _____ Total _____

FLOPPY DRIVE A: ❏ 5.25" ❏ 3.5" ❏ Single-sided ❏ Double-sided ❏ High Capacity _____ KB
FLOPPY DRIVE B: ❏ 5.25" ❏ 3.5" ❏ Single-sided ❏ Double-sided ❏ High Capacity _____ KB

INTERNAL HARD DISK 1: _____

INTERNAL HARD DISK 2: _____

Ref	Name/Description	Option No.	Int. Line (IRQ)	I/O Base Address	DMA Line	RAM/ROM Addresses	Notes
LAN INTERFACE BOARD DRIVERS							
A							
B							
C							
D							
HARD DISK CHANNEL DRIVERS							
0							
1							
2							
3							
4							
"OTHER" DRIVERS							

RESOURCE SETS AND RESOURCES

Set	Res						

Figure 10-4 A   Advanced NetWare 286 Installation Worksheets

NetWare Workstation Configuration Worksheet
FOR USE WITH SFT AND ADVANCED NETWARE 286 (v2.15)

■ **CONNECTED TO FILE SERVER** _____ INSTALLER _____

   LAN ❏ A ❏ B ❏ C ❏ D   SYSTEM SUPERVISOR _____

■ **WORKSTATION HARDWARE INFORMATION**

❏ IBM PC   ❏ IBM PC Compatible_____

❏ IBM PC XT   ❏ IBM PC XT Compatible_____

❏ IBM PC AT   ❏ IBM PC AT Compatible_____

❏ IBM Personal System/2 Model _____   ❏ Other_____

MEMORY: Base _____   Extended _____   Total _____

FLOPPY DRIVE A: ❏ 5.25" ❏ 3.5" ❏ Single-sided ❏ Double-sided ❏ High Capacity_____ KB

FLOPPY DRIVE B: ❏ 5.25" ❏ 3.5" ❏ Single-sided ❏ Double-sided ❏ High Capacity_____ KB

INTERNAL HARD DISK:_____

Name/Description	Option No.	Int. Line (IRQ)	I/O Base Address	DMA Line	RAM/ROM Addresses	Notes
■ **LAN INTERFACE BOARD DRIVER**						

■ **RESOURCE SETS AND RESOURCES**

Set	Res							

■ **BOOT INFORMATION**

❏ Boot from Floppy Disk   ❏ Boot by ➤ Remote Reset

DOS Version _____

FILES COPIED TO MASTER SHELL DISKETTE

❏ IPX.COM

❏ NET4.COM, ❏ NET3.COM, OR ❏ NET2.COM

❏ NETBIOS.EXE

❏ INT2F.COM

❏ OTHERS _____

_____

Additional Information
for Remote Boot Workstations Only

Remote Reset Enabled ❏ Yes ❏ No

❏ Remote Reset PROM(s) _____

  Installed on LAN Board _____

❏ LAN Board Set to Configuration Option 0

Network Address_____

Station (Node)   Hex _____

Address   Decimal _____

Remote Boot Filename_____

Figure 10-4 B   Advanced NetWare 286 Installation Worksheets

NetWare Installation Parameters Worksheet
FOR USE WITH SFT AND ADVANCED NETWARE 286 (v2.15)

■ **FILE SERVER NAME**_____ INSTALLER_____

OS OPTION: ❏ SFT Level II   ❏ SFT Level II with TTS   SYSTEM SUPERVISOR _____
❏ Advanced Dedicated   ❏ Advanced Nondedicated

SERIALIZATION: OS SERIAL NO. _____

■ **LAN SUMMARY**

LAN	LAN Interface Board Drivers	Config. Option No.	Network Address
A			
B			
C			
D			

Number of Communication Buffers _____   File Server Node Address _____

■ **SYSTEM CONFIGURATION PARAMETERS**

Number of Open Files_____   Number of Indexed Files_____

(TTS Only) Transaction Backout Volume_____   Number of Transactions_____

Limited Disk Space ❏ NO   ❏ YES ➡ Number of Bindery Objects_____

■ **UPS INFORMATION**

Type of UPS_____   Rating_____   ❏ W   ❏ VA

UPS monitored by: ❏ Disk Coprocessor Board (Channel____)   ❏ Keycard   ❏ Standalone UPS Board

I/O Address _____   Down Time_____ min. Wait Time_____ sec.

Battery Low Input Setting   ❏ Open Contact (no current)   ❏ Closed Contact (current)
Battery Online Input Setting   ❏ Open Contact (no current)   ❏ Closed Contact (current)

■ **NETWORK PRINTERS**

Device	Printer No.	Type of Printer	Baud Rate	Word Size	Stop Bits	Parity	Xon/Xoff
COM1							
COM2							
LPT1							
LPT2							
LPT3							

■ **DISK SUBSYSTEMS**

Type of Subsystem	Model Number	Disk Channel Attached to	Controllers/Drives Contained in the Disk Subsystem

Figure 10-4 C   Advanced NetWare 286 Installation Worksheets

NetWare File Server LAN Worksheet
FOR USE WITH SFT AND ADVANCED NETWARE 286 (v2.15)

■ **FILE SERVER NAME** _____ INSTALLER _____

LAN INTERFACE BOARD_____ SYSTEM SUPERVISOR _____

LAN ❑ A ❑ B ❑ C ❑ D   NETWORK ADDRESS_____

■ **WORKSTATIONS CONNECTED**   (For Remote Reset Only)

Workstation ID	Type of Computer	DOS Version	Type of LAN Interface Board	Station (Node) Address Decimal	Hex	Remote Reset Boot DOS Image File

■ NETWORKING HARDWARE	Description	Vendor
Main Network Cable		
Drop Cables (if applicable)		
Other Types of Cable Used		
Connectors		
Other Hardware Used		

Figure 10-4 D   Advanced NetWare 286 Installation Worksheets

NetWare Hard Disk / Volumes Worksheet

FOR USE WITH SFT AND ADVANCED NETWARE 286 (v2.15)

■ NETWORK HARD DISKS

				NetWare Partition on System Hard Disk (Ref No _____)		Start Cyl	End Cyl	Size (MB)		

| | | | | | | Hot Fix | | Mirroring (SFT only) | | |
Ref No.	Channel	Controller	Drive	Controller Type	Drive Name	Logical Size (in 4K Blocks)	Prim/ Sec	Mirrored with (Ref No.)	Removable Media?	

■ VOLUMES

Disk Ref No.	Volume Name	Size (MB)	Number of Directory Entries	Directory Cached?	Disk Ref No.	Volume Name	Size (MB)	Number of Directory Entries	Directory Cached?
	SYS								

Figure 10-5   Advanced NetWare 286 Hard Disk/Volumes Worksheet

Configuring the Network Operating System for the Server

As we have said earlier in this book, you can have more than one server on a Novell network. You can also have a nondedicated server (one that doubles as a workstation). There are several reasons not to use a server as a workstation. Most of these have to do with performance and security. Except in the smaller configurations, like ELS NetWare, we heartily advise against nondedicated servers for most installations. If you have a serious installation, you'll want the performance a dedicated server can give you. Also, the workstation user of a nondedicated server will experience slow-downs in performance during heavy network activity.

We are going to install this example server as a dedicated server. Also, as we said at the beginning, we are going to use the Standard Floppy Disk installation method. That method is best suited if you plan to install one network server and it's your first installation. You can, however, install NetWare from the server's hard disk, from a RAM disk or from a network drive. These options are appropriate for experienced installers and when you are adding servers to your LAN. In some cases, these other methods will speed up your installation. But, for learning purposes and to avoid confusion, we'll use the Standard Floppy Disk method.

To begin with, be sure that your server has 640K of memory, that you are running no memory resident programs, that you have your hard disk ready and partitioned, and that you have a DOS bootable partition for DOS 3.X or 4.X (If your hard disk was not prepared by Novell or your Novell dealer in advance, you won't have or need this partition. Use your DOS floppy disk to boot the server during the first phase of NETGEN instead.) Get out your worksheets with drive and other system information on them. We're ready to begin.

There are two levels at which you can install NetWare 286. The first, and easiest, is the default level. Default installation is the one you'll use most often and we plan to use it here. But if you will need to make additions to your network, or add exotic peripherals with special interrupts or addresses, you will need to use the custom installation. In any event, we suggest that you use the default installation parameters the first time you install a Novell LAN.

Installing networks can be rather complex. If you are getting the idea that we want you to walk before you run, you're right on target. Even if you end up reinstalling your LAN with custom configurations, it would be easier than getting all tangled up in problems on your first installation.

And that is what can happen if you move too quickly with advanced installation options.

You will find it easier to run NETGEN if you have two floppy disk drives. There are a lot of reasons to use two floppies on the server in the future as well. We'll assume that you have two and they are the A: and B: drives respectively. Insert your NETGEN disk in drive A:. Place the SUPPORT disk in drive B: (if you are using 5 1/4" disks. If you are using 3 1/2" disks the files you will need are on the AUXGEN diskette.) From time to time NETGEN will ask you to insert other disks. You'll need to follow the prompts since the program will be updating your disks with configuration information which you will use later.

The first command you will enter at the DOS prompt starts the NETGEN program. The syntax of that command is

```
A:NETGEN [-[N] [D] [C] [S]]
```

where the [N] option means generate a new system, [D] means use the default configuration, [C] means use the custom configuration and [S] means use the Standard Floppy Disk installation method. The hyphen [-] must precede the first option switch and there is no space between each letter. Notice that two of the options are mutually exclusive. You couldn't use both the [D] and [C] options at the same time. Also, don't type the brackets ([ ]).

We'll start our NETGEN session by typing

```
A:NETGEN -NDS <Enter>
```

The next screen you'll see will be the Network Configuration Options Screen as shown in Figure 10-6.

You will highlight the Select Network Configuration choice. All NetWare menus offer you an option of quitting (exiting) at any time. So if you get into trouble, quit before you get into more. You can usually step back and start over if necessary. This is preferable to making wrong installation steps.

You will see a NETGEN Run Options menu. Select Standard Floppy Disk and press ‹Enter›. The next menu you will see is the NetWare Generation Options Menu. Choose Select Network Configuration. You will then see the Available Options menu as in Figure 10-7.

Select the Set Operating System Options choice and then either the Advanced NetWare 286/Dedicated or /Nondedicated choice depending upon which configuration you want for your server. Remember we said we were installing a dedicated server so we'll make that choice.

```
┌─────────────────────────────────────┐
│ Network Generation Options           │
├─────────────────────────────────────┤
│ Select Network Configuration         │
│ NetWare Installation                 │
│ Exit NETGEN                          │
└─────────────────────────────────────┘
```

```
┌──────────────────────────────────────────────────────────────┐
│ Use the arrow keys to highlight an option, then press the SELECT key. │
└──────────────────────────────────────────────────────────────┘
```

Figure 10-6   Network Generation Options Menu.

At this point, if you selected the default level you'll begin to define the server configuration in terms of the various drivers and hardware you have installed. You can have certain specified numbers of drivers of each type, however, the default configuration assumes one LAN driver and one disk driver. If you are using the Custom configuration, you can have four LAN drivers, five disk drivers and one other driver such as a backup tape drive.

```
┌─────────────────────────────────────┐
│         Available Options            │
├─────────────────────────────────────┤
│ Set Operating System Options         │
│ Select LAN Drivers                   │
│ Select Disk Drivers                  │
│ Select "Other" Drivers               │
│ Save Selections and Continue         │
└─────────────────────────────────────┘
```

```
┌──────────────────────────────────────────────────────────────┐
│ Use the arrow keys to highlight an option, then press the SELECT key. │
└──────────────────────────────────────────────────────────────┘
```

Figure 10-7   Available Options Menu

From the Available Options Menu highlight the Select LAN Drivers choice. Next choose the Select Loaded Item line and press ‹Enter›. When you first ran NETGEN, it loaded a number of files into your server's memory. Now you will select one (or more) of those drivers for permanent storage as part of your server configuration. You'll see the available drivers when you make the above choice. Now your menu looks like Figure 10-8.

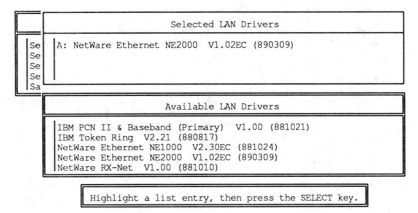

```
                    ┌──────────────────────────────────────────────┐
                    │            Selected LAN Drivers              │
┌──┬─────────────────────────────────────────────────────────────┐
│Se│A: NetWare Ethernet NE2000  V1.02EC (890309)                  │
│Se│                                                              │
│Se│                                                              │
│Se│                                                              │
│Sa│                                                              │
└──┴─────────────────────────────────────────────────────────────┘
      ┌──────────────────────────────────────────────────────┐
      │               Available LAN Drivers                   │
      ├──────────────────────────────────────────────────────┤
      │IBM PCN II & Baseband (Primary)  V1.00 (881021)        │
      │IBM Token Ring  V2.21 (880817)                         │
      │NetWare Ethernet NE1000  V2.30EC (881024)              │
      │NetWare Ethernet NE2000  V1.02EC (890309)              │
      │NetWare RX-Net  V1.00 (881010)                         │
      └──────────────────────────────────────────────────────┘

          ┌──────────────────────────────────────────────────┐
          │ Highlight a list entry, then press the SELECT key.│
          └──────────────────────────────────────────────────┘
```

Figure 10-8   Available LAN Drivers Submenu

If you select more than one driver, they will be assigned in order to LAN A, LAN B and so on. The drivers correspond to the network interface cards you have installed in your server. We installed the NE2000 Ethernet card so that's the choice we'll make. The LAN driver you selected will appear in the window. Press ‹Enter› and return to the Available Options menu. Your LAN driver is installed.

Our next task is to select a disk driver. This gets a bit more complex than selecting LAN drivers. Remember we referred casually to disk channels at the start of this chapter? Well, it's time to dive into that aspect of the installation procedure. Although there are five disk channels, in most cases (at this point, anyway) you'll only be concerned with the 0 channel. That is the channel used to define the server's internal hard disk. As you add external drives to your growing system, you'll need the other channels. A channel is really just a way of describing a group of physical drives that are similarly configured for a particular type of installation and keeping individual drives separate from each other. For the moment, we will use Hard Disk Channel 0 as our choice.

Go back to your Available Options menu (which is where you should be now) and choose the Select Disk Drivers line and press ‹Enter›. Your menu will look like Figure 10-9.

Use a similar approach to selecting LAN drivers. Highlight the Select Loaded Item to bring up a list of the disk drivers loaded into your server's memory when you started NETGEN. When you see the Channel: prompt, type 0 ‹Enter›. This will bring up the Select Driver Type window as in Figure 10-10.

Here you will need some help from a friend. The friend could be the instruction manual that came with your hard disk or, in extreme cases,

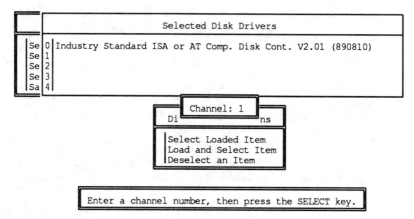

Figure 10-9   Select Disk Drivers Submenu

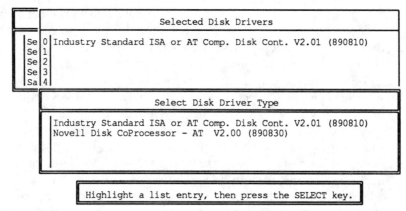

Figure 10-10   Select Driver Type Submenu

your Novell dealer. The problem is this: Each hard drive has unique requirements for its driver. In most cases, the driver you need will be evident from the choices on the submenu. In some cases the obvious driver will not be on the list. There are a couple of possible reasons for this. One is that you selected the wrong channel for the type of disk you are installing. For example, we selected channel 0. But if you were using an external drive, channel 0 wouldn't work since it is for the server's internal hard drive. There is a chart in the NetWare manual which we have reproduced here in Figure 10-11 for your convenience. It shows the available channels and drivers for particular configurations.

If all else fails and you can't make a selection, contact your Novell representative and describe your configuration.

Hard Disk Channel	TYPE OF FILE SERVER				
	IBM PS/2 30 IBM PC & Compatibles	386 AE 150 X 1	386 AE 150 X 2	IBM PS/2 50, 60, 70	IBM PS/2 60, 70, 80
0	AT Hard Disk Controller — Internal Drive	Not Available	Not Available	PS/2 MFM Controller — Internal Drive	PS/2 ESDI Controller — Internal Drive
1	Novell Disk Coprocessor — External Drive	Novell Disk Coprocessor — External Drive Internal Drive	Novell Disk Coprocessor — External Drive Internal Drive	Not Available	Not Available
2	Novell Disk Coprocessor — External Drive	Novell Disk Coprocessor — External Drive	Novell Disk Coprocessor — External Drive Internal Drive	Not Available	Not Available
3	Novell Disk Coprocessor — External Drive	Novell Disk Coprocessor — External Drive	Novell Disk Coprocessor — External Drive	Not Available	Not Available
4	Novell Disk Coprocessor — External Drive	Novell Disk Coprocessor — External Drive	Novell Disk Coprocessor — External Drive	Not Available	Not Available

Figure 10-11   Possible Disk Drivers for Hard Disk Channels (courtesy Novell)

Our next task is to define the file server hardware information. To get to this step of our installation, we press ‹Enter› to install the hard disk driver and then choose the Save Selections and Continue choice from the Available Options menu. When we press ‹Enter› we'll see the File Server Information window as in Figure 10-12.

At this point your NetWare Installation Parameters worksheet becomes important. Any information that you will need should be on it and information the NETGEN program creates should be recorded. This worksheet becomes a hard copy record for future reference. The first task we have is to assign network addresses.

Network addresses are simply designations for each individual string of cable from the file server. If you have one network adapter card installed in your server (LAN Board A) you have one cable leaving your server, going to network workstations. In order for a workstation to know how to talk to that server and the server to know how to talk to that workstation, we need to give LAN Board A a unique address. If we had two LAN adapter cards (A and B) in our server, we would need unique addresses for each of them. Information in the server destined for workstations on A would know where to go to get to that workstation and information returning to the server would be recognized as having come from a LAN A workstation.

```
+--+------------------------------------------------------------+
|  |               File Server Information                      |
|  +------------------------------------------------------------+
|Se| A: NetWare Ethernet NE2000  V1.02EC (890309)               |
|Se|     Network Address: 1986B00B                              |
|Se| B: NetWare RX-Net  V1.00 (881010)                          |
|Se|     Network Address: 1987B00B                              |
|Sa| Communication Buffers: 250                                 |
+--+------------------------------------------------------------+
```

```
+------------------------------------------------------------------+
| Use the arrow keys to highlight the desired field, then type in the |
| desired data.  Press the ESCAPE key to save selections and continue. |
+------------------------------------------------------------------+
```

Figure 10-12   File Server Information Window

We assign the address as an 8-digit hexadecimal number. That means we can use any combination of numbers from 0 through 9 and characters from A through F. The address we assign to the LAN card on the server must also be assigned to all of the adapter cards in all of the workstations on that cable (network). In other words, all of the adapter cards, workstation or server, that are on the same cable must have the same address.

The first entry you will make is the network address for the A LAN adapter board. When asked for the network address make your 8-digit entry as we described above and press ‹Enter›. Then make the same entry on your Installation Parameters Worksheet. You may not include any character except 0–9 and A–F in your address. Other than that, you may choose any combination of characters you wish as long as it makes a valid hexadecimal number. If you have doubts, you can stick to using 0–9 only and you won't go wrong.

The next entry is the number of communications buffers. You can have from 10 to 150 buffers. The default is 40. For most networks you should not reduce the default. There are some tradeoffs to selecting the number of buffers you install. Here are some rules of thumb. For each workstation on the network add one buffer to the default of 40. Since each buffer requires 500 bytes of memory, you add 1 K every time you add two buffers. The default 40 buffers, therefore, requires 20 K of server memory.

After you enter the number of buffers you need, choose the Save Selections and Continue option on the menu. At this point NETGEN will choose a configuration for you. Since you selected the Default configuration, this should be satisfactory. If you use an IBM PS/2, however, you will want to check the configuration carefully and refer to your Novell manual for further information. If you wish at this point you can alter the default configuration. We don't recommend that you make any changes this time, though, since this is, in part, a learning session for you.

Make sure you have recorded all of the information on your screen in the File Server Configuration worksheet. You'll need the information later. Leave the Selected Configuration window by [ESC]aping and answer Yes when you are asked if you wish to use the selected configuration.

We will now generate the network operating system. Since you are using the Default installation, this procedure is automatic. Your configuration information was saved by NETGEN in the Config.dat file in either the Support directory or the Netgen directory on your hard drive. NETGEN reads the configuration and creates a complete executable network operating system file, configured for your LAN called Net$os.exe.

This is a unique part of the NetWare operating system. Unlike many other networks which provide a preconfigured operating system, NetWare generates one that is unique to your network requirements. If you ever need to add additional peripherals or change your configuration, you can do so by reinstalling, regenerating and relinking the operating system file. During the latter stages of this process you may be prompted to insert other disks for linking to your custom operating system. Simply follow the prompts as they appear. These prompts will be different for every installation, since your selections will be unique to your LAN.

At this point you are through with generating the network operating system on the server. Remember, you have created a set of master disks containing your network operating system for a particular server. If you are going to install additional servers, you need separate operating systems generated for them as well since each server has a unique address.

It's time to perform your final hookup between workstations and the server and test them. As we suggested earlier, you should connect one workstation first. Note that if you are using any topology but Ethernet, you'll have to connect the entire network at this point. Since our example is an Ethernet bus configuration, we can start with a single workstation and add new ones one at a time until the entire bus is installed. A word of caution, though. Ethernet needs to see a terminated line at both ends. This prevents reflections and garbled data. Terminate one end with a termination resistor or directly into the adapter card and the other with a grounding terminator plug.

However, for the COMCHECK test we're about to perform, you'll need to connect the entire network, at least for a brief time. We're going to validate the actual cable connection to all the workstations and insure that they can communicate "across the wire." After this test, you can disconnect all but your own workstation so that users can go back to using their

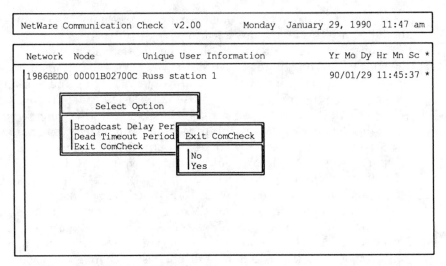

```
┌─────────────────────────────────────────────────────────────────┐
│  NetWare Communication Check  v2.00      Monday  January 29, 1990  11:47 am │
├─────────────────────────────────────────────────────────────────┤
│                                                                   │
│ │ Network  Node          Unique User Information        Yr Mo Dy Hr Mn Sc * │
│ │                                                                 │
│ │ 1986BED0 00001B02700C Russ station 1                 90/01/29 11:45:37 * │
│ │         ┌─────────────────────────┐                             │
│ │         │     Select Option       │                             │
│ │         ├─────────────────────────┤                             │
│ │         │ Broadcast Delay Per│                                  │
│ │         │ Dead Timeout Period│ Exit ComCheck │                  │
│ │         │ Exit ComCheck      ├───────────────┤                  │
│ │         └───────────────────┤ No            │                  │
│ │                             │ Yes           │                  │
│ │                             └───────────────┘                  │
│ │                                                                 │
│ │                                                                 │
│ │                                                                 │
└─────────────────────────────────────────────────────────────────┘
```

Figure 10-13   COMCHECK Utility Menu

computers in single-user mode. Any workstations that are not currently assigned to users can, of course, remain on the LAN.

Before we actually finish setting up the server's hard disk, we will want to check each network connection to insure that our cable and workstations are properly installed. We will use the COMCHECK utility and it doesn't matter that the server is not completely configured.

Running the COMCHECK Utility

In order to run COMCHECK you need the master shell disk and the NetWare 286 Diagnostic disk. Here's what COMCHECK does. It checks the configuration of the workstation, its ability to connect to the network and its ability to connect to other workstations on the network. You will be able to test each of the workstations.

The server, however, is not part of the test. Here's a trick, though, to insure that the server will connect to the LAN. Assume, for the moment that it is a workstation, not a server. Be sure that it has a network interface card that is compatible with you master shell. Now, treat it as if it were a workstation instead of the server. You'll at least validate the network connection.

Go to each workstation and, using the master shell disk, type A:IPX ‹Enter›. If you can't load IPX, you have a mismatch in the master file and the interface card's configuration or you have a bad interface card.

Once you have brought up each workstation, use the Diagnostic disk and type A:COMCHECK ‹Enter›. You'll bring up the menu shown in Figure 10-13. Type in a label that identifies the workstation you are on (this won't stay with the workstation—it's just for the COMCHECK test) where the menu asks for Unique User Information.

Now move on to each of the workstations on the LAN in turn and repeat the process. Eventually, you'll see screens on each station that show the other workstations on the network. If a workstation is missing, try running COMCHECK on it again and if it still doesn't register check the cable. By using the various displays you can isolate the section of cable that is bad between any two stations. Another possible, but unlikely, problem is a duplicate or bad interface card address. If that occurs you must replace the interface card.

Setting Up the Server Hard Disk

Having established that the workstations and the server (tested as if it were a workstation) can communicate over the LAN it is now time to complete our server installation and initialize the hard drive for use on the network. Again we will use NETGEN and select the Default level of installation. Before we continue we must insure that our server has a Config.sys file in its boot directory and that the file shows at least a FILES entry of 10 and BUFFERS of 20.

Now, insert the NETGEN disk into drive A: and the SUPPORT disk (or the AUXGEN disk for 3 1/2″ installations) in drive B:. Type A:NETGEN -D to select the Default configuration. Do not include the [N] option this time since it would take you back to the beginning of your NETGEN session and cause you to create a new operating system from scratch, replacing the one you have already generated.

The Run Options menu will appear. From it you will select Standard Floppy Disk method since that was the method we used earlier to build the network operating system. You will now see the Network generation Options menu. Select the NetWare Installation choice and press ‹Enter›. The program will then examine your hard diver and system. When it is finished, it will present a list of the drives it found on the server. This list looks like Figure 10-14.

Compare the list with your worksheet and press [Esc]ape. You will be offered an opportunity to verify, reexamine or correct the list. Be sure the list is correct before you assent and press <Enter>. If you are using an unusual disk you may be asked by NETGEN to run a utility called COMP-

```
┌────────────────────────────────────────────────────────────────────────┐
│                        Selected Configurations                           │
├────────────────────────────────────────────────────────────────────────┤
│Disk Chan. 0: Industry Standard ISA or AT Comp. Disk Cont. V2.01 (890810) │
│          Option 0: ISADISK      PRIMARY      Verify=ON     I/O=1F0h       │
│              IRQ=14                                                       │
│Disk Chan. 1: Industry Standard ISA or AT Comp. Disk Cont. V2.01 (890810) │
│          Option 2: ISADISK      SECONDARY    Verify=ON     I/O=170h       │
│              IRQ=11                                                       │
│                                                                          │
│Resource Set  1: ISA or AT Compatible File Server                         │
│    Resource  1: AT Auxiliary ROM                                         │
│             Option  0: Mem E000h-EFFFh                                    │
│    Resource  2: Western Digital Floppy Controller                        │
│             Option  0: IRQ=6, I/O Base=3F0h, DMA=2                        │
└────────────────────────────────────────────────────────────────────────┘
```

```
┌──────────────────────────────────────────────────┐
│     Use the arrow keys to scroll the display.      │
│  Press ESCAPE to leave this window and continue.   │
└──────────────────────────────────────────────────┘
```

Figure 10-14   List of Disk Drives Found by NETGEN

SURF before you can continue. Any disk not prepared in advance by Novell or your Novell supplier will fall into this category.

To run COMPSURF, press [ESC]ape and select the Analyze Disk Surface choice. COMPSURF destroys all data on the hard disk and reformats it. So, if you prepared your disk as we suggested earlier, all your partitions will be lost.

Select the disk you want to test and format. At this point, if the disk has never been prepared with COMPSURF you will be prompted through a series of steps after which your disk will be formatted. These are all pretty automatic except one. If you are asked if you want to enter bad blocks into the bad block table answer Yes. You will need a bad blocks list, in some cases, which the drive manufacturer usually attaches to the drive itself. You'll need that list if you are going to manually enter the bad blocks. It is important that the bad blocks be on record since the system will avoid writes to a designated bad block.

Once the COMPSURF utility is finished preparing your hard drive, you can return to the NETGEN NetWare Installation Menu. Select the Default installation options. The default installation will progress automatically and will

- Set up a default partition table,
- Install the Hot Fix feature, and
- Display the default volumes on the screen.

The volumes will have labels assigned by NETGEN. Record the volume labels on your Hard Disk/Volume worksheet.

The next step is naming the file server. You can have any name you wish for the server as long as it is 2–24 characters long and does not start with a period (.) or contain any of the forbidden characters. These characters are:

```
space ( ), "", *, comma (,), /, \, |, :, ;, =, <, >, ?,[, ]
```

Also, you must be sure that the name does not duplicate any server name to which your server might connect. At this point you will have an opportunity to see your default configuration. Record it on your worksheet and press ‹Enter›. Now it's time to define the network printers. You will be asked several questions about which ports to use for network printers. The answers are on your NetWare Installation Parameters worksheet where you entered them earlier. Answer the questions as you are prompted and [ESC]ape when you are finished. You must make an entry at each available port. The entry can be Yes or No, but an entry must be made.

We're almost finished. Select Continue Installation from the Installation Options menu and answer Yes when asked if you want to install the Networking Software on the File Server. You will be prompted to insert the appropriate disks and when you are finished you will see the message:

```
System files successfully installed
Strike a key when ready....
```

You will be returned to the Network Generation Option menu. Select Exit NETGEN ‹Enter›. When you have exited you can reboot the server by typing ‹Ctrl› ‹Alt› ‹Del› simultaneously. You will then see the boot process terminating in the network prompt (:) on the screen. You can enter any of the server commands from this prompt.

Now That You Know How—A Faster Method of Generating the Network Operating System

Now that we've shown you the basics of building a network operating system using NETGEN and the Standard Floppy Disk method, you should have noticed a few things. First, the files and programs delivered as NetWare 286 or SFT NetWare are, for the purpose of creating a customized network environment, peculiar to each individual installation.

Although this is not particularly common in the PC world, it is the normal course of events on mainframes and minicomputers. Operating systems usually need to match the hardware configuration of the platform. So operating system developers have been creating programs that generate operating systems on larger computers almost as long as there have been computers. The PC world has not needed this level of sophistication until relatively recently. Today, however, the complexity of personal computers demands that the network be individually generated if users are going to realize the full power of their systems. In this regard, the NetWare system will give you the most flexibility and power.

The second thing you probably noticed is that there has to be an easier and faster way to get the job done than a floppy disk at a time. Well, you're right. So now, we're going to take you on a brief tour of installing and generating the operating system using the Hard Disk method. To start with you will need a separate PC—not the server yet. This PC must have 640K of memory, a hard disk with at least 8 MB available disk space and two floppy drives.

Start by booting the computer upon which you will generate the operating system. This is not the server as we said above. What we are going to do, simply, is use the speed and storage space of the hard disk to generate the system. Then we'll transfer the system to our floppy disks and load them onto the server. By doing this we'll avoid the time and effort we expended taking out and replacing floppy disks when we used the Standard Floppy Disk method. However, the process, from the standpoint of the computer is the same. And, when we are finished, we will prepare our server and load the system exactly as we did before.

Once the utility computer is booted, we need to create a directory called GENERATE. We will generate the new operating system in this directory. GENERATE should be a first level directory under the root. We won't go into quite as much detail this time because you have already generated and loaded an operating system. Once you have created the GENERATE directory, switch to that directory and place the NETGEN disk in drive A:. Type

```
A:NETGEN -ND
```

to generate a new operating system using the NETGEN defaults. The program will respond with a menu of NETGEN Run Options. Select Hard Disk from this menu and, when asked, respond with the drive on which you created the GENERATE directory.

Next, you will be asked to insert the GENDATA disk in any drive. After the program is through with the GENDATA disk it will tell you to replace it with the NETGEN disk followed by several other diskettes. What the program is doing now is creating several directories and subdirectories and loading files from the various diskettes into them.

When all of this uploading is finished you'll have one last chance to add any additional drivers that were not uploaded as part of the standard configuration. These drivers might be additional LAN drivers, Disk drivers or Other drivers. If you have any of these (LAN drivers named LAN_DRV_nnn where nnn is any number except 001 or 002, Disk drivers named DKS_DRV_nnn where nnn is any number except 001, or Other drivers named OTH_DRV_nnn where nnn is anything) load them now.

Now it's time to select the network configuration. This procedure is much the same as the one we used with the Standard Floppy Disk method. The big difference is that it goes much faster and we don't need to keep inserting and removing disks. Just follow the same prompts you saw before. You will go through the selection of operating system options, defining the server's hardware, selecting LAN and disk drivers (and Other drivers, if you have them) and entering the default server information such as network address.

Once you have made your selections, confirmed them and entered them in your worksheets, you can proceed to generating the operating system and the server utilities. Since we are using the Hard Disk method, this part of the job is pretty automatic. There is little for you to do but wait until the program is done.

When the program is done linking the new operating system, you will ned to copy it to your floppies for transfer to the server. Remember what we've done. First, we copied a bunch of files from the NetWare distribution disks onto a hard drive on our utility PC.

Then the NETGEN program asked us how our network was to be configured. Armed with that information and the files from the distribution disks, NETGEN generated (created) a customized network operating system in two pieces. These files, called NET$OS.EX1 and NET$OS.EX2 are combined together on the server in a final file called NET$OS.EXE. This is the executable network operating system file that controls your network server. When we used the Standard Floppy Disk method, we created the same files. So this method gets us to the same point as the other. It's just faster and easier.

To exit NETGEN and copy the files we will be using later, we simply select the Yes choice when asked if we wish to exit. Be sure to answer Yes when asked if you want to download the needed files to floppy disk. The program will then prompt you for the disks it needs to download the files you prepared during the configuration procedure. Now it's time to install the operating system on the server.

At this point the installation and preparation of the server and the network drives is exactly the same as we used in our first example. Remember, you will need to restart NETGEN using the command

```
NETGEN —DS
```

to use the default configuration and the Standard Floppy Disk method. You must use the Standard Floppy Disk method from this point on no matter how you generated the operating system.

Getting Brave—Custom Configurations

Although we won't go into great detail regarding the custom configuration options, there are a few things you should know. First, the custom configuration is not much more difficult than the default configuration option. Second, the NETGEN program prompts you through each step.

Why might you choose to use the custom options instead of the default options? The main reason is that with the custom options you'll have a bit more control over the configuration. If you want to fine tune your network installation, this is the way to go. Remember, though, that you can make changes to your configuration right up until the final steps before NETGEN links your selected options together.

You select the custom configuration in one of two ways. You can select it from the start when you add the [C] option instead of the [D] option to the NETGEN command. Or, if you enter NETGEN without any options selected you'll make your choice on the first menu that NETGEN presents. All will then proceed as you have seen before up until you start selecting the server hardware.

Now, you'll start selecting resources for the file server. A resource is anything that communicates directly with the server's cpu. A resource might be an add-in board, a disk drive, a printer or any other device that communicates with the internals of the server.

Resources are grouped together in resource sets. These sets are usually a single device. But they can be a collection of devices which you would normally think of as a unit. For example, a file server is really several devices connected together. But we generally consider them collectively as a server. The server, then, is an example of a resource set. If this confuses

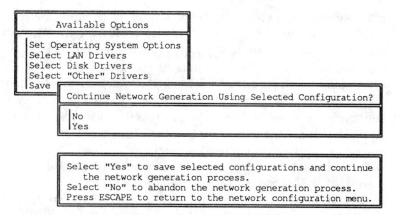

Figure 10-15   The Select Resource Sets Submenu

you, don't worry too much. NetWare has several diskettes with common resources and resource sets already grouped together for you to use.

Because resources and resource sets are static in nature (you can't usually configure them) you need to configure the server around them. This may mean that you need to write down all of your resources and the interrupt lines, I/O addresses, etc., before you start your configuration. In most cases you'll be asked by the menu to select from several resource sets. To get to that menu, select the Select Resource Sets in the Network Configuration Available Options menu. It will look like Figure 10-15.

You'll be shown the available sets and you can make your choices. If you make an error, you'll have a chance to deselect your mistake before you save. Next, you will select LAN drivers just as you did in the default configuration. Remember that you can have up to four separate network interface cards in each server. You'll need a LAN driver for each one.

Next, it's time to install the disk drivers. This is done exactly as you did in the Default configuration and you can have up to five hard drives here too. Other drivers can be installed now, too. An example of an Other driver is a tape backup unit. Here again the procedure is the same as the Default. The next place you'll see a difference in the Custom and the Default configurations is if you need to configure a resource set. I know we said that resources sets aren't usually configurable, but there are a few times when a resource such as a LAN driver or disk driver needs to be configured. In either of these cases you'll be prompted through the procedure.

Next you'll need to enter server information for network addresses (each LAN interface card needs one) and the number of communications buffers. Remember that the default configuration assigned these for you but now you can do it yourself. You'll have much more control over your LAN's performance. However, you may recall that we did some of this even when we were using the Default configuration. Like all of the configurable options, you have a chance to modify the number of communications buffers even with the Defaults before you save your settings. If you make errors you simply use the appropriate Release option on the menus before you save your settings. All configurations and resource sets can be released up until the last few steps. From this point on you will proceed exactly as you have in earlier configurations.

The only real difference between Custom and Default configurations, then, is that you can make your selections as you go with the Custom configuration, whereas with the Defaults you take what NETGEN gives you and make your changes just before you save. The difficulty with that, though, is that you may not have the resource sets available at that point, or you may need to reconfigure to avoid address or interrupt conflicts. If you think that the defaults won't do the job for you, then, go straight to the Custom configuration and do it right.

SFT—Keeping the Data on the LAN Safe

As we pointed out earlier, the SFT level of NetWare is similar in most respects to NetWare 286 except that SFT NetWare has some built-in provisions for system redundancy. That means, as we explained earlier, that the system supports uninterruptable power supplies, disk mirroring and some other safety measures. These facilities install as you configure your operating system.

Since you will be using an SFT version of NETGEN, you'll get an extra menu when you select the Set Operating System Options in the Available Options menu. This menu looks like Figure 10-16.

You'll have two choices to select from here, SFT Level II with or without TTS. TTS is the Novell Transaction Tracking System. We mentioned it earlier in conjunction with our discussion of databases. If you are using a lot of database manipulations on your Novell LAN you'll need TTS.

Once you select the level of SFT protection you want to install, you'll have appropriate choices available to you on the various menus as you configure your system. The SFT choices only appear when you run the Custom configuration options. It is assumed that, since you are installing SFT NetWare, you want some level of SFT protection. So you'll be exposed to the SFT issue any time you install SFT NetWare.

```
        ┌─────────────────────────────────┐
        │        Available Options        │
        ├─────────────────────────────────┤
        │Set Operating System Options     │
        │Select LAN Drivers               │
        │Select Disk Drivers              │
        │Select "Other" Drivers           │
        │Save Selections and Continue     │
        └─────────────────────────────────┘

                    ┌──────────────────────────────────────┐
                    │      Set Operating System Options      │
                    ├──────────────────────────────────────┤
                    │SFT NetWare 286 with TTS               │
                    │SFT NetWare 286                        │
                    │Advanced NetWare 286 / Dedicated       │
                    │Advanced NetWare 286 / Nondedicated    │
                    └──────────────────────────────────────┘


        ┌──────────────────────────────────────────────────┐
        │ Highlight an option, then press the SELECT key.  │
        └──────────────────────────────────────────────────┘
```

Figure 10-16   SFT Set Operating System Options Menu

Summary

In this chapter we have shown you how to use the default installation to install an Advanced NetWare file server and workstations and how to test the network before final network installation. There are several advanced options for installing network servers and workstations. They vary considerably depending upon the actual hardware configuration you install. A fair amount of experience is required before installing some of the more exotic configurations and we recommend that you start with the default installation. You'll get familiar with the way NetWare performs an installation and what options NETGEN assigns automatically.

Part III
NetWare 386

11

NetWare 386 Version 3.0

Novell introduced its new version of NetWare, designed specifically for computers using the Intel 80386 and 80486 processors late in 1989. Initially, the primary changes visible to the user were the ability to support 250 users per LAN instead of 100, and the ability to support memory resident programs in the file server. These memory resident programs are called NetWare Loadable Modules, and they can be loaded and removed from the file server while the server is running. There is no need to take the file server down while loading these processes, unlike the situation with the Value Added Processes used by earlier versions of NetWare.

Of course, there were other significant changes as well. The new version of NetWare is far easier to install. It's much faster than older versions, and it supports vastly more disk space. Of equal importance is the fact that NetWare 386 will coexist on the same LAN with earlier versions of NetWare, and it uses the same user interface as earlier versions.

As a result, using NetWare 386 is very much like using the NetWare 2.1X that we've discussed elsewhere in this book. There are differences, though. Some of the utilities covered earlier are gone, some have been changed, and some new utilities and commands have been added. These changes will be referenced in the next chapter.

In addition to changes in commands, there are other differences in NetWare 386. Passwords can be encrypted in such a way that decryption is unlikely. There is now a new class of supervisor called a Workgroup Manager, who can have control over limited portions of a server, thus allowing control over the activities of a specific work group. Finally, NetWare now uses MS-DOS to load, eliminating the cold boot loader of earlier versions, and you can exit to MS-DOS on the file server when you're done using NetWare.

The Big Changes

The most significant changes are those that help NetWare 386 move into the world of corporate computing. These include the great expansion in the capacity of the server, and the greater sophistication in the design. Specifically, the changes include:

- Supports up to 4 gigabytes RAM.
- Addresses up to 32 terabytes of disk storage.
- Supports up to 250 simultaneous users (this will increase later).
- Allows up to 100,000 files to be open simultaneously.
- Handles memory dynamically.
- Single volumes containing as many as 32 hard disks.
- Up to 32 disk volumes.
- Up to 1,024 hard disks.

In addition, NetWare 386 contains some major architectural enhancements. These enhancements affect the way NetWare interacts with other networks, file systems, and computer designs. They include what Novell calls an Open Systems Architecture, which means that the new version of NetWare will allow multiple protocols and will support a form of server-base terminate and stay resident (TSR) software called a NetWare Loadable Module. The security improvements are also part of the new design philosophy. One of the security items, encrypted passwords, made rewrites of many of the utilities and commands mentioned in Chapter 7 necessary.

The move to an Open Systems philosophy had the greatest effect on the design for NetWare 386. Novell's stated intent is to move out of the proprietary environment that the company has occupied since its inception, and shift to industry standards where possible. Novell is making this move because its largest corporate customers, as well as the U.S. government, are demanding that network operating software meet published standards. This has resulted in the Open Systems Architecture.

Open Systems Architecture

The recent move away from proprietary operating systems, especially by the U.S. Government, has led a number of vendors to design their systems so that they no longer work only with their own software. Users of personal computers probably won't find this too unusual, because personal computing has been reasonably open for the last several years. This has not been the case with larger systems.

Traditionally, mainframe and minicomputer manufacturers designed their hardware and software to be as proprietary as possible. This locked the customer into buying everything from them, and assured that sales would continue well into the future. This changed when minicomputer manufacturers began adopting the Unix operating system, developed by AT&T. Unix was designed to be an open system, and for that reason there is a version of Unix available for nearly every computer, from the IBM-PC/AT through the supercomputing world of the Cray.

When the government announced that they were going to adopt standards, the assumption was that the government would choose Unix. They nearly did, settling on something called "POSIX" which results in an operating system that looks very much like Unix. Companies that deal with the government are expected to use computer systems that are compliant with the POSIX standard. This has led the commercial world into the adoption of standards, and in turn has created an atmosphere where standards and open systems are expected.

Novell's attempt at an open system is NetWare 386. While the software is still based on earlier versions of NetWare, it has moved much closer to meeting POSIX standards, including adopting some portions of the Unix operating system. It also has adopted other methods of making the operating system as open as possible, both for software that will run in the server, as well as for networks that must attach to the server.

The NetWare Open Systems concept is based on three major parts. They are the NetWare Loadable Modules, the Open Data-Link Interface, and the Streams Interface. The Streams Interface is a direct port from AT&T's Unix System V.

- NetWare Loadable Modules—If you're familiar with earlier versions of NetWare, or if you read the part about Value Added Processes earlier in this book, these took the place of the VAPs. The NLMs are terminate and stay resident programs that you can load from the console in NetWare in exactly the same way as you load a TSR program in MS-DOS. The NLMs support special functions, peripheral devices, and customized equipment. You might use one to support signalling from your uninterruptable power supply, for example. One major change from the VAPs in earlier versions is that you can unload an NLM from the file server's memory when you are done using it. This is particularly useful when you are using one for diagnostics and want to free up the server's memory when you are through. Novell has made the necessary information available to developers so that anyone can create an NLM to support their software or device.

- Open Data Link Interface—As you will recall from earlier in this book, the data link is one of the seven OSI layers. The Open Date Link Interface allows a file server to support multiple LAN protocols from the same machine and even the same network adapter. This means that you can run an IPX and a TCP/IP network from the same server and same network interface card at the same time. The Open Data Link Interface is an important step in moving NetWare 386 into an open environment that meets most organizations' requirements for standards. The full implementation of the Open Data Link Interface will be available with version 3.1 of NetWare 386.

- Streams Interface—The Streams Interface is ported from AT&T's Unix System V. It allows multiple file systems to exist in the same file server. This means that an application that is being used on a workstation will be able to understand the file system on the server, in spite of the fact that the workstations may sometimes use completely different native file systems. This is why you can use a Unix workstation that communicates through TCP/IP to communicate with the same file server as an MS-DOS workstation communicating with IPX. Normally, these workstations and their applications would use file systems that are completely incompatible, but the Streams Interface translates things so that they can communicate.

As you might imagine, all of this extra capability comes with a price. That price is memory. NetWare now requires more system memory and more mass storage than before. On the other hand, it also comes with the ability to manage more memory. This allows NetWare to take advantage of the larger hard disks that are available now, as well as the greater flexibility in managing system memory that the 80386 processor permits.

Storage

NetWare 386 essentially eliminates all system memory and disk drive restrictions. There are limits, of course, but they are well beyond what is available under current or near-term developmental technology. For example, NetWare 386 will allow addressing of up to 4 gigabytes of system memory, even though there are no 80386-based computers that can even approach supporting that much memory. Likewise, the ability to access up to 32 terabytes of mass storage is well beyond the capabilities of any current hardware.

System Memory

Novell NetWare 386 requires at least 2 M of system memory to operate. Larger disks, additional disks, and additional NLMs past the minimums will increase this requirement. The NLMs require memory in which to reside. In addition, NetWare 386 uses cache buffers for the disk drive space and the disk directories, and for some of the NLMs.

The size of the cache buffers can be changed when you install NetWare 386. The default size is 4 K, but you can also choose 8 or 16 K. Larger hard disks will require larger cache buffers. In some cases, such as with buffers assigned to NLMs, the memory assigned as a cache buffer can be returned to the system. When an NLM is terminated, for example, the memory assigned to it is vacated and returned to system use.

NetWare 386 also allows dynamic allocation of memory, based on the amount of memory you have installed in the server, and the requirements of the operating system. In addition to the cache buffers mentioned above, NetWare 386 also sets up buffers for indexes, packet receiving, routing, and the like. These are assigned sections of memory when they are needed. Otherwise, this memory is available to the operating system. As is the case with many other operating systems, NetWare 386 will often function better with more than the minimum configuration. The reason for this is that when memory is held to the minimum, many operations must use the server's hard disk, rather than performing operations in memory, and the hard disk is much slower.

Mass Storage

NetWare 386 differs significantly from earlier versions in the manner in which it handles disk space. As mentioned above, these differences include the ability to handle larger disks and much more total disk space. In addition, NetWare 386 handles disk space differently in that it allows a single volume to spread across more than one disk drive. When it sets up volumes with multiple disk drives, it allocates data evenly across all drives, so that they fill up at an even rate.

Each volume can contain as many as 32 hard disks, and each server can have as many as 32 volumes. This means that you can have as many as 1,024 hard disks. This currently exceeds the capacity of existing disk controllers, but it also means that NetWare 386 won't be your limiting factor when you need to expand your network.

One factor that controls the size of a NetWare 386 volume is the disk allocation block size. The maximum size of a volume with the smallest 4 K block size is less than that available to one with a 64 K block size. You get to choose the disk allocation block size when you install NetWare 386, according to what you plan to use the particular volume for. You might choose a smaller block size if you plan to have a large number of small files, and a larger block size for a volume that is handling very large files.

There are some differences between the ways that NetWare 386 handles the file system and the directories compared to the way that MS-DOS and earlier versions of NetWare handle them. The Turbo-FAT is a good example, in that it indexes the file allocation table to speed up searches of FATs with more than 64 entries. Likewise, NetWare handles sparse files by only writing the actual data in a sparse file to disk, and having the server generate the empty data from the sparse file.

Because NetWare 386 supports many different operating systems, it also supports multiple directory entries. This means that each file will have a directory entry for each operating system using the server. The directory entry for each operating system reflects the proper format, so each operating system sees the directory entry as a user would normally expect to see it. In addition, the directories will support multiple byte characters, allowing directory entries to be in alternate character sets, including Kanji.

The final change, a negative one to some users, is that NetWare 386 no longer writes over erased files until there is no other space available on the disk. This means that you can go back and recover files that you erased by mistake, even if it was some time ago. Unfortunately, that also means that the files continue to take up disk space, and they are available to an unauthorized user who may chance across them. You can eliminate erased files by using the PURGE command, and you can set NetWare 386 to automatically purge all files as soon as they are erased. Setting the immediate purge option to "on" will boost performance and security, but will make it impossible to restore any files that were erased by mistake. With the exception of this need to purge files explicitly, security with NetWare 386 has been generally improved.

Security

Password encryption is a feature of NetWare 386. The encryption is performed at the workstation, and the encrypted password passes through the network in that form. Prior to this, a person with a device called a "sniffer" (a type of network diagnostic tool) could read passwords as they were sent to the server. Now, only the operating system can decode the encrypted passwords. Because you may be working with a network that has both NetWare 386 as well as earlier versions, the encryption can be defeated if you need to log into a server that does not support it.

A new supervisory level has been added to users rights. The new level, called Workgroup Manager, allows limited supervisory rights to a user who can then control the accounts of a specific group of people. This new level became necessary because NetWare 386 allows many more people to use a specific LAN, making it impractical for a single supervisor to handle it all.

Because Workgroup Manager(s) can control only specific user accounts, they need not be given full supervisory rights. This makes the LAN more secure, while at the same time making it easier to manage. As a Supervisor, you assign a Workgroup Manager to a specific group on the server, and then assign users to that group.

The Supervisor also has some additional control over the rights granted to users. This includes the ability to grant rights to specific files, as well as to directories and subdirectories. With these changes, you can assign different rights to the same file to different users. You can also have different rights to different files in the same subdirectory. This is particularly useful where you might want to restrict the rights to executable programs, while allowing users to create data files in the same directory.

The Supervisor also has more control over the file attributes than before. You can, for example, keep users from renaming specific programs or directories, even though they have the right to modify files in that directory. In a similar fashion, you can protect files from being erased or copied.

Using NetWare 386

You will notice some changes as soon as you turn on your file server. The most noticeable is that NetWare 386 no longer boots from the NetWare cold boot loader, but instead starts up with MS-DOS. You can assign a small partition on the server's hard disk specifically to contain the copy of MS-DOS used for booting the server, or you can boot from a floppy disk drive. The floppy method is easier to install, and it may be the only method with some types of hard disk controllers.

The file server still tells you it's ready with a colon prompt, just as it did in earlier versions. You run the Monitor program by loading an NLM, however, rather than just issuing a command. On the other hand, Monitor is much more informative than before, giving connection information in addition to the information on the progress of work on the other stations. Because the NLMs are terminate and stay resident programs, you can switch between them from a menu on the server. Other NLMs that you might load are the print server, the network interface card driver, or the UPS driver.

From the viewpoint of the workstation, NetWare 386 is not a lot different from earlier versions. You still see the familiar DOS prompt, usually one that includes the complete path. You may notice that NetWare 386 responds somewhat faster, and you will notice that a few of the programs, including the Help system have had major changes.

The Help system is really a complete set of on line documentation. You can use it to find out proper command syntax, to get added information on what a utility or command is supposed to do, or to find added information on the capabilities of commands related to the one you are using. To a considerable extent, the NetWare Help system eliminates the need for bound documentation. This is just as well, because the NetWare documentation is more limited than that shipped with earlier versions.

Unless they were dependent on the existence of a value added process, or some other specific attribute of an earlier version of NetWare, your applications should be unaffected by the change to NetWare 386. This means that applications that run on your workstation and simply use the LAN as disk storage may never know the difference. On the other hand, applications that are more tightly integrated into the LAN environment may not work. Examples of the type of packages that might have problems include LAN-based scheduling and electronic mail packages. LAN backup packages frequently depend on a VAP to support the process, so you should confirm whether they will work with NetWare 386.

Printing from NetWare 386

The NetWare 386 package includes a remote printing utility that allows a printer attached to a workstation to be used as a network printer. This is a significant improvement over earlier versions that used only printers attached to the file server. While third-party remote printing packages have been available for NetWare for some time, this is the first such package from Novell. The remote printing utility, PSERVER, (for dedicated print servers) and RPRINTER, (for nondedicated print servers) is now available for NetWare version 2.15 also.

You can run the remote print server two ways. One is to dedicate a workstation for use only as a print server. The other is to have network printing work in the background. If you plan to use the print server for a great deal of printing, it's probably best to dedicate a workstation to the task. It's not required that you use anything more advanced than an old PC/XT compatible computer for this task, but running the print server in the dedicated mode reduces the risk that the user of a nondedicated workstation might do something that would cause the printing to be interrupted. In addition, background printing requires some of the resources of the workstation, so things will run more slowly if it's running in the nondedicated mode.

Once the print server is set up and installed properly, you use it just like a printer attached to the file server. It has the advantage of allowing printers to be located more conveniently than if they had to be connected directly to the file server. You simply assign a print queue to the remote printer and it's ready for use.

Unfortunately, setting up the remote printer in the first place is not particularly easy. Part of the reason is that one critical step, the assignment of SPX buffers, is hidden in a different place in the manual. The other is that the installation process requires a great deal of changing from menu to menu in the PCONSOLE program in a manner that is less than intuitive.

In order to make the print server installation work, you have to follow the steps in the manual exactly as they are written. You have to be careful not to skip anything or perform any functions out of order, or the software won't work—but it won't tell you WHY it won't work. The steps in the manual are correct, however, and you can follow them cookbook fashion. If you make a mistake and the print server doesn't work, you can delete the partially installed server and start again.

The hidden step is the creation of the text file, SHELL.CFG. This file must be in the same directory as the IPX.COM file, and it must be created exactly as follows:

1. Type the following: COPY CON SHELL.CFG
2. You will find the cursor on a blank line. Type the following exactly, including the placement of spaces: spx = 50
3. Press the carriage return, then type a CTRL-Z and press return again. You will have created a file called "SHELL.CFG" which will contain the line "spx = 50."
4. Make sure that this file is in the same directory as the IPX.COM that you use to attach your workstation to the network. Once that is finished, you may continue with the installation of the remote print server. This file must exist on every workstation that is going to be doing remote printing.

Once the print server is installed, you invoke it either by running the dedicated server software, or by loading the print server NLM at the server, and then running the remote printer software at the workstation. The command for the dedicated server is:

```
PSERVER print server name
```

To run the nondedicated server requires two steps. First, you load the NLM, then run the workstation software:

From the file server console:

```
LOAD PSERVER print server name
```

From the workstation:

```
ATTACH file server name
RPRINTER
```

Installing NetWare 386

The installation process for NetWare 386 has been simplified considerably over previous versions. In addition, the new version comes on high density disks, which eliminates the disk swapping that took place in earlier versions. Still, you have to be careful and follow the steps in order if you plan to use NetWare 386.

Think carefully about the method you wish to use for booting the server. Once you decide, you can't change your mind without reinstalling the server completely. The choices are the floppy disk method, which is easier to accomplish and dedicates the entire hard disk to NetWare use, and the hard disk method, which requires that you allocate 1 M of hard disk space to MS-DOS. In addition, only hard disks using a standard disk controller can use the hard disk method. If you have a disk coprocessor board, you must use the floppy disk method.

The floppy disk method is more secure than the hard disk boot method. This is because the file server cannot be booted without the boot disk. If you lock the boot disk away, the file server can't be booted, and the information on it can't be tampered with. In addition, creating the 1 M partition is more time consuming and difficult than creating a boot floppy.

If you have a choice, and security is not a serious consideration, the hard disk boot method results in a server that boots much faster. In addition, floppy disks are much more prone to failure than are hard disks, so you must maintain a backup boot floppy if you don't use the hard disk boot method. Of course, you may not have a choice, so before you decide you must determine what sort of disk controller your file server has.

Once you have determined your preferred boot method, check to make sure that your network interface card is supported by NetWare 386. As of this writing, relatively few third-party boards are supported, but the number is being added to constantly, so you should check. The manufacturers of network interface cards can normally supply the necessary driver software, and it is usually supplied with the board when you buy it. Incidentally, this requirement for driver software also applies to workstations that will be using the NetWare 386 workstation shell, but in that case have an option, since a NetWare 2.15 workstation shell will also work with the NetWare 386 server.

Installation of the file server requires the following steps. They are explained in detail in the manual, which must be followed carefully when you are doing the actual installation. This will tell you what to expect:

1. Decide which boot method you plan to use. (See the description above regarding this).
2. Record the configuration of your file server. This means that you will need to write down the type of disk drive controller, network interface card, and hard disk drive. You should also record the memory address and interrupt of these items where appropriate, because you will need it when you begin the installation.
3. Create a boot disk. You may use either the file server or another PC/AT or PS/2 class computer for this, but you **MUST** use a high density disk. This disk must be blank except for the boot files and COMMAND.COM. Use this boot disk to boot the file server from its A: drive.
4. Alternatively, you may use FDISK to create a one megabyte DOS partition, format that, and make it bootable. You can only do this if you have a hard disk controller that will allow DOS to be booted from it. If you have a disk coprocessor board, you can't do this, and have to use the floppy disk method. Once you have created a DOS partition and installed DOS, boot with the partition.
5. Create the AUTOEXEC.BAT file. Using either the COPY CON command or a text editor, create an AUTOEXEC.BAT file containing the single command: "SERVER." Place the AUTOEXEC.BAT file onto the boot disk or the boot partition.
6. Copy the following files from the System diskette to the boot floppy or the boot partition:

```
SERVER.EXE
VREPAIR.NLM
*.DSK
*.NAM
```

7. Run SERVER from the floppy disk or the DOS partition. SERVER will prompt you for information it needs.

8. Name the server. You have 47 characters, including underscores and other characters except spaces. The name must be at least two characters long. If you share a network with other servers, pick a name that is unique. If you are on a network server that is by itself on the network, you can pick whatever makes you happy. Remember that you might have to tell the Novell technical support staff what the name is when you call for help, so try not to pick something that's too embarrassing.

9. Pick an internal network number. You can pick any hexadecimal number you like, up to eight digits long. If you are attached to an existing network, you will have to avoid the number that's already assigned to that LAN. Otherwise, pick your favorite number.

10. Load the disk driver NLM. You do this by typing the following: LOAD disk driver. Replace the words "disk driver" with the name of the actual disk driver on the boot partition. That name will be one of the following:

   • ISADISK—For standard PC/AT controllers.
   • ESDI—For PS/2 or compatible ESDI disk controllers.
   • DCB—For disk coprocessor boards.

   You may be prompted for I/O addresses and interrupts at this point. If you are, answer the questions with the information you recorded earlier. Users of PS/2 compatibles may not have these questions. If you have an external disk drive, you will use the LOAD DISKSET command instead of the above. You will be given a list of supported external disk drives from which to select.

11. Load the LAN driver NLM. As I mentioned before, you don't have a lot of choice here. If your network interface card isn't supported by NetWare 386, check to see if your card came with a disk containing the NLM. Or you might need to contact Novell for this. If your board is not supported, your only other choice is to buy a card for your server that is supported.

12. Load any other NLMs. This might include drivers for the Macintosh, for your UPS, or for an alternate file system. Use the LOAD command, followed by the name of the module for this.

13. Bind IPX to the LAN driver. If you have more than one network interface card in your server, you will need to do this with each one. You will also need to assign the network number, which is different from the internal network number discussed above. If you have an earlier version of NetWare running on the same LAN, you must use the same number as the network number on that LAN.
14. LOAD INSTALL. This is the installation program that will perform the rest of the process. You will be presented with a menu of choices for tasks that must be accomplished. They are as follows:

   A. Select "Disk Options" from the "Installation Options" menu. Select the "Format Disk Drive" option. You will be warned about destroying data, and asked to confirm that you really do want to format the disk.
   B. Select the "Partition Tables" option. If you have created a DOS partition for booting the server, you will see it here. If you see any additional DOS partitions, remove them using the "Delete Partition' choice. If you have multiple disk drives, you will need to choose which one you want to partition.
   C. Select the "Create NetWare Partition" choice from the "Partition Options" menu. You will be prompted for changes to the standard partitioning, then prompted to confirm that you really want to partition the disk. You'll complete the partitioning process for each disk drive you have on the server.
   D. Select the disk for mirroring, if any, from the "Disk Options" menu. You will be prompted to choose the primary and secondary disk. The secondary disk must be as large or larger than the primary disk. If it's larger, you will be asked to confirm that you know this. You'll also be asked to select partitions again for the secondary disk drive.
   E. Create volumes. NetWare automatically creates a volume named SYS. You can create additional volumes if you want them. If you plan to do this, you must indicate the intended segment size when prompted by the Volume Options menu. You will be prompted to press the escape key to initiate the volume creation.
   F. Copy files. Select "System Options" from the "Installation Options" menu, then select "Copy System and Public Files." Make sure the System disk is in drive A: when you do this. You will be prompted when to change disks.
   G. Create the AUTOEXEC.NCF file. Select the "Create AUTOEXEC.NCF File" from the "System Options" menu.

This creates a text file that is placed in your boot partition or on the boot floppy. It tells NetWare what environment to expect when it loads.

H. Create the workstation shell. You will do this on a workstation rather than the file server. Again, you will need to know the configuration of the computer, but this time it will be the workstation computer. To do this, you create a subdirectory on your workstation hard disk called NETWARE with an additional subdirectory beneath it called SHGEN-1. You copy the SHGEN.EXE file from the SHGEN-1 disk to the NETWARE directory, then copy the contents of the SHGEN-1 disk to the SHGEN-1 subdirectory. When this is done, change to the NETWARE directory, and type SHGEN. You will be asked to select a LAN driver from the list. If your network interface card is not listed, you will be asked to insert a floppy disk containing it into the floppy disk drive. SHGEN will create the workstation drivers.

Once you have completed the generation of the file server and the workstation shell, you are done. Of course you will need to add applications, users and additional directories, but you already know how to log on as the Supervisor and do that. The process is identical to that covered earlier in this book. If you have problems creating the workstation shell, remember that you can also use shells from NetWare versions 2.1 on.

Upgrading to NetWare 386

The process of upgrading an existing file server running NetWare 2.1 or later to NetWare 386 is very similar to setting up a new server. The major differences are that the Upgrade utility will allow you to back up your server first, and then it will attempt to transfer the bindery and user information to the new operating system. You will need to take the file server down during the Upgrade process.

Upgrading is a complex process. In fact, it's more complex than performing a new installation. Before you do anything, perform a complete backup of your file server. The Upgrade process will do this also, but you need this backup in case something goes wrong with the process. Once you have done that, continue upgrading.

As in the case of the installation process above, you need to follow the steps in the manual in order. In the case of an Upgrade, however, it's probably best to read the process through before proceeding. As you do that, keep in mind that you need to select an Upgrade process and a backup device, as well as the other selections you have to make otherwise.

A detailed explanation of the Upgrade process is beyond the scope of this book; however, we will discuss the major steps. This will alert you to steps that may require preparation before you actually start.

1. Choose the Upgrade method. You have a choice of performing the process using the transfer method or the DOS device method. The transfer method requires you to have at least two file servers. If you don't have two, you must use the DOS device method.
2. Back up the file server. The Upgrade utility will do this for you. You can use a workstation hard disk, if you have one with enough room, or you can use a tape or a WORM drive. If you are using the transfer method, you will not need to do the backup, since the other file server still contains the data.
3. Install the file server. Use the instructions above to install the file server.
4. Pick either the "Transfer" choice or the "Restore' choice from the Upgrade main menu. If you are using the Transfer method, choose "Transfer." If you are using the DOS device method, choose "Restore." You will need to choose whether to transfer or restore all directories or just some of them, and you will need to choose whether to restore or transfer the bindery information. During this process, logins will be disabled. You will have to type "Enable Login" at the file server console before you can continue.
5. Once the upgrade is complete and logins enabled, you will need to run Install again, and copy files to the system and public directories. This works just as it did above. Once you have completed the copying, you will need to check that the user security information is still correct, and you will need to check the login scripts.

The Upgrade process should be performed by an experienced supervisor, and it should be done only after the file server has been backed up. If you can't get the upgrade process to work, you can reinstall your original version until the problem is solved. The most common problem with upgrades probably is a network interface card not supported by NetWare 386. You can eliminate this as a possibility if you confirm that your selection of LAN cards will work, or that you have the necessary support software.

Because of the risk to your data, and because of the requirement to transfer bindery information, upgrading is more difficult and time consuming than a new installation. If your LAN is fairly small, and if you can reinstall your applications easily, you might want to consider merely backing up the data, then performing a new installation rather than an upgrade. You will have to enter the user data again, but if you only have a few people, this should not be difficult. Remember though—back up your server before you do anything else.

Once NetWare 386 is installed, you will have some new commands and utilities, as well as some changes in old commands. Some utilities will have been eliminated. The next chapter will provide a command reference for the new commands and will explain the changes to the commands that remain.

12

NetWare 386 Commands

As we mentioned in the last chapter, using NetWare 386 isn't greatly different from using earlier versions. Still, there are differences. Some commands from NetWare 2.15 have been removed, others have been changed. Many of the changes aren't obvious, and, in some cases, the only changes are to support the added capabilities of NetWare 386.

In addition to the changes, there have been several commands that are new with NetWare 386. These commands follow earlier NetWare commands in their approach to syntax, but, as is always the case, they do have their requirements for proper use. Finally, you should know that most of the NetWare 2.15 utilities will work on a NetWare 386 file server, but in some cases they will not be fully functional. Unless you really need a special command, it's best to leave it in its intended environment. Of course, as you will find out, many NetWare 386 commands will also work from a file server with an earlier version of NetWare.

Eleven commands that were supported by earlier versions of NetWare have removed. A list of these commands follows. For the most part, the functions of these commands are now supported elsewhere. The only exception is MAIL, which is no longer provided as standard by Novell. If you want electronic mail for your Novell network, you'll have to buy it separately. The commands that were removed are:

HIDEFILE
HOLDON
HOLDOFF
LARCHIVE
LRESTORE
NACBACK

MAIL
MARCHIVE
NRESTORE
PSTAT
SHOWFILE

There are seventeen commands that are still supplied as a part of NetWare 386, and are unchanged. The options, syntax and results of these commands are just as you will find them in Chapter 7. The commands that are unchanged are:

ATOTAL
BRGEN
CASTOFF
CASTON
COLORPAL
DOSGEN
ENDCAP
MENU
PAUDIT
RENDIR
SEND
SETPASS
SETTTS
SMODE
SYSTIME
USERLIST
VERSION

The remaining commands are modified in some manner, or they are completely new. For the most part, the modified commands are used in exactly the same manner as before, the changes being restricted to support for the changes to the file system or to support password encryption. Four of the five new commands are replacements for commands that were in earlier versions of NetWare, while one, UPGRADE, is completely new.

In the section that follows, we will discuss the new commands in their entirety, using the same format as we used in Chapter 7. For commands that have changed, we will discuss only the changes, if any, that will affect you as the user. If there are no changes to the way that you use the command, we will tell you that.

You should, of course, refer to the appropriate Novell NetWare 386 manual for official information on using NetWare. Depending on the function of the command or utility in question, you will find it explained in one of three manuals. Command line utilities have their own manual as do commands and utilities used for system administration. All utilities are explained in the Utilities manual, but command line utilities are explained more briefly than they are in the Command Line Utilities manual. Are you clear on that?

The Utilities manual, meanwhile, tells you at the beginning of each reference section whether it refers to a command line utility, a console command, or something else. If you keep all three books in front of you, you should be able to find whatever you want. We weren't able to convince Brady Books to print three books, so the information for all of the commands is right here in one book, but explained a little more briefly so that it will all fit.

ADD NAME SPACE

Format:

ADD NAME SPACE module_name [TO [VOLUME] volume_name]

Command Function:

Because NetWare 386 now supports file systems in addition to MS-DOS, it needs to have a way to add the additional file systems if they are needed. The ADD NAME SPACE command does this by telling NetWare 386 to allow naming conventions for non-MS-DOS machines, such as the Apple Macintosh. To use the command, replace module_name with the name of the module that is supporting the desired file system. Replace volume_name with the name of the NetWare volume on which you want the supported file system to reside.

Using ADD NAME SPACE

This command is simple to use. If you want to add support for another file system you must first LOAD the appropriate loadable module. Once that is done, you can add the name space. For information about the LOAD command, see page 301 later in this chapter. Once you have done that, simply invoke the command, followed by the name of the module and the volume, as follows:

```
ADD NAME SPACE MACINTOSH TO VOLUME SYS
```

You should note that the words "Volume" and "To" in the example are optional. The command will work just as well if you leave them out. If you want to see if you have already loaded support for a particular file system, simply type ADD NAME SPACE without further modifiers. The utility will tell you that you forgot to add the space name, and then it will tell you what space names are already added.

ALLOW

Format:

ALLOW [path [TO INHERIT] rightslist]

Command Function:

The ALLOW command can be used to view, set or modify the inherited rights of a directory path or of a file. Any user can see the rights they have in a particular area with the ALLOW command, but it requires supervisory privileges to change anything with it. When using the command, replace "path" with the directory path about which you want to query, or that you want to change. Then follow it with the rights you want every user to have. You may use the initial letter of the following rights:

ALL

Allows all eight of the following rights to users.

Supervisory

Gives users supervisory rights to the path or the file.

Read

Allows users to open and read files.

Write

Allows users to open files and write to them.

Create

Gives users the ability to create new files and to write to the files they've created.

Erase

Permits users to delete files, directories or subdirectories.

Modify

Allows users to change the attributes and/or the names of files, directories and subdirectories.

File scan

Shows the users the directory listing if they want to see it.

Access control

Allows users to modify trustee assignments and their inherited rights. If a user has Access control capability, they can still only affect the rights they have been given.

Nothing

Revokes all rights except supervisory rights.

Using ALLOW

ALLOW by itself will simply tell you the rights that you are allowed in a given file or directory. You can follow it with a file name or a directory name for information about that specific item. If you have the necessary rights to a file or directory, you can also give those rights to someone else. A supervisor can remove rights to a file or directory. Using the N option will remove all rights to the directory for all users who are not supervisors. If you follow ALLOW with an explicit list of rights (from those above) users will be granted only those rights. This means that any additional rights they may have that are not in the list you are entering will be removed.

Here are some examples of how ALLOW might be used:

```
ALLOW SYS:DATA/GOSSIP TO INHERIT R F
```

This will allow all users to look at the directory listing in the DATA/GOSSIP subdirectory, and to read any files that might be there. If some of those users had Write or Create rights to this subdirectory, that capability would be removed.

```
ALLOW DATA/GOSSIP N
```

This command will eliminate all rights for all users except the supervisor.

ATOTAL

This command is unchanged for NetWare 386.

ATTACH

This command has been changed only to the extent required to allow encrypted passwords and to support up to 250 users per server. There are no changes in the manner in which this command is used from its description in Chapter 7.

BIND

Format:

BIND protocol [TO] driver [dparameter(s)] [pparameter(s)]

Command Function:

BIND is used to link LAN drivers into NetWare for the support of the network interface cards installed in the server. BIND will support multiple cards, but you must use the driver parameters (dparameter) to tell BIND about them. At this point, the protocol will always be IPX, but Novell will be shipping protocol drivers for TCP/IP and others. Only a few network interface card drivers are supplied by Novell. The others must be obtained from the manufacturers of the cards or separately from Novell.

If you have more than one network interface card installed in the server, you must list the appropriate driver parameter after the BIND command. You have the following list to choose from, but you will not need to use all of these for any card. You should only choose the parameter that makes the card different, such as the DMA channel, interrupt level, memory address, etc.

DMA=n   This identifies the DMA channel that the board will be using. Replace n with the proper channel number.

INT=n   The interrupt level is used by some cards, especially Ethernet cards, as an identifier. You should make sure that this number will not conflict with other devices, such as serial ports, hard disks, and so forth, that are installed in the file server. Replace n with the proper interrupt level.

MEM=n   Many cards, including some ARCnet cards, use a specific memory address. Replace n with the proper address.

PORT=n   Some boards communicate through an I/O port. Use this parameter for those network interface cards. Replace n with the port address number.

SLOT=n   Network cards installed in Microchannel-based file servers are identified by their slot number. As the new EISA machines began to show up, it may be that they also have their boards identified this way. Replace n with the slot number.

Protocol Parameter

The following protocol parameter may also be used:

NET = n   This allows the file server to identify which physical cabling system it is using. If the network already has a number assigned to the cable that is being used, then replace n with that number. If this is the first server on this cabling segment, then assign n a unique hexadecimal number.

Using BIND

Normally, BIND is run as a part of the file server's AUTOEXEC file. You can run it from the file server console if needed, however. An example of a typical BIND command follows:

```
BIND IPX to NE2000
```

You can follow this with any parameters you need. For example:

```
BIND IPX to TOKEN DMA=5 NET=10
```

This would tell NetWare that you wanted to use a Token Ring card, and you wanted the DMA channel set to five, and it would be attached to network number ten.

BINDFIX

This command is unchanged in syntax from earlier versions of NetWare.
WARNING: Some earlier versions of BINDFIX would corrupt the bindery on NetWare 286 file servers, making the file server useless. Unless you are confident that your copy of BINDFIX has been updated, do not use this utility with any server on which NetWare 286 resides.

BINDREST

This command is unchanged from earlier versions of NetWare, except that support for password encryption and support for the NetWare 386 bindery has been added. There is no change in the syntax from that discussed earlier.

BROADCAST

The BROADCAST command is identical to the version in NetWare 286.

CAPTURE

The CAPTURE command has been changed to support encrypted passwords and to support the NetWare 386 print server facility; however, there are no changes in the syntax from the earlier versions.

CASTOFF

The CASTOFF command is identical to the version in NetWare 286.

CASTON

The CASTON command is identical to the version in NetWare 286.

CHKVOL

CHKVOL has had support for larger volumes added, but there have been no changes in the syntax or usage from NetWare 286.

CHKDIR

Format:

CHKDIR [path]

Command Function:

The CHKDIR command allows you to check a volume or directory path for the amount of space in use and available. The package displays the following statistics about the target path or volume:

Directory space limits—How much space is available for *your* use on the file server, volume and directory. This may be less than the total available space.

Storage capacity—How much *total* space is available on the file server, volume or directory.

Space in use—The number of kilobytes in use already on the volume and directory.

A typical example would be:

```
CHKDIR F:
```

This would show you the statistics on the portion of the file server that is assigned as drive F: on the file server.

CLEAR STATION

Format:

CLEAR STATION n

Command Function:

The CLEAR STATION command allows the supervisor to immediately drop a workstation from the network, regardless of what the workstation might be doing. If the station is involved in a transaction, the files are closed in their current state, and the temporary files removed. You might want to do this if a workstation began to malfunction and in the process began to tie up the network with meaningless requests. If the work station is logged in to a single server, they will need to log in again. If they are connected to multiple servers, the drive mappings for the cleared server will disappear.

Using CLEAR STATION

```
CLEAR STATION 10
```

This command will immediately drop the connection with work station 10. You will need to use the correct station number, which you can find with the MONITOR console display, or with USERLIST.

CLS

Command Format:

CLS

Command Function:

CLS clears the console screen. If you'd rather, you can use the OFF command to do the same thing.

COLORPAL

Command Format:

COLORPAL

Command Function:

COLORPAL will allow you to change the colors in the NetWare menus to some that you like better. It will affect all of the menus on the system. If you have a monochrome monitor, you should approach this command with caution, because some combinations of colors on some monitors can result in the text and background looking the same, which in turn makes it impossible to use anything. There is no way to predict exactly what combinations will cause this, since the effect is dependent on the monitor and the video adapter.

Normally, the menus all use the default colors in NetWare. When an individual user runs COLORPAL, it will change only the colors of the menus they create. To change the colors of the standard NetWare menus, the supervisor will have to change the system's default colors.

The COLORPAL command uses NetWare menus to operate. For further information on menus, see the menu instructions in Chapter 8. Make sure you remember to save your changes when exiting the menu.

CONFIG

Command Format:

CONFIG

Command Function:

The CONFIG utility shows the current configuration of the NetWare 386 file server. You might want to use this command prior to making changes to the server so that you will know the current settings before you have to change them to support file server changes. CONFIG will give you the following information:

File server name
Internal network number of the file server
LAN drivers that are currently loaded
Hardware settings on all network boards. This will allow you to install additional boards without creating a conflict in settings.
Node addresses of the network interface cards
Communications protocol(s) bound to the network interface cards
Network number(s) of the cabling attached to the file server.

There are no parameters or arguments that follow CONFIG. It only applies to the server from which it is run. If you need information about additional network numbers, disk drivers or loadable modules, you will have to use the DISPLAY NETWORKS, INSTALL, and MONITOR commands respectively.

DISABLE LOGIN

This command is unchanged from the previous version of NetWare.

DISABLE TTS

This command is unchanged from the previous version of NetWare.

DISKSET

Command Format:

LOAD [path] DISKSET

Command Function:

DISKSET is a loadable module that is used to set up and install external hard disks attached to a disk coprocessor board. This utility allows a network installer to save configuration information prior to installing a NetWare Ready hard disk, to place disk configuration information into the DCB's EEPROM, and to create or change disk configuration information where necessary. The operation of the DISKSET module is beyond the scope of this book, and the command itself should only be used by qualified, experienced installers who have been through the proper training.

DISMOUNT

Command Format:

DISMOUNT volume

Command Function:

The DISMOUNT function allows you to take a volume out of service so that you can perform maintenance without taking the server down. Once you have run DISMOUNT, users will not have access to the volume. You would do this if you needed to make a repair on the file system, add disk drivers and the like. You replace "volume," above, with the actual name of the volume you want to dismount.

DISPLAY NETWORKS

Command Format:

DISPLAY NETWORKS

Command Function:

You can see all of the networks that the router in your file server knows about with the DISPLAY NETWORKS command. When you run the command, you will be shown a listing with network number and the number of intervening networks.

DISPLAY SERVERS

Format:

DISPLAY SERVERS

Command Function:

This command is similar to the DISPLAY NETWORKS command above, except that you get a listing of all servers that the router is aware of, along with the number of any intervening networks.

DOWN

This command, which shuts down the file server, is unchanged from the previous version of NetWare.

DSPACE

Command Format:

DSPACE

Command Function:

This is a menu utility that allows the supervisor to set limits on the amount of space available to a user. You can limit space either in a directory or a volume. To use this command, refer to the instructions on using menu utilities elsewhere in this book.

ENABLE LOGIN

This command, which permits user logins, is unchanged from the previous version of NetWare.

ENABLE TTS

This command is unchanged from the previous version of NetWare.

EXIT

Command Format:

EXIT

Command Function:

The EXIT command returns you to MS-DOS after you have shut down the file server by using the DOWN command. If you have used the REMOVE DOS command, then EXIT will not work.

ENDCAP

This command is unchanged from the previous version of NetWare.

FCONSOLE

Command Format:

FCONSOLE

Command Function:

FCONSOLE is the NetWare file server console. The primary changes from NetWare 286 are the ability to support encrypted passwords and the ability to handle a greater number of workstations. In addition, FCONSOLE will now allow you to purge files that have been erased but not removed, and it will provide LAN driver information.

As you will recall from the previous chapter, NetWare 386 flags a file as erased, but does not actually remove it from the file server's disk until all other available space is used up. The ability to purge these files results in their removal from the disk so that they cannot be recovered. The use of the FCONSOLE menu system remains unchanged from the previous versions, with the exception of offering choices for the new capabilities.

FILER

This menu utility remains unchanged from the previous version of NetWare except for the ability to support the new file attributes, rights, and disk size under NetWare 386. The syntax is the same as it was in earlier versions, and the menu works in the same fashion.

FLAG

Command Format:

FLAG [path (or filename) [option]]

Command Function:

You use FLAG to change the attributes of a file. The command is used exactly as it was in Chapter 7, but the options are different now, because the attribute list in NetWare 386 is also different. The new list of options follows:

Read Only	Shareable
Hidden	SYstem
Transactional	Purge
Read Audit	Write Audit
Copy Inhibit	Delete Inhibit
Rename Inhibit	**ALL**
Normal	SUBdirectory

In addition to the change in options, FLAG now allows you to add or delete options to a file. You can, for example, add the Purge attribute to a file by using FLAG +P. You can delete an existing option in the same way. For example, removing the Transactional attribute would be done by using this syntax: FLAG −T. The + and − constants can be used in conjunction with any option except Normal, ALL and SUBdirectory.

FLAGDIR

Command Format:

FLAGDIR [path[options]]

Command Function:

FLAGDIR works like FLAG, above, except it changes the attributes of a directory. The syntax is unchanged from the preceding version, except that the option list has changed slightly to reflect the new attributes supported by NetWare 386. The options are:

Normal	Delete Inhibit
Hidden	Rename Inhibit
SYstem	**HELP**
Purge	

GRANT

Command Format:

GRANT rights [FOR path] TO [USER (or GROUP)] name

Command Function:

As above, the only changes with GRANT are those that reflect the changes in the rights that are available in NetWare 386. The syntax of the command has not changed from that found elsewhere in this book. The new rights supported by GRANT are:

ALL	**C**reate
No Rights	**E**rase
Supervisory	**M**odify
Read	**F**ile Scan
Write	**A**ccess Control

As with other command options, only the letters in bold should be used.

HELP

Command Format:

HELP

Command Function:

NetWare 386's new HELP facility is really a complete set of on line documentation. To enter the HELP program, you only need to enter the word, and you will be led through a learning environment that presents the text in windows and allows you to explore related topics. You move around and among the windows of the HELP program using the standard editing keys on your keyboard. You can control direction with the arrow keys, for example. If you follow the HELP command with the name of a specific command that you need to learn more about, you will be presented with the information on that command.

Some subjects are linked together with square blocks called Link Tokens. If you go to these, you will find information on a topic related to the kind of help you are currently using. You can move between the Link Tokens by using the <TAB> key. HELP also includes a search facility that will allow you to search the entire database for a particular word or phrase. The searches can include a specific word or phrase, or it can contain proximity searches, wild cards, and combinations of words.

The HELP facility includes help on itself, so you can always find out how to use it. In short, this is a point and shoot menu system, so all you have to do to look at a topic is move the highlight to the subject in question, and press <ENTER>. The HELP facility will give you complete examples of each command and function in NetWare 386, along with a number of examples to illustrate proper use.

INSTALL

Command Format:

LOAD [path] INSTALL [parameter]

Command Function:

The INSTALL loadable module is one of the more useful system administration tools available in NetWare 386. You use INSTALL during the initial setup of the file server, and then you continue to use it when you reconfigure the server or install additional hardware or implement additional functions.

INSTALL performs a variety of functions that have become necessary with the increased capabilities of NetWare 386. Those functions include the ability to add disks to an existing server, to mirror and unmirror disks, and to create and modify volumes and partitions. In addition, INSTALL will perform a surface test on a new hard disk and then format the disk.

The INSTALL program is based on the NetWare menu system. You can find additional information on how to use NetWare menus elsewhere in this book. Here is a brief description of the functions that INSTALL will support:

- Add a Hard Disk to the Network—When you need to add more space to the network, you can use INSTALL. You do this by designating a partition on the new hard disk and assigning it to a volume that needs more space. As you will recall, a NetWare volume can now span multiple hard disks. If you need to replace, repair or format a hard disk, INSTALL will allow this also.
- Create and Delete Partitions—Install will allow you to add partitions to existing or newly-added hard disks, or to remove existing partitions. You might want to do this if your needs change, and you want to rearrange the manner in which your disks are divided.
- Mirror or Unmirror Hard Disks—Because NetWare 386 supports disk mirroring, you need to have a way to tell it to begin mirroring a disk. This will happen when you start the file server up for the first time, and whenever you need to add additional disks that need to be mirrored. You will also need this capability when you replace one hard disk in a mirrored set.
- Create or Modify Volumes—As we discussed earlier in this book, NetWare identifies its hard disks by volume names. While a volume

can span more than one hard disk with NetWare 386, you still need a way to create new volumes, or to change existing volumes. You might, for example, add a new disk, and either call that a new volume or add its capacity to the available space on an existing volume.

- Create, Delete or Modify Boot Files—NetWare 386 uses a pair of text tiles, AUTOEXEC.NCF and STARTUP.NCF in much the same way that your MS-DOS computer uses AUTOEXEC.BAT. You can use INSTALL to make changes in these files. Of course, like AUTOEXEC.BAT, you can also use any ASCII text editor.

- Format a Hard Disk—While some hard disks come already formatted for Novell NetWare, normally you will need to format them before you can use them. INSTALL will do this for you.

- Run the Surface Test—The condition of the hard disk surface is critical to the operation of a file server. For that reason, you need to do a comprehensive test of the disk's recording surface. Many disks are sold with this already done, but if it hasn't been, you can do it with INSTALL.

- Load NetWare 386 Disks—Install will also copy the contents of the NetWare 386 distribution disks to the file server's hard disks when you set up the file server, or later, as you need to add more capabilities.

LISTDIR

The LISTDIR command has not changed since the previous version of NetWare.

LOAD

Command Format:

LOAD [path] module [parameter(s)]

Command Function:

The LOAD command is used to invoke the loadable modules in NetWare 386. Loadable modules include LAN and hard disk drivers, name space and NLM utilities. Loadable modules are terminate and stay resident programs that reside in the file server and can be loaded and unloaded as needed. In addition, you can load several types of loadable modules at the same time. If the loadable modules are utilities, you can switch between them as needed.

You have to load one loadable module at a time, but you can load as many as you need to support your requirements, provided you have enough memory. Unless you specify otherwise, LOAD expects to find its loadable modules in the System directory of volume SYS.

Specific instructions for loading each loadable module are included in the entry in this chapter for that module. For example, the instructions for LOAD MONITOR will be found in the MONITOR heading of this chapter.

LOGIN

Format:

LOGIN [/option(s)] [server/[name]] [script options]

Command Function:

The LOGIN command is unchanged in this version, with the exception that you can now add script parameters. The script parameters will allow you to log on with a special login script, rather than the default login script or system login script. The script options follow:

/Script

Use this option to indicate an alternate login script to use rather than the system and user login scripts on the file server. You will need to follow the /S with a complete path to the script you want to use.

/NoAttach

The NoAttach option allows you to run a login script without logging out of the server and logging in or attaching again.

/Clearscreen

This option clears your screen immediately after you enter your password.

LOGOUT

The LOGOUT command is unchanged from the previous version of NetWare.

MAKEUSER

While there are a few differences in the contents of the user files that MAKEUSER creates and processes in order to reflect the changed user rights in NetWare 386, the syntax described in Chapter 8 is unchanged.

MAP

The syntax of the MAP command is unchanged from the previous version of NetWare.

MENU

The syntax of the menu utility is unchanged from the previous version of NetWare.

MODULES

Command Format:

MODULES

Command Function:

The MODULES command is used to display the name and description of all loadable modules currently in use by the file server.

MONITOR

Command Format:

LOAD [path] MONITOR [parameter]

Command Function:

The MONITOR utility has changed greatly from its existence as a console command to menu-driven loadable module. The new version of MONITOR gives you a standard NetWare interface that you can use to find out the following:

- File server activity
- Utilization
- Users connected and their activity
- Disk drives attached
- Volumes on resident drives
- LAN drivers loaded
- NetWare loadable modules currently in use by the file server and the amount of memory they require
- File lock status
- Memory status

In addition, you can use MONITOR as a way to lock the console. MONITOR has two parameters that you can use to affect the operation of the MONITOR program. They are:

ns   no saver—Turns off the screen saver utility on the file server.
nh   No help—Keeps the MONITOR help file from being loaded. This saves the memory that the help file would take otherwise.

Unless you disable it (see above) the MONITOR program has a screen saver that clears the screen after one minute if the console is locked or after ten minutes if the console is not locked. When the screen is cleared, it is replaced with an "activity snake" that moves around the screen. The snake's speed and the length of its tail reflects the activity of the server. The more active the server is, the faster the snake moves and the longer its tail grows.

The NetWare 386 version of MONITOR does *not* provide the familiar screen divided into six squares for monitoring the activity of six stations at a time. Instead, it is based on the standard windowing interface of a NetWare menu. You can monitor any one station as you desire, and you can monitor the activity of the LAN as a whole.

When MONITOR loads initially, it presents a screen that gives some basic information about the current NetWare session. This information will include the amount of time that the file server has been operational, the status of cache buffers, current server utilization, and the status of the network and the attached disks. You will also be presented with a standard NetWare menu that will allow you to access the functions listed earlier. You use these menus following the directions for menu utilities in Chapter 8.

MONITOR is a terminate and stay resident program, which means that you can load it into the file server's memory, and then exit with the <ALT> <ESCAPE> key sequence. This will bring you to another menu that will give you the option of entering a different TSR, or of going to the console command prompt. You can reenter MONITOR at any time with the same <ALT> <ESCAPE> key sequence. You can also leave MONITOR by choosing the appropriate choice from the main menu, or by pressing <ESC> until you exit.

MOUNT

Command Format:

MOUNT volume
or
MOUNT ALL

Command Function:

You use the MOUNT command to make a volume attached to the file
server available to the network users. You might do this if you had just
created a new volume, or if you had earlier dismounted a volume for
repair or backup, and want to make it available again. You can perform
the MOUNT command while the server is up and running.

If you want to MOUNT a specific volume, then you follow the MOUNT
command with the name of the volume you want to mount. You can also
mount every volume attached to the server by using the MOUNT ALL
command. If you tell the file server to mount a volume that is already
mounted, the file server will tell you that this is the case.

NAME

Command Format:

NAME

Command Function:

You use the NAME command to find out the name of the server you are presently using. When you run the command, you will receive a message telling you what server you are using.

NBACKUP

Command Format:

NBACKUP

Command Function:

NBACKUP is Novell's network backup utility. It will allow you to back up the network file server's disk, including system files and the bindery data. You can also use NBACKUP to perform backups on servers running NetWare 2.15 or even the local hard disk on your workstation. NBACKUP will work with Macintosh and other non-DOS directories and files.

There are a couple of important rules that you must observe if you are going to have successful backups. First, MS-DOS directories and files must have valid DOS names if they are to be backed up. You will remember that earlier versions of NetWare allowed names that were longer than normally allowed by DOS. In addition, you must restore to exactly the same environment that you were running when you backed up. This means that you can only restore a local drive backup to a local drive. Likewise, if you were running a Macintosh VAP or had a Macintosh volume mounted, the conditions must be the same when you restore.

You can back up to any DOS device. This includes removable hard disks and optical disks. You can also back up to floppy disks at the workstation (assuming that you are extremely patient) or to a tape drive. NetWare 386 also supports backups to some non-DOS devices such as tape drives for which special software drivers exist.

NBACKUP is a menu driven utility that will prompt you for the appropriate action. You will have to choose between backing up your entire server in a single session, or whether to do it in multiple sessions. If you choose a single session, you will need to be sure that you have sufficient space on the DOS device that is holding the backup data. Multiple sessions allow you to back up the bindery information and the directories separately.

When you enter the NBACKUP utility, you will have to choose what type of device will be receiving the backup information. Once that is done, you may be prompted for items such as directory names and session descriptions. You may use the default values. You will also have the opportunity to decide whether to back up all files on the server or only those that have been modified since the last backup, as well as specific files to include or exclude. Normally, you will be either doing a full backup or a backup of only the files that have changed.

NBACKUP will not backup system or hidden files from NetWare version 2.15. If you are backing up from such a file server, you will have to change the attributes of system and hidden files if you want them backed up. NBACKUP will back up hidden and system files from NetWare 386.

Proceeding with the backup session is as easy as following the prompts. Normally, the backup session is quite fast, and you will be done in a few minutes. Of course, the backup of a large server will take longer than that of a small server, and a partial backup will take less time than a full backup.

NBACKUP creates a text file called the Error Log while it is proceeding with the backup. In this file, you will find a series of messages if there were problems during the backup. Not all of these messages are serious problems. Some merely indicate that a file was not backed up because it was in use, which you would expect of a few system files on NetWare 2.15.

NBACKUP will also restore previously backed up data from disks where it is stored or from a tape device. To start the restoration, you will choose the "Restore" menu from the Main Menu. That will lead you to the restore operation, and among the choices will be one that will start the restoration process. Restore allows you to choose whether or not you want to overwrite existing directories and files.

NCOPY

Command Format:

NCOPY [path1] [TO]path2] [option(s)]

Command Function:

You can use NCOPY to copy network files from one place to another. To use the command, you replace the name of the file and path for the file you want moved with path1, and the destination with path2. You don't need to use the word "TO" but you can if it makes you feel better. The options allow you to further modify the copy process in the following ways:

/Subdirectories	Use this if you want to copy subdirectories.
/Empty subdirectories	This option allows you to also copy empty subdirectories. This option MUST be used with the /S option.
/Force sparse files	Forces the operating system to write to sparse files.
/Preserve file attributes	Makes sure that any existing file attributes remain with the file when it is copied. The Purge attribute is not copied. NetWare specific attributes will not be copied to a local drive.

The NCOPY command is otherwise like the MS-DOS copy command, and with the exception of supporting options, it has the same syntax. NCOPY supports wild card characters such as * and ? if you want to copy multiple files.

NDIR

Command Format:

NDIR path [option(s)]

Command Function:

The NDIR command's syntax is unchanged from that discussed in Chapter 7. The changes Novell introduced to this command include the ability to support Macintosh and other non-DOS file types, new rights, and the changes in the disk size available under NetWare 386. NDIR now also has an imbedded interactive help file that will assist you in using the program.

NPRINT

The NPRINT command uses the same syntax as that used in the previous version of NetWare.

OFF

Command Format:

OFF

Command Function:

OFF is used to clear information from the file server's screen. It is entered at the console's keyboard.

PAUDIT

Command Format:

PAUDIT

Command Function:

PAUDIT is used to display the accounting audit trail. You must have Novell Accounting Services installed on your file server for this to work. The accounting system keeps track of user activity on the file server, including login and logout, connect time, and disk activity. You can print the results of PAUDIT by redirecting output to a file using the MS-DOS redirection capability, and then printing the resulting text file. An example of this process would look like this:

```
PAUDIT > printfile
NPRINT printfile
```

PCONSOLE

Command Format:

PCONSOLE

Command Function:

The PCONSOLE command is very similar to the same command in NetWare version 2.15. The biggest difference is that the new version now supports remote print servers directly, instead of as a third-party solution in earlier versions of NetWare. Incidentally, as of this writing, Novell has begun shipping print server support to purchasers of NetWare version 2.15C also.

Print server support is the only difference that the user will see in this utility, which is a NetWare menu-based program. Otherwise, it runs as described in Chapter 8. Installing a print server is a complex process that must be performed by the system administrator and, as such, is beyond the scope of this book.

It's important to point out, however, that there are some significant decisions that must be made if you are considering using a print server on your network. First, you will have a choice of using a dedicated print server or a nondedicated print server. As you can tell from the names, a dedicated print server performs only that function. It is best used when there will be heavy printing requirements and several printers. A nondedicated print server can also be used as a workstation, but because the print server software takes up a portion of the workstation's memory, not all software will be able to be used in that workstation.

It is not necessary to use a high performance computer as the platform for the print server. Even computers such as IBM-PC/XT clones that are otherwise obsolete will work fine in this application. Setting up the print server requires strict observance to the step-by-step procedure in the NetWare 386 Installation Manual.

PCONSOLE also allows you to control network printing. You can see what jobs are scheduled for which print queue, and you can remove jobs or change priorities if you need to do so. You can also see information about network printing, including the print server and/or printer attached to each queue. That's helpful, because if you find a printer with a problem (which you can tell if there's a sudden increase in the number of print jobs in the queue) you can at least tell specifically which printer it is. The single biggest reason for problems with print queues seems to be an "out-of-paper" condition on a laser printer.

Because PCONSOLE is a NetWare menu program, you can operate it by following the directions in Chapter 8.

PRINTCON

Command Format:

PRINTCON

Command Function:

The only changes in PRINTCON for NetWare 386 were those required to support a larger number of users and to support encrypted passwords. There is also now support for print servers in PRINTCON. The use of PRINTCON is unchanged.

PRINTDEF

This command, which allows you to set up printer definitions for the printers attached to the LAN, in unchanged in use from the previous version of NetWare.

PROTOCOL

Command Format:

PROTOCOL [REGISTER] [protocol] [media] [id number]

Command Function:

The PROTOCOL command is run from the file server console, and is used to display the protocol identification numbers that are registered with the file server. Protocol identification numbers reflect the communications protocol and the media type.

NetWare currently supports IPX, AARP and Appletalk as protocols. You will need to find the protocol ID number of additional protocols in the documentation for the protocol you are planning to install. You must also list the media type, which would be the type of LAN that you are adding a protocol to. Examples of this might be RXNET or TOKEN. If you were going to add a new protocol called TCP to your Ethernet LAN, for example, you might enter the following after you had used LOAD to install the loadable module for TCP:

```
PROTOCOL REGISTER TCP ETHERNET_802.3 999.
```

In this example, TCP is the new protocol name, Ethernet_802.3 is the media type, and 999 is the protocol ID number. Once you do this, you must BIND the TCP protocol to Ethernet_802.3 using the BIND command found earlier in this chapter.

PSC

Command Format:

PSC PS = printserver P = printer_number flag(s)

Command Function:

PSC performs on the command line many of the same functions that are available with PRINTCON. You can use it to see the status of a print server attached to the network and their printers, and the print server operator can use it to control the operations of those same printer servers and printers. To use PSC you must replace printserver with the name of a print server, and you must replace printer_number with the number of a printer that is attached to that print server. The flags are listed below:

STATus	FormFeed
PAUse	**MO**unt form = n
ABort	**PRI**vate
STOp	**SH**ared
STARt	CancelDown
Mark	

Most of these commands are self-explanatory. PRIvate allows you to keep network users from using a printer attached to your workstation. SHared cancels the PRIvate command. If you ABort or STOp a print job, you have the ability to keep the document in the print queue by following with the K option.

PSERVER

Command Format:

PSERVER [file server] [print server]

LOAD PSERVER print server

Command Function:

As you can tell from the format above, PSERVER exists as both a DOS executable file and as a loadable module. You can handle a print server on the network with either, but using the loadable module means that you will end up with a nondedicated server, and using the DOS executable will mean that you will have a dedicated server.

Other than telling PSERVER which print server you want to use (and possibly what file server it's attached to with the DOS command) there are no arguments. The print server software loads, and you are presented with a screen showing eight blocks that contain information about print servers. In the case of the DOS command, the print server status screen will show up on the workstation that's being used as the dedicated server. If you are using the loadable module, the screen will show up on the file server.

The loadable module is handled like other loadable modules that will reside in the file server's memory. You can leave the print server status screen at any time and you can remove the module from memory if you need to. The only way to leave the print server function on the dedicated print server is to reboot the workstation that it is running on.

The status screen will show you the current operating state of each printer connected to the print server. If you are printing, the status block for that printer will say what you are printing. Otherwise, you will be told that the printer is waiting for a job or that it's not connected.

When you are running in nondedicated mode, the workstation must run the RPRINTER program before your workstation can function as a print server. If you define new printers, you must UNLOAD the loadable module and then reload it so that it can load the new printer information.

PURGE

Command Format:

PURGE [filename or path] [/ALL]

Command Function:

As you will recall in the last chapter, NetWare 386 now does not actually erase a file from the hard disk unless it's told explicitly to do so. The PURGE utility is the program that does the removing. PURGE will remove files and directories that are marked for deletion, and recovery of the information will be impossible.

If you simply run PURGE by itself from the root directory, it will remove all erased but recoverable files anywhere on the disk. If you follow PURGE with the name of a file, it will purge a specific file. If you enter it from within a directory, it will purge all recoverable files within that directory. Adding the /ALL switch will also clear out all subdirectories below the current directory.

The system supervisor can PURGE files from anywhere on the disk. Other users can PURGE only files that they own. In some cases, such as when the disk is getting full, NetWare will purge files itself, starting with the oldest. Purge is usually used to insure that sensitive files are not available for recovery.

REMOVE

Command Format:

REMOVE [USER or GROUP] name [[FROM]path] [option(s)]

Command Function:

The remove command remains substantially unchanged from the previous version, with the exception that there are now two options that are available to the system supervisor to support changes in the rights assignments in NetWare 386. Because of the fact that you can now have inherited rights, you can also now remove trusteeship from an entire path. Also, the ability to assign trusteeships to a specific file means that you can also remove them from a specific file. The options are as follows:

[-SUBdirectories]

This option allows you to remove trustee rights from all of the subdirectories in a path.

[-Files]

This option allows you to remove a trustee from a file or group of files.

To use REMOVE you must have access control to the area being affected. This means that you must be the supervisor or workgroup manager, or must otherwise have been granted access rights. You can also remove a trustee from a directory or a file by using SYSCON or MAKEUSER. You can use REVOKE to remove trustee rights to a directory or a file, but even though the rights may have been revoked, the trustee's name will remain on the trustee list. REMOVE will take both the trustee (and the actual rights) off the list altogether.

The arguments USER and GROUP above are optional, except in the case where a user and a group have the same name. In that case, you must specify which one you are using. For example, if you have a user named "Fred" you can insert the following:

```
REMOVE FRED
```

In the case above, Fred will be removed from the trustee list of the directory that you are currently in. If you follow it with the -SUB, then he will also be removed from all of the subdirectories of the directory you are currently in.

If you wish, you can specify a particular directory of volume:

```
REMOVE FRED FROM F:SYSTEM
```

A group is removed in the same manner, such as with the group "janitors" below:

```
REMOVE JANITORS
```

If you had both a user and a group named "janitors" you would need to specify which you were using:

```
REMOVE USER JANITORS
```

REMOVE DOS

Command Format:

REMOVE DOS

Command Function:

You can regain the memory taken up by DOS to the file server cache with the REMOVE DOS command. This command is entered at the file server console, and is only needed if the available memory is getting low. If you remove DOS, you will not be able to EXIT to DOS from the file server console after you DOWN the file server.

RENDIR

Command Format:

RENDIR

Command Function:

The RENDIR command, which is used for renaming directories, has the same syntax that it had in the previous version of NetWare.

RESET ROUTER

Command Format:

RESET ROUTER

Command Function:

The file server's router table may become corrupted if several other file servers or bridges on the network go down. When the command is issued, the file server advertises for updates to its router table to the other servers and bridges on the network. Normally, the file server will update its router tables every two minutes.

REVOKE

Command Format:

REVOKE rights [FOR path] FROM [USER or GROUP] name [option(s)]

Command Function:

REVOKE operates in the same manner as it did in previous versions of NetWare. There are some differences because the rights have changed and because there are now inherited rights. As in the case of REMOVE above, you now have the option of revoking rights from specific files or from subdirectories of the current directory. The rights that you can revoke are the same as those discussed in the last chapter. They are:

ALL	Erase
Supervisory	Modify
Read	File scan
Write	Access Control
Create	

As above, you also have the option to specify subdirectories or files:

[**-SUB**directories]
[**-Files**]

You can also remove trustee rights with the SYSCON utility or with REMOVE. REVOKE will eliminate the specified rights from the user or group, but will not actually remove them from the list of trustees. In addition, REVOKE will let you control specific rights (as will SYSCON) while REMOVE simply removes the trustee and all the trustee's rights.

RIGHTS

Command Format:

RIGHTS path

Command Function:

The RIGHTS command, which will show you your rights in a specified area, has the same syntax as previous versions. Because the list of rights has changed, you will get a listing reflecting current rights for the specific file server involved.

RPRINTER

Command Format:

RPRINTER [print server] [printer number] [-r]

Command Function:

RPRINTER works with the PSERVER loadable module to allow a remote workstation to become a nondedicated print server. You run RPRINTER to connect the print server to a remote printer. You can specify those items if you know them, or you can run RPRINTER by itself, and you will get a menu to choose from. You can disconnect a remote printer with the -r option.

SALVAGE

Command Format:

SALVAGE

Command Function:

SALVAGE is used to recover files that have been erased, as long as they have not been PURGEd. SALVAGE presents a menu interface that allows you to view deleted files and decide if you want to recover them or remove them from the server entirely. When you erase a file that is located in a directory, it remains in that directory unless the directory is also deleted. In that case, deleted files are placed in the DELETED.SAV directory. In either case, they are available to SALVAGE.

SALVAGE is a standard NetWare menuing program. Refer elsewhere in this book for instructions on how to use NetWare menus. SALVAGE will show you a list of all deleted files, and give you the opportunity to mark the file by using the F5 key. A marked file can be recovered or purged.

SALVAGE also has other display and file management capabilities, including the ability to sort the file display. You will be presented with menu choices for each of these capabilities.

SEARCH

Command Format:

SEARCH [parameter]

Command Function:

The SEARCH command is used at the file server console to tell the file server where to find its loadable modules and .NCF batch files. Normally, the search path is set for the SYS:SYSTEM directory; however, you can add other directories to the list. There are two parameters that you can use to add or remove search paths from the list. They are:

ADD [number] [path]

You can use this parameter to add a new search path to the file server's list. If you follow ADD with a number, the search path is added at that number.

DEL [number]

This parameter will allow you to delete a specific search path. To find the number of the search path, first run SEARCH without options, and all of the search paths will be displayed along with their priority number. This is the number that you tell SEARCH to remove from the search path.

SECURE CONSOLE

Command Format:

SECURE CONSOLE

Command Function:

SECURE CONSOLE helps protect against the possibility of Trojan Horse loadable modules. While anyone can create a loadable module that would bring about a security violation, the SECURE CONSOLE command prevents their being loaded into the file server. It does not lock the console keyboard, although you can do that with the MONITOR loadable module. It does prevent loadable modules from being loaded from a directory other than SYS:SYSTEM. It also prevents entry into the OS debugger, and it removes DOS, so that a DOS program designed to access data on the NetWare hard disk cannot be used.

SECURE CONSOLE also prevents any user besides those with supervisory privileges from copying anything into the SYSTEM directory. Finally, SECURE CONSOLE prevents the date and time from being changed by anyone other than the system supervisor.

While SECURE CONSOLE is not a total solution to security, it does help prevent tampering and Trojan loadable modules. Additional security is gained by using the locking feature of MONITOR, by making sure that the file server is physically secure, and by making sure that more traditional security measures, such as passwords, are used. The SECURITY command will help make sure that proper security procedures are being followed.

SECURITY

Command Format:

SECURITY

Command Function:

The SECURITY command will check for, but not correct, potential security violations. The violations that it checks for include accounts with no password or an insecure password. Existing passwords are checked to make sure that they are changed often enough and not reused, and that the grace period after password change is not unlimited. Finally, SECURITY will report any users who have Supervisor equivalence or who have been granted access rights to the root directory of a volume, and it will report unnecessary rights that have been granted in the standard directories.

Because SECURITY will frequently find enough of such violations that there will be more than one screen full of information, normally you should redirect the output to a file, using the DOS redirection capability. Once the file is created, you can print it using the NPRINT utility.

SEND

Command Format:

SEND "message" [TO] [server/][USER or GROUP or CONNECTION or CONSOLE]

Command Function:

With the exception of adding the ability to send to the console or to a connection number, the SEND command has not changed from earlier versions. Users who do not want to be interrupted by messages from other users should use CASTOFF ALL.

SERVER

Command Format:

SERVER [parameter]

Command Function:

As you will recall from the previous chapter, NetWare 386 now boots with MS-DOS, from which the SERVER command is run. SERVER, in turn, installs NetWare 386 on the file server. SERVER normally resides on the floppy disk or on the hard disk segment that you use to boot MS-DOS initially. When SERVER executes, it performs a number of functions as it is loading NetWare 386. Those functions are:

- Execution of STARTUP.NCF—This is the file server's initial start-up batch file. It tells NetWare to load the disk drivers.
- Mounting of volume SYS—Once NetWare 386 knows it has a disk drive, you have to tell it to mount one of them. The first to be mounted is SYS.
- Execution of AUTOEXEC.NCF—This provides the remainder of the data necessary to bring up the NetWare 386 file server. AUTOEXEC.NCF contains the file server name and LAN drivers, as well as any NLMs that must be present at startup. The rest of the volumes are mounted, and any other commands that are to be executed on startup are executed.

The parameters control the operation of the SERVER command as NetWare 386 is loaded. You can tell NetWare to load an alternate startup file, or none at all. The parameters include:

-S file

The -S parameter tells NetWare to use an alternate startup file name. Replace file with the name of the file that you wish to use instead of STARTUP.NCF.

-NS

This parameter tells NetWare not to use either STARTUP.NCF or AUTOEXEC.NCF. You might want to use this when you are installing a new cabling system, and need to change the file server boot process.

-NA

The -NA parameter tells NetWare not to use the AUTOEXEC.NCF file.

-C cache_size

This parameter allows you to change the size of the cache buffer. This size must be equal to or smaller than the block allocation size, or SERVER won't mount that volume.

SESSION

Command Format:

SESSION

Command Function:

SESSION is the NetWare user's console. It allows users to perform common functions relating to NetWare and networking in general. The menu choices available under SESSION are all duplicated as command line utilities or NetWare commands, but SESSION provides a menu-operated way of making them work. This can be helpful, because some NetWare commands are less than intuitive, and a user who is not completely familiar with them is likely to feel intimidated.

SESSION supports the following functions:

- Drive mapping and file server attachments—SESSION will allow you to view or change your drive mapping, your default drives, and your file server attachment. You can use it to change or add servers, or to drop servers currently being used.
- View and send messages to groups and users—You can duplicate the capability of the SEND utility with this function. Instead of having to type out a command line, SESSION will prompt you for the information needed to send messages to users or to groups. You can also view the available groups and see which users are using the server.

SESSION is a NetWare menu program, so you will use it as you do the others that are described elsewhere in this book. Briefly, you can choose a menu item that presents the action you want to perform, and you will be presented either with an additional menu, or prompted for information to make the command work. You can leave the program by pressing <ESC> until you're asked if you want out.

SET

Command Format:

SET [parameter]

Command Function:

SET allows you to view or change operating system configuration parameters. The default parameters are set when the file server is installed, but you can use SET in some cases to improve the performance of the file server. Parameter changing by using SET must be done by an experienced system installer, and, as such, is beyond the scope of this book. You can, however, simply type SET into the console keyboard and see what the parameters are. If you follow SET with the name of a parameter, you will see the setting of that specific parameter. If you add a value to the parameter, and the value is one that is appropriate to the parameter being set, the parameter will be changed to the new value.

The values introduced into the system through the SET command are implemented immediately, but, unless the values are saved into the AUTOEXEC. NCF files the original values will be used the next time the server is booted. The complete list of parameters and acceptable limits are given in the NetWare 386 System Administration manual. Inexperienced administrators should approach changes through the use of SET with caution.

SET TIME

Command Format:

SET TIME [month/day/year] [hour:minute:second]

Command Function:

SET TIME is used to adjust the time and date settings of the file server's internal system clock. You can set either parameter or both at the same time, and you can set them in any order. Dates can be entered as slash-separated numerals, in traditional date format, or in military date format. Here are some typical examples:

```
SET TIME 23 March 1990
SET TIME 3/23/90 8:41 PM
SET TIME 20:41 March 23, 1990
```

If you just enter SET TIME by itself, NetWare will tell you the current time.

SETPASS

Command Format:

SETPASS [server]

Command Function:

You can change your password with SETPASS. If you add the name of a file server after the command, it will change the password on that file server, provided you are attached to it. Your password can be up to 127 characters long, and it cannot contain control characters. If you are attached to more than one file server with the same user name, you will have the opportunity to synchronize passwords on each server.

You will be prompted to enter your old password, and then the password that you want to be your new password. SETPASS requests your old password first to prevent your password from being changed by someone else if they should find your workstation unattended.

SETTTS

Command Format:

SETTTS [logical level[physical level]]

Command Function:

The syntax of SETTTS has not been changed from the previous version, except the levels now number 0 through 254 rather than 1 through 255. As before, dBASE III Plus version 1.0 with copy protection is the **only** commercial software package that requires the use of SETTTS.

SLIST

Command Format:

SLIST [server] [/Continuous]

Command Function:

SLIST, which lists the file servers on your LAN, has not had its syntax changed since the previous version of NetWare.

SMODE

Command Format:

SMODE [path [option] [/SUB]]

Command Function:

With the exception of the /SUB switch, SMODE has not been changed from the previous version of NetWare. SMODE specifies the method that a program will use to search for a data file. The /SUB switch specifies that all subdirectories of a specified directory will also be searched.

SPEED

Command Format:

SPEED

Command Function:

The SPEED command, when typed into the file server console, will report the speed at which the processor is running, as well as the type of processor and the number of wait states.

SPOOL

Command Format:

SPOOL n [TO] [QUEUE] name

Command Function:

Print spooler mappings can be displayed, as well as created or modified with the SPOOL command. SPOOL only requires that you specify the number (n) of the spooler and the name of the print queue for it to work. The words "TO" and "QUEUE" are not necessary, but can be used if they make you more comfortable. If you simply enter the word SPOOL, you will be shown the mappings. If you follow SPOOL with a spooler number and valid queue name, you will set up print spooling to that queue.

SYSCON

Command Format:

SYSCON

Command Function:

NetWare's system console is SYSCON. Although SYSCON is of most use to the system administrator, all users have access to it. SYSTIME will show file server information and allow users to change file servers. In addition, you can see lists both of all groups and of all individual users entitled to use the server. For users, the User Information choice is the most important, because this is where they are able to record their full name and to set their password. The group and user information will also show such diverse items as the list of workgroup managers and group ID numbers.

As you can see, SYSCON is rarely used by users other than the system administrator. While it might be interesting to see what the LAN address of the file server is, it's not the sort of information that most users frequently need.

The system administrator, on the other hand, will use SYSCON frequently. SYSCON will allow supervisors to install and modify the accounting system, add, change and delete users, groups and workgroup managers, and install user and system login files. The supervisor can use SYSCON to add individual new users, and to modify the trustee assignments of existing users. Most of the security settings, including allowed login locations, operating hours, disk space allocation, intruder detection, password requirements and rights assignments are (or can be) performed with SYSCON.

SYSCON is a standard NetWare menu program, and using it is like using all of the others described in this book. Refer to Chapter 8 for further information on using NetWare menus. Because SYSCON is intended primarily for the support of the system administrator, detailed descriptions of the operations are beyond the scope of this book. You will find, however, that you only have to contend with menu choices and prompts for specific information, so using the menus is not difficult. As in other NetWare menus, you can leave at any time by pressing the <ESC>key until you are asked if you want to leave SYSCON.

SYSTIME

Command Format:

SYSTIME [server]

Command Function:

SYSTIME, which reports the file server's time and date and then resets the workstation's time and date settings, is unchanged from previous versions.

TIME

Command Format:

TIME

Command Function:

TIME reports the file server's internal time and date, just as SYSTIME above does, but it does not reset the workstation's clock.

TLIST

Command Format:

TLIST [path [USERS or GROUPS]]

Command Function:

The syntax of TLIST, which shows you the trustee assignments of a user or a group, is unchanged from previous versions.

TRACK OFF

Command Format:

TRACK OFF

Command Function:

The console command TRACK OFF turns off the Router Tracking Screen which was turned on by TRACK ON. The Router Tracking Screen displays the network and server advertising packets on the file server console screen.

TRACK ON

Command Format:

TRACK ON

Command Function:

The console command TRACK ON turns on the Router Tracking Screen and makes it the active screen. The Router Tracking Screen displays the server and network advertising packets as they are received by the file server. You turn it off with the TRACK OFF console command.

UNBIND

Command Format:

UNBIND protocol [FROM] driver [parameter(s)]

Command Function:

UNBIND will remove a previously bound communications protocol from the LAN driver of a network interface card. You can also use UNBIND to change the network number assigned to your cabling plant. You only need to use the parameter for the driver when you have more than one network interface card of the same type in the file server. The parameter will be the same one you used when you bound the protocol originally (see BIND).

You can change the network number by first issuing the UNBIND command and then the BIND command. You will be prompted for the new network number. You will need to edit the AUTOEXEC.NCF file to reflect the new network number.

UNLOAD

Command Format:

UNLOAD module

Command Function:

You can remove a loadable module from the file server's memory with the UNLOAD command, which is typed into the console's keyboard, just as you used the LOAD command to put it into memory in the first place. You should be careful to have all users log off before you UNLOAD modules such as LAN drivers, disk drivers or name space drivers. Other loadable modules that do not affect user access to the file server can be unloaded at any time.

UPS

Command Format:

LOAD [path] UPS [type] [port] [discharge] [recharge]

Command Function:

NetWare 386 includes the ability to monitor the status of the uninterruptable power supply, but to do that you need a loadable module and you need to tell the module how to do the monitoring. This is the purpose of the UPS loadable module. You use LOAD to place UPS into the file server's memory. The path defaults to SYS:SYSTEM and the type assumes a disk coprocessor board. Before installing the UPS NLM, you will need to look at the documentation that came with your UPS, and with the UPS monitoring board (if they were sold separately), and determine the information needed below:

type = n

Replace n with one of the UPS interface board types below. Most monitor boards are either part of the DCB, or they are a keycard, since Novell NetWare required one of these until recently. If you try two and that doesn't work, you might find that you have a keycard, so try three, instead.

    1 = DCB
    2 = Standalone
    3 = Keycard
    4 = Mouse
    5 = Other

I/O Port = n

Replace the I/O Port number with the address that matches the jumper setting on your UPS monitor card. You will need to look at the card to see what this is. Mouse boards do not require a port number.

Discharge = n

This is your estimate of the time that the UPS can support the file server and anything else that is drawing power from the UPS. Replace discharge with the number of minutes the UPS can run before the network has to start shutting down.

Recharge = n

This is the time it will take your UPS to recharge after supporting the network on batteries. Enter the time in minutes.

If you simply issue the command LOAD UPS you will be prompted for the proper values of each of the items above.

UPS STATUS

Command Format:

UPS STATUS

Command Function:

You can check to see the status of the UPS, including whether the server is on battery power or not, and how long the UPS will be able to support the server in its current condition. To use the UPS STATUS command, you must have loaded the UPS NLM into the server's memory before you type UPS STATUS into the file server console keyboard. If the file server is running on battery power, you will be told how many minutes remain before the server begins shutting itself down.

UPS TIME

Command Format:

UPS TIME [discharge] [recharge]

Command Function:

If you need to adjust the time settings for UPS, above, you can do it with UPS TIME. The UPS NLM must be loaded before you can type this command into the file server console. Replace discharge and recharge with the revised number of minutes. If you only type in UPS TIME you will be prompted for the appropriate numbers.

USERDEF

Command Format:

USERDEF

Command Function:

There are several ways in which you can create new users within NetWare. Two of those ways, MAKEUSER and SYSCON have already been covered. USERDEF is another. This method is designed for entering multiple users through the use of a template that allows you to enter the appropriate information into a form on the workstation screen. You must have DOS loaded into your file server to use USERDEF, so if you routinely remove DOS, you will be prompted to load it.

Before you can use USERDEF, you must have already installed the accounting system using SYSCON, print device definitions using PRINTDEF, and print job configurations with PRINTCON. The print job definitions must be available to the supervisor.

If you do not intend to install the accounting system, or if you plan to add groups in addition to EVERYONE, or if you plan to otherwise customize your server installation, you may set up USERDEF to meet your needs with the EDIT TEMPLATE menu choice.

When you want to create users with USERDEF you start by selecting the Add Users choice from the main menu. This selection will prompt you for the template you wish to use if there is more than one available. Once that is done, you will be presented with a list of users. Begin entering new users by pressing the <INSERT> key, typing the user's full name, and pressing <ENTER>. USERDEF will pick a login name which you can either accept or change. You do this for each user you intend to add.

Once you have completed your additions, review the list of users to make sure you haven't forgotten any, and then press <ESC>. You will be asked if you want to create the new users using the template. Select "Yes" to let the program proceed.

As a part of the creation process, USERDEF will create passwords for each user. If the user name is longer than five characters, the user name and the password will be the same. If the user name is less than five characters, USERDEF will make up a password. You will be asked to approve the passwords for users with fewer than five characters in their user name. You can either accept or edit the password. Passwords created by

USERDEF are for the initial log on only. They must be changed by the users the first time they log on.

Once you have finished creating your list of users, USERDEF invokes the MAKEUSER utility, which actually does the adding of the users to the file server. When this process is finished, you will have the opportunity to review the MAKEUSER Results Screen, which will show you any errors that MAKEUSER encountered when creating the users. When you have finished reviewing this screen, press <ESC> to return to the menu.

You can create a custom template for USERDEF by selecting the appropriate choice from the main menu. When you do this, you will be requested to provide a name for the template. Your choice should reflect the type of user who will be created with it. After that, you will be presented with a window containing the default settings. By moving among them with the arrow keys, you can change those that need to have different values.

USERLIST

Command Format:

USERLIST [server/] [user] [/Address or /Object] [/Continuous]

Command Function:

As in the USERLIST command in the previous versions of NetWare, this command will show you the users who are currently logged in or attached to the file server. This list will include the user name, connection number and login time. You can also request the network node address and a list of attached objects. Those optional displays are invoked with one of the following switches:

/A   Includes the network node address.
/O   Includes attached object type at that connection.
/C   Displays the user list in a continuous scroll, rather than stopping at each screen.

VERSION

Command Format:

VERSION

VERSION [path] file

Command Function:

There are two versions of VERSION (confusing, huh?) one of which runs as a console command that you must type into the file server's console keyboard, and another which is a command line utility. The console command will tell you the version of NetWare that is running on that server. The command line utility will tell you the version of other Novell utilities. It will not work with anything that didn't come from Novell.

To use VERSION, you follow the command with the path to the utility (if you're not already in the same directory) and the name of the utility in question. VERSION will report the utility's version number, along with a brief description of the utility's function.

VOLINFO

Command Format:

VOLINFO

Command Function:

The VOLINFO command will tell you how much space and how many directories have been used and what remains. It will do this for all volumes attached to the server. You can change to a different server and see volumes attached to that one also. You must be attached to a file server before you can view information about it.

VOLINFO presents a screen that shows the volume name, kilobytes used and remaining, and directories used and remaining. The display is organized in groups of eight volumes. If you have more volumes than this, you can view additional pages. You can toggle between kilobytes and megabytes in the display by pressing the <F2> key. Up to 32 volumes can be viewed with VOLINFO.

VOLUMES

Command Format:

VOLUMES

Command Function:

You can type VOLUMES into the file server console keyboard and be shown a list of the volumes currently mounted on the server.

VREPAIR

Command Format:

LOAD VREPAIR

Command Function:

If your file server's hard disk suffers minor problems such as data corruption to one of the file allocation tables (FATs), VREPAIR may be able to correct the problem by copying information from a mirrored or secondary FAT to the primary one. You can use VREPAIR on the problem volume while the remainder of the file server is functioning.

To use VREPAIR, first run MONITOR to check for users on the volume that must be repaired, then close out their open files, and DISMOUNT the volume. At that point, LOAD VREPAIR and confirm which volume you want to repair (if more than one is dismounted.)

VREPAIR will begin repairing the FAT, and it will pause after each item is repaired so that you can see it, and then press <ENTER> for the process to continue. If there are a great many errors, you can press <F1> and tell VREPAIR not to pause after each error. The time it takes for VREPAIR to perform its work varies according to the size of the disk. Large disks (over 200 M) may take more than a half hour. When VREPAIR is done, it will show you a list of the repairs and ask you to confirm that they should be written to the FAT. Enter "Yes" to continue. You can exit from the Options menu.

If the damage to the disk or the FAT was extensive, VREPAIR may not be able to fix everything. You will know this because you will not be able to MOUNT the volume after the repair is finished. In that case, you must recreate the volume with the INSTALL NLM, and restore the volume contents from your backup tape.

WHOAMI

Command Format:

WHOAMI [server] [option(s)]

Command Function:

The syntax of the WHOAMI command, which reports the user name you are logged on with, is unchanged from previous versions, with the exception that the /SY option has been added. This option allows you to view general system information.

Glossary

Abort   To stop a process or to make a program to stop execution.

Accounting   A service within Novell NetWare that permits the system administrator to determine usage of the network by each user. Normally this is used for billing network expenses, but may also be used for security.

Accounts   The information that the network operating system maintains about a user, including the users name, password, rights, and trusteeships.

ACS   Asynchronous Communications Server. A software package that works with a multi-port serial communications board to permit asynchronous serial communications through the LAN.

Adapter   A device that installs in the computer which allows communications with a peripheral device or outside service. A network interface card is a type of adapter.

Address   A specific numeric description of a location within the computer's memory. It is normally represented by a hexadecimal (base 16) number.

Administrator   The person (also called the "system administrator") who is responsible for the overall operation of the network. This person may also be the network supervisor, but also may be the supervisor's boss.

Amplifiers   A device that increases the amplitude of an electronic signal. On a LAN, an amplifier may be used to boost signal strength to allow the LAN cable to run a greater distance.

API   Application Programming Interface. A routine in a computer program that is designed to allow information transfer with another program.

Apple   A computer company originally known for its early computers, but now known for a computer known as the Macintosh.

Appleshare   Networking software used by Apple Computers.

Appletalk   Networking protocol used by Apple Computers.

Application   A program that is designed to support user work requirements. Word processing and spreadsheet programs are examples of applications.

Archive   In a computer, the process of storing information outside of the computer itself to protect it against loss.

ARCNET   A token passing network protocol developed and supported by Datapoint.

Argument   In computer terminology, the statements or information that follows a command on the same line as the command.

ASCII   American Standard Code for Information Interchange. Numeric representations of characters, numbers, punctuation, and other symbols.

Asynchronous   A form of communications signaling that does not require specific timing. Virtually all personal computers use this form of communication with their connection to the outside world.

Attach   To connect with a file server without logging on.

Attribute   Characteristics of a file or directory, such as whether they are read only, designated for system use, hidden, etc.

Autoexec   A file in MS-DOS (and some other operating systems) that executes automatically when the computer starts up.

Backbone   A network used to connect other networks. Ethernet is most commonly used for backbone LANs.

Bandwidth The total capacity for information transfer available to a communications medium.

Banner In computer printing, the first sheet of a printed file that contains information about the file, such as the origin, time it was printed, etc.

Baseband A type of network that can carry only one channel of data traffic at a time.

Baud A measurement of communications speed. Usually taken to mean bits per second.

Benchmarks Standardized measurements of performance that can be compared.

Bindery The files in the NetWare System directory that contain the information about the system users, connection information, etc.

Bit The basic unit of digital information. A bit may be either a 1 or a 0.

BIX The Byte Information Exchange. An online service of Byte Magazine. You can communicate with the authors on BIX.

BNC A type of connector for coaxial cable that attaches in a quarter turn.

Boot To cause a computer to start running.

Bootable A disk or partition that contains the information necessary to cause a computer to boot.

Borland A manufacturer of microcomputer language compilers and related products. Also known for productivity tools and applications, including Sidekick, Quattro, Paradox and Sprint.

Bridge A device to connect two LANs, or two different segments of the same LAN. A bridge will isolate traffic to the portion of the LAN for which it is intended, unless it is intended to cross the bridge.

Broadband A type of network that will carry multiple data channels, as well as voice and video information. Broadband LANs are frequently based on cable TV technology.

Broadcast   To send a message to all users on a LAN.

Buffers   Segments of memory intended to hold information temporarily.

Bus   A standardized method of transferring signals, either within a single computer or on a network. A bus consists of one or more physical conductors which carry various types of electrical signals in a single direction. In a LAN, bus also refers to a specific topology consisting of a single end-to-end signal path.

Byte   Eight bits of information. Usually a single character is represented by a byte.

Calendaring   A type of application or process that automates an appointment calendar.

Card   In computers, a printed circuit board.

Carrier   A high frequency signal in the medium being used by a LAN. A lower frequency signal representing data being transferred is usually imposed upon the carrier.

CCITT   An international communications standards committee.

CD-ROM   Compact Disc—Read Only Memory. A method of storing large amounts of data on a Compact Disc for use by a computer.

Client   A computer that is dependent upon and receives information from, a server.

Coaxial   A type of cable, the conductors of which share a common axis.

Collision   Events on an Ethernet in which two stations attempt to transmit information at the same time.

Compaq   A major manufacturer of IBM-PC compatible computers.

Compliant   Meeting specifications.

Compsurf   A low-level data formatting process used on Novell file servers.

CompuServe   An online service operated by H&R Block.

Console   The workstation used to operate the file server on a NetWare LAN.

Controller   A device that operates a peripheral and acts as an interface.

Cooperative   As in Cooperative Processing, a form of data processing where portions of the process are performed on separate computers which are connected by a network.

Coprocessor   A device that assists the central processing unit in carrying out an operation. It may be specialized to perform calculations, disk operations, graphics and the like.

Cray   A computer manufacturer that makes the fastest mainframe computers in the world.

CRC   Cyclical Redundancy Check—A mathematical method of checking the accuracy of transmitted data.

Cylinders   Concentric tracks of data on a hard disk.

Database   An organized collection of information.

Datapoint   A minicomputer manufacturer that developed ARCNET and continues to support the protocol.

dBASE   The generic term for a family of well-known file managers manufactured by Ashton-Tate. More correctly, the database language and its extensions used in those products.

DCB   Disk Coprocessor Board. An intelligent SCSI disk controller designed for use with Novell NetWare.

DMA   Direct Memory Access

DOS   Disk Operating System. Usually taken to mean MS-DOS when referring to personal computers.

Dot-matrix   A type of printer that creates characters from dots arranged in a matrix.

Driver   A program that acts as an interface between an application of operating system and an external device.

E-mail   Short for electronic mail. A method of sending messages between users.

EEPROM   Erasable Electronically Programmable Read Only Memory. A method of storing digital information in non-volatile form.

EISA   Enhanced Industry Standard Architecture. A type of very high capacity computer bus developed by manufacturers of IBM compatible microcomputers.

Emulation   The process of appearing to be something else. Usually meant to mean a method of making a personal computer appear to be a proprietary terminal to a mainframe or minicomputer.

ESDI   Enhanced Small Device Interface. A type of interface for disk drives originally developed for minicomputers, but now used for high performance hard disks on microcomputers.

Ethernet   A LAN protocol developed by Xerox corporation, and now embodied in the IEEE 802.3 network specification. This is the original LAN protocol, and one of the most widely used.

Executable   A computer program in a form that the computer can load it and begin running it.

FAT   File Allocation Table. A method of telling the computer's operating system where to find data on a disk.

Fiber-optic   A method of communications that uses LASER transmissions through a glass or plastic fiber as a medium.

Firmware   Programs stored in non-volatile memory. See EEPROM.

Flag   An indicator that an event has taken place or that a condition exists.

Gateway   A device for connecting a network to an external service or device.

Gigabytes   1024 Megabytes.

Global System-wide or program-wide.

Groupware Applications or groups of applications designed to enhance workgroup productivity.

Gupta Technologies Manufacturer of database SQL server software often used with NetWare.

Handles A method used by MS-DOS to manage files used in or by an application. The number of available file handles for an application running in MS-DOS is determined by the line: Files=XX in the PC's Config.sys file where XX is the number of handles. A value of less than 20 will not usually allow most applications to function properly.

Host A computer that supports centralized processing.

Housekeeping The process of making sure that extraneous information is cleared from a computer.

Hub A device that permits cables leading to other workstations or other hubs to be interconnected.

Hz Abbreviation for Hertz, the measurement for cycles per second.

I/O Abbreviation for Input-Output.

IBM International Business Machines. A computer manufacturer based in Armonk, NY.

IEEE Institute of Electrical and Electronic Engineers.

Intel Manufacturer of the most widely used central processor chips in the microcomputer industry.

Intelligent In computing, this means that the device has a central processing unit.

Interface The area of interconnection between dissimilar systems.

Internet A network of smaller networks.

Interrupt   A process that stops operation of the processor, and causes it to take some action.

Intruder   An unauthorized user on a network.

Invoke   To begin operation.

Ipx   The Novell NetWare workstation shell which allows communication between the workstation's operating system and NetWare.

Kanji   The form of Japanese text originally based on Chinese characters.

Kilobyte   1024 bytes.

LaserJet   A type of laser printer produced by Hewlett-Packard.

Log   To sign on to a computer or network server. Also a journal of activities on the network maintained automatically by NetWare.

Lotus Development Corporation   A manufacturer of spreadsheet software based in Cambridge, MA.

Macintosh   A computer produced by the Apple computer company which is incompatible with MS-DOS computers, and many LAN operating systems. NetWare supports the Macintosh.

Map   The process of assigning areas on the file server as disk drive equivalents.

Megabyte   1024 kilobytes.

Microchannel   A type of microcomputer bus developed by IBM, similar in function to the EISA bus, above.

Microprocessor   A central processing unit on a single integrated circuit.

Microsoft Corporation   A major manufacturer of operating system software, based in Redmond, WA.

Mirroring   The process of having disk drives on a file server automatically copy each other for backup purposes. If the primary disk drive fails, the mirrored drive takes over automatically.

Motherboard   The primary circuit board in a computer.

Mouse   A input device that controls pointing through movement.

MS-DOS   The Microsoft Disk Operating System.

Multiplex   The process of allowing two signals to occupy a single medium.

NetWare   Novell's LAN operating system.

NOS   Network Operating System.

Novell   A major manufacturer of LAN operating systems and LAN related hardware, located in Provo, Utah.

Ontrack   A manufacturer of data recovery software for NetWare.

Oracle   A manufacturer of multiuser database software.

OS/2   Operating system/2. Designed as the replacement for MS-DOS.

OS   Abbreviation for operating system.

OSI   Open Systems Interface. A standard for LAN organization consisting of seven theoretical layers, each with individual functions to perform within a LAN.

Owner   The user who created a file and retains control over it.

Packet   A discrete segment of data.

Password   A group of characters that you use to prove to the computer that you are who you say you are.

Peer-to-peer   A LAN design where all nodes communicate at an equal layer on the OSI model.

Port   An interface to a peripheral, such as a printer or modem.

Posix   The US government's standard for a Unix-like operating system.

Program   A collection of organized instructions for a computer.

Protocol   A common pattern for communication between two computers or similar devices.

PS/2   A type of personal computer developed by IBM that uses the Microchannel bus.

Queue   A list of processes waiting for the computer or a peripheral to handle them.

Read-only   A device or storage medium that can be read, but not written to.

Record   A line of data in a database.

Recoverable   A file that is capable of being repaired and returned to use.

Redirect   The process of sending data to a location other than where it would normally go. You can have data redirected from the screen to the printer, for example.

Reset   A method of causing a computer to reboot.

Router   A device that decides what the destination for a specific packet of information is, and then sends it.

Rxnet   Novell's name for ARCNET.

Scheduling   An application or process that coordinates the appointment calendars of several people. See Calendaring.

Script   A listing of commands that the file server will execute when a user logs on.

SCSI   Small Computer Systems Interface. A method of connecting with a variety of storage devices and peripherals, including disk drives, tape drives, and optical disks.

Serial   A method of data transmission in which the bits which make up characters are sent sequentially.

Server   A primary hub of a Local Area Network. NetWare resides on the file server. In database applications, the database may reside on a database server. There are also print servers which support network printing and communications servers which allow users on the network to communicate outside of the network.

SNA   Systems Network Architecture. IBM's network protocol for wide area networks.

SQL   Structured Query Language. A database language developed by IBM, and now in use on a variety of systems.

SubLAN   A type of communications medium based on RS-232 serial connections.

Supervisor   The user on a NetWare LAN who controls the operations of the LAN. The supervisor has complete freedom to access anything on the LAN.

Tcp/ip   Transport Control Protocol/Internet Protocol. A protocol used for interconnecting dissimilar network systems (such as NetWare to UNIX) by interconnecting at the transport layer of the OSI model.

Terabyte   1024 gigabytes.

Token   A special packet of data that contains information about other packets moving on a token passing network.

Topology   The physical or electrical layout of a network.

Transaction   A single database action between a client and a database server where data is either added to the database, modified or retrieved.

Transceiver   A device that both transmits and receives data from a network.

Transparent   In computing, a circumstance where the existence of an interface is not obvious to the user.

Trustee   A user or group that has limited control over a file or group of files on the file server.

TSR Terminate and Stay Resident. A program that loads into a computer's (or server's) memory, and is invoked without having to load it again.

Tymnet A world-wide public packet-switching data network owned by British Telecom.

Unix An operating system developed by Bell Labs which is now available for nearly any computer sold.

VADD Value Added Disk Driver—a special hard disk driver for NetWare 2.1X file server.

VAP Value Added Process—A program that runs in a NetWare version 2.1X file server, and adds additional capabilities.

VAX A type of minicomputer produced by Digital Equipment Company.

Virus A program which attaches itself covertly to an executable file and causes damage to other programs or data within a computer or network. A virus, unlike a worm, can reproduce itself and attach to other programs.

VMS The operating system used by VAX computers.

WAN Wide Area Network

Windows A graphical user interface developed by Microsoft.

WordPerfect The name of a major word processing package, and of the company that produces it.

Workgroup Several people working on a common assignment.

Worm A type of computer virus that invades a computer and then creates multiple copies of itself. A worm usually does its damage by reproducing until it has used up all available disk and or memory resources within the system.

Xerox The company that developed Ethernet. They also make copiers and laser printers.

Xircom   A company that makes portable Ethernet and other network interface cards.

Zenith   A manufacturer of IBM compatible computers, and the leading manufacturer of laptop computers.

Index

G

H

I

About the Authors

Wayne Rash, Jr. writes about networks frequently in his column "Down to Business" which appears monthly in *Byte Magazine*. He also writes the weekly column "Rash's Judgment" which appears in *ByteWeek*, and he writes a monthly column for *Computer Digest*. Rash is the Technical Director of American Management Systems' Network Integration Group, where he designs, integrates, and installs local and wide area networks for a wide variety of federal and private clients. He is listed in Who's Who in the East, has spoken about networks to audiences throughout the US, and in Europe and Asia, and he appears frequently in radio and television interviews on the subject of personal computers and networking.

Peter Stephenson is vice president of Stephenson and Associates Marketing Services Inc., a consultancy specializing in software products with database management, data security or connectivity applications. In addition to authoring several books, his writings have appeared in such well-known computer publications as *InfoWorld*, *Byte*, and *Government Computer News*. He is a columnist and contributing editor for *Computer Buyers Guide and Handbook*, producing the Networking 101 column monthly. He is also the monthly local area network columnist for *MIS Week*, *LAN Times*, and *Federal Computer Week*. Mr. Stephenson is the editor of *Andrew Seybold's Outlook on Database Management*, a monthly newsletter covering database management issues.

Winn Rosch and Chet Heath Together for the first time!

The Micro Channel™ Handbook

0-13-583493-7
$29.95

If you care about multiprocessing and multitasking performance and what it means to you in getting the most out of your computer; or you simply want a straightforward, no-nonsense introduction to IBM's advanced new Micro Channel technology: then *The Micro Channel Handbook* is the perfect solution!

Chet Heath, IBM Senior Engineer and principal designer of the Micro Channel, joins forces with PC journalist and Brady best-selling microcomputer author Winn Rosch to provide the premier guide to the Micro Channel. Inside you'll find everything you'll need to know to take full advantage of the Micro Channel's great potential. It's all here at your fingertips— from the easy-to-understand introduction and overview, to an unintimidating detailed look at every discrete function found in the IBM PS/2 Model 50 through the new RS/6000 Workstations and beyond.

The dynamic combination of expert authors and IBM technology truly makes *The Micro Channel Handbook* the single most valuable Micro Channel accessory money can buy!

Master Paradox® with
Understanding and Using Paradox 3.5

Leading computer journalist and well-known microcomputer book author, Rob Krumm, adds to his successful Brady *Understanding and Using* series with this latest tutorial. His easy-to-follow style thoroughly details Borland's phenomenal database program, Paradox.

Organized to provide a structured series of lessons, Rob Krumm's *Understanding and Using Paradox 3.5* develops a master Paradox application throughout the book. All of the program's techniques and procedures are seamlessly unified in the sample application to provide the most effective discussion possible of the program's powerful new features.

Included are:

- all of Paradox's extensive 3.5 capabilities
- programming with the Paradox Application Language
- networking
- designing menus
- numerous example screens and sample code listing
- a wealth of hints, tips, and ideas for better performance

Don't hesitate—put Paradox 3.5 to work for you with Rob Krumm's *Understanding and Using Paradox 3.5.*

ISBN: 0-13-946328-3
$29.95

Look for this and other Brady titles at your local book or computer store. To order directly, call 1 (800) 624-0023. Visa/MC accepted.